Buddhists, Shamans, and Soviets

O | R | S

OXFORD RITUAL STUDIES

THE PROBLEM OF RITUAL EFFICACY
Edited by William S. Sax, Johannes Quack, and Jan Weinhold

PERFORMING THE REFORMATION
Public Ritual in the City of Luther
Barry Stephenson

RITUAL, MEDIA, AND CONFLICT
Edited by Ronald L. Grimes, Ute Hüsken, Udo Simon, and Eric Venbrux

KNOWING BODY, MOVING MIND
Ritualizing and Learning at Two Buddhist Centers
Patricia Q. Campbell

SUBVERSIVE SPIRITUALITIES
How Rituals Enact the World
Frédérique Apffel-Marglin

NEGOTIATING RITES
Edited by Ute Hüsken and Frank Neubert

THE DANCING DEAD
Ritual and Religion among the Kapsiki/Higi of North Cameroon and Northeastern Nigeria
Walter E.A. van Beek

LOOKING FOR MARY MAGDALENE
Alternative Pilgrimage and Ritual Creativity at Catholic Shrines in France
Anna Fedele

The Dysfunction of Ritual in Early Confucianism
Michael David Kaulana Ing

A DIFFERENT MEDICINE
Postcolonial Healing in the Native American Church
Joseph D. Calabrese

NARRATIVES OF SORROW AND DIGNITY
Japanese Women, Pregnancy Loss, and Modern Rituals of Grieving
Bardwell L. Smith

MAKING THINGS BETTER
A Workbook on Ritual, Cultural Values, and Environmental Behavior
A. David Napier

AYAHUASCA SHAMANISM IN THE AMAZON AND BEYOND
Edited by Beatriz Caiuby Labate and Clancy Cavnar

HOMA VARIATIONS
The Study of Ritual Change across the Longue Durée
Edited by Richard K. Payne and Michael Witzel

HOMO RITUALIS
Hindu Ritual and Its Significance to Ritual Theory
Axel Michaels

RITUAL GONE WRONG
What We Learn from Ritual Disruption
Kathryn T. McClymond

SINGING THE RITE TO BELONG
Ritual, Music, and the New Irish
Helen Phelan

RITES OF THE GOD-KING
Śānti, Orthopraxy, and Ritual Change in Early Hinduism
Marko Geslani

BUDDHISTS, SHAMANS, AND SOVIETS
Rituals of History in Post-Soviet Buryatia
Justine Buck Quijada

Buddhists, Shamans, and Soviets

Rituals of History in Post-Soviet Buryatia

JUSTINE BUCK QUIJADA

OXFORD
UNIVERSITY PRESS

Oxford University Press is a department of the University of Oxford. It furthers the University's objective of excellence in research, scholarship, and education by publishing worldwide. Oxford is a registered trade mark of Oxford University Press in the UK and certain other countries.

Published in the United States of America by Oxford University Press
198 Madison Avenue, New York, NY 10016, United States of America.

First issued as an Oxford University Press paperback, 2020

Library of Congress Cataloging-in-Publication Data
Names: Quijada, Justine B., 1973– author.
Title: Buddhists, shamans, and Soviets : rituals of history in post-Soviet Buryatia / Justine Buck Quijada.
Description: New York : Oxford University Press, 2019. | Includes bibliographical references and index.
Identifiers: LCCN 2018030292 (print) | LCCN 2018034587 (ebook) | ISBN 9780190916800 (updf) | ISBN 9780190916817 (epub) | ISBN 9780190916824 (online content) | ISBN 9780190916794 (cloth) | ISBN 9780197536421 (paperback)
Subjects: LCSH: Buriats—Religion. | Buddhism—Russia (Federation)—Bur?i?ati?i?a—Rituals. | Shamanism—Russia (Federation)—Bur?i?ati?i?a—Rituals.
Classification: LCC BL2370.B87 (ebook) | LCC BL2370.B87 Q45 2019 (print) | DDC 200.957/5—dc23
LC record available at https://lccn.loc.gov/2018030292

Contents

Acknowledgments

THIS BOOK WOULD not exist without the assistance of a great many people. They should get most of the credit and none of the blame. This project would not have been possible without the generous support of several funding agencies. Pre-field research was supported by a Leiffer Pre-dissertation Fieldwork Grant from the Department of Anthropology, University of Chicago. Dissertation fieldwork was generously funded by a Fulbright-Hays Doctoral Dissertation Fellowship and an IREX Individual Advanced Research Opportunity Grant. Dissertation writing was supported by a Charlotte W. Newcombe Fellowship, and reworking that into this book was made possible by a post-doctoral research Fellowship at the Max Planck Institute for the Study of Religious and Ethnic Diversity, and a faculty fellowship at the Center for the Humanities at Wesleyan University. I am deeply grateful for all their support. All conclusions are my own.

I owe a great deal to a great many people in Buryatia. First and foremost, I must thank Nikolai Tsyrempilov for his friendship, inspiration and endless support. I would also like thank Inge Tsyrempilova, Zhargal and Natasha Badagarov and their sons, Bair Sundupov and Alessia and Darima Ardanovna Batorova and her family (especially her grandmother) for making us at home in Ulan-Ude. I am deeply grateful for the friendship and intellectual support of Margarita Maximovna Boronova and to Tsimzhit Badmazhapovna Bazarova, for her infinite patience in teaching me Buryat. I am deeply grateful to Erzhena Alexandrovna Bazarova and Sveta Sergeevna Khabinova. They first introduced me to Ulan-Ude and their long-standing friendship is a big reason why I return to Buryatia, time and again. I must also thank Sveta's sister, Valentina Sergeevna Antropova, and all of their family for their welcome and help.

My research would have been impossible without the support and cooperation of local scholars in Ulan-Ude. Special thanks go to Tatiana Skrynnikova and her colleagues at the Academy of Sciences, at the National Archives of the Republic of Buraytia, and the faculty and staff of the Buryat State University.

I especially thank Dashinima Dugarov for introducing me to Tengeri, and Anatolii Dambaevich Zhalsaraev for putting up with me.

None of this would be possible without the enthusiastic cooperation of the Local Shaman's Organization Tengeri and the Etigelov Institute. I thank Ianzhima Dambaevna Vasil'eva at the Etigelov Institute for her time, her generosity and openness, Pandito Khambo Lama Damba Aiusheev for allowing me at the datsan, and giving permission to photograph Etigelov, and to all the monks, whose names I did not know, but who shared their thoughts with me. Many of the members of Tengeri have since gone their separate ways, and I hope that if and when they read these chapters they remember their time together as fondly as I do. I must thank Bair Zhambalovich Tsyrendorzhiev, Victor Dorzhievich Tsydipov, Budazhab Purboevich Shiretorov, Tsitsik Batoevna Garmaeva, Aldar Andanovich Rampilov, Oleg Dongidovich Dorzhiev, Valerii Viktorovich Khodoshkinov, Marina Schoetschel, and all the members of Tengeri, their friends and family, who welcomed us and took the time to explain their lives to us. Victor Dorzhievich Tsydipov, deserves to be mentioned twice for all of his patience, time and enthusiasm. I would also especially like to thank Yuri Nikolaivich Baldanov, his wife Larissa, and his mother Nellie Inokentievna, for sharing Yuri's initiation with us. I also thank the many people I met in Ulan-Ude over the course of my time there.

I have incurred many debts, intellectual and otherwise, at home as well. At the University of Chicago, my dissertation committee, Susan Gal, Elizabeth Povinelli, Adam T. Smith and Danilyn Rutherford generously shared their time and their wisdom. I am deeply grateful for their mentorship, as well as that of Jean and John Comaroff, Michel-Rolph Trouillot and all of my teachers at Haskell Hall. I would also like to thank Sheila Fitzpatrick for allowing me to hang around with the historians. Raymond T. Fogelson, and especially E. Valentine Daniel, deserve special mention for their mentorship and support. I am deeply grateful to Anne Chien for everything she does at Haskell Hall. I want to thank Melissa and Janis Chakars, Kathryn Graber, Eleanor Peers and Naj Wikoff for many productive discussions in the field, and all my fellow Buryat studies colleagues, including Manduhai Buyandelger, Tatiana Chudakova, Melissa Chakars, Tristra Newyear, Kathryn Metzo, Joseph Long, and Ivan Sablin. Feedback and support from Bruce Grant, Alaina Lemon, Laurel Kendall, Catherine Wanner, Serguei Oushakine, Sonja Luehrmann, Neringa Klumbyte, and Doug Rogers at various stages was deeply appreciated.

I am likewise grateful to all my colleagues and mentors at the Max Planck Institute for the Study of Religious and Ethnic Diversity in Goettingen, Germany, especially Peter van der Veer, Tam Ngo, Vibha Joshi and Sophorntavy Vorng. I am deeply grateful to my wonderful and supportive colleagues at

Wesleyan University, including Elizabeth McAlister, Peter Gottschalk, Mary-Jane Rubenstein, Ron Cameron, Dalit Katz, Yaniv Feller, Victoria Smolkin, Priscilla Meyer, Susanne Fusso, Peter Rutland, Betsy Traube, J. Kēhaulani Kauanui, and all the members of the Indigenous Studies Research Network, as well as Sergei Bunaev, Anna Gelzer, Jenny Caplan and Ryan Overbey, all of whom gave much needed feedback and encouragement. I need to thank Marc Eisner for his support, and Ethan Kleinberg for my time at the Center for the Humanities, and for helping me frame my ideas about history. Thanks go as well to Rhonda Kissinger, to Sheri Dursin, and to Eric Stephen for all his help. A special thank you goes to Meaghan Parker, who is the best friend and the best editor. I would also like to thank Jim Lance, Cynthia Read and Ronald Grimes and the anonymous readers at Cornell and Oxford, whose feedback was transformative.

I would not have been able to complete this without the support and encouragement of all my family and my friends, both those I have known most of my life, and those I have met along this path. I especially need to mention Regina Shoykhet, Kimberly Arkin, Greg Beckett and Christina Trier.

I am deeply grateful to my aunt, Eva Maria Perrot, for first taking me to Russia as a teenager in 1989, just before it ended, beginning my fascination with all things Soviet. I would like to thank my grandmother, Frida Johanna Mathes, for urging me to 'not let anything get in the way', my uncles, Fritz Phillip Mathes and Alexander Perrot for their support, my parents-in-law, Maria and Juan Astudillo for all their help over the years, and my father, Bill Buck, for encouraging me to question everything. I wish you could have seen the final version. I am eternally grateful to my mother, Waltrudis Buck, for cat-sitting, for fieldnote hauling, for hours of baby-sitting and undaunted cheerleading.

Last, but never least, I would like to thank my husband Roberto Quijada, whose photos grace these pages, who was with me every step of the way, who never faltered in his support, and who makes all things seem possible. There is no way I could have done this without you. I give daily thanks for my children Eva Maria and Esme Maja, who make life worth living, and who remind me that if I get my work done I get to play with them. They voted this their least favorite book ever. I love you.

May all of your roads be open.

Note on Transliterations, Translations, and Photographs

ALL TRANSLITERATIONS OF Russian and Buryat words and names follow the Library of Congress transliteration standards for Russian, except in cases where another spelling is commonly used in English. For example, I write Buryatia and Buryat instead of Buriatiia and Buriat because this is how most Buryats spell their ethnonym when writing in English. In the text I have included native terms where I thought additional meaning might be gained from knowing the original term or where a translation fails to capture the meaning of the original. The source language (Russian or Buryat) is marked by using *Russ.*— or *Bur.*— before the term. When using original terms in the text, I have rendered transliterated terms plural by using an -s at the end, to facilitate reading by an English speaking audience. For example, when referring to ancestral shamanic spirits, I use *ongon* (sing.), *ongons* (pl.). instead of *ongonuud*, as it would be in Buryat, or *ongony*, as it would be in Russian.

Buryats follow the Russian convention with regard to personal names, using a first name, patronymic, and family name. As per Russian convention, I use the first name and patronymic to refer to most speakers, except a few speakers with whom I, and the reader, become well acquainted.

The archival materials used are from the National Archive of the Republic of Buryatia (NARB) and are identified by Fond, Opis, Delo, and List as is standard for Russian archives. All translations are my own except where noted in the text. All photographs were taken by Roberto Quijada.

Chronology of Relevant Dates

ca. 1162–1227	Chinghis Khan
1652	Patriarch Nikon's reforms produce a schism in the Russian Orthodox Church
1666	The fort of Udinskoye (later Verkhneudinsk, then Ulan-Ude) founded
1689	Treaty of Nerchinsk establishes border between Russia and China
1703	Delegation of Khori Buryat clan leaders visit Peter I
1727	Treaty of Kiakhta solidifies border between Russia and China
1741	Buddhism recognized by Empress Elizabeth I as an official religion of the Russian empire
1764	Damba Dorzha Zaiaev (1711–1776) becomes the first Pandito Khambo Lama of Buryatia
1852	Birth of Dashi-Dorzho Etigelov
1911–1917	Etigelov elected and serves as Pandito Khambo Lama of Buryatia
1914–1917	World War I
1917	Russian Revolution, followed by the second, Bolshevik Revolution in October
1917–1923	Russian Civil War, during which the Bolshevik forces (the Red Army) fight a coalition of anti-Bolshevik forces (the White Army) for control of the country
1922	Stalin (1878–1953) becomes General Secretary of the Communist Party
1923	Buryat-Mongolian Autonomous Soviet Socialist Republic established
1924	Lenin dies and is embalmed
1927	Dashi-Dorzho Etigelov "leaves"

1928–1932	The First Five Year Plan and the beginning of agricultural collectivization
1930	Buryat language reform requires Buryat to be written in the Latin alphabet
1934	The city of Verkhneudinsk is renamed Ulan-Ude
1937	Stalin's purges
1938	Buryat language reform requires Buryat to be written in the Cyrillic alphabet
1940	All Buddhist monasteries in Buryatia have been closed
1941	Hitler invades Russia, and Russia enters World War II
May 9, 1945	Victory Day
1946	Ivolginsky Buddhist monastery (*datsan*) opened
1985	Gorbachev becomes General Secretary of the Communist Party. He initiates *perestroika* (reconstruction/renovation), a policy intended to reform the Communist Party and the government of the USSR
1991	The USSR is dissolved. The Union Republics become autonomous countries and the remaining territories (including Buryatia) become the Russian Federation. The Buryat Autonomous Soviet Socialist Republic becomes the Republic of Buryatia
1991	Boris Yeltsin (1931–2007) becomes President of Russia
1992	Nadezhda Stepanova founds the first shaman's organization in Buryatia, Bo Murgel
1995	Damba Aiusheev elected Pandito Khambo Lama
1997	Law on Freedom of Conscience and Religious Associations legally distinguishes traditional and new religions
1999	Vladimir Putin becomes President of Russia
2002	Etigelov is exhumed and brought to the Ivolginsky monastery
2003	"Local Religious Organization of Shamans, Tengeri" [Mestnaia religioznaia organizatsiia shamanov Tengeri (MROSH)] officially registered as a religious organization in the Republic of Buryatia
2008	Ust-Orda and Aga Buryat Autonomous Okrugs are merged into Irkutsk and Chita oblasts, respectively

Buddhists, Shamans, and Soviets

MAP 0.1 Map of Russia showing the Republic of Buryatia. Map courtesy of Eric Stephen, 2014.

MAP 0.2 Map of the Republic of Buryatia, showing Ust-Orda and Aga Buryat okrugs. Map courtesy of Eric Stephen, 2014.

Introduction

"IF YOU WANT TO HAVE A FUTURE YOU HAVE TO HAVE A GOOD RELATIONSHIP TO YOUR PAST"

I MET BORIS and Svetlana in 2012 outside the Tengeri shamans' offices in Ulan-Ude, the capital city of Buryatia, a republic located in south-central Siberia along Russia's border with Mongolia (Map 0.1–0.2). The city of Ulan-Ude has nearly half a million residents, but the suburb where Tengeri built their offices still has enough open space for them to hold rituals.[1] I was waiting to speak to someone about attending an upcoming initiation, and they were waiting for their shaman to finish meeting with a client.

Boris and Svetlana, a Buryat couple in their fifties, were friendly and eager to tell me about their experiences with the shamans. They lived and worked in Yakutia, another indigenous republic farther north in Siberia, for most of the year. Boris had grown up in Yakutia; his parents were scientists who had been sent there during the Soviet years. They had started coming back to Buryatia every summer to hold clan offering ceremonies with a shaman at Tengeri. Their children were in their early thirties, they explained, but did not yet have children of their own. At this rate, they were afraid they would never have grandchildren, so they had turned to the shamans to remedy the situation. They did not explain why this was a problem; they did not need to. Every Buryat with childless, adult children that I had ever met expressed similar concerns. Given the uncertain post-Soviet economy, young Buryats were marrying and having children later than their parents, causing their families untold stress.

Friends had told Boris and Svetlana that the shamans at Tengeri might be able to help them. But for the shamans to help, they had to contact Boris's ancestors and find out if they were the cause. As educated, urban children of the Soviet era, neither Boris nor Svetlana knew their genealogies. Their own parents did not know much more than they did, so they turned to the state census and tax records, but these only listed the first few generations. They asked every relative they could find, until finally an uncle revealed that he had the family's *un bichig*, a genealogical chart from the 19th century, showing all ten patrilineal generations. He had saved it for just such an occasion. "Can you imagine how lucky we are?" Svetlana said. "No one has these anymore. We were sure all this was completely gone."

The shaman they worked with at Tengeri then channeled his own ancestor spirit (*ongon*). This ancestor spirit served as an intermediary for Boris's ancestors, to find out whether they were causing their descendant's fertility problems. Knowing whom to ask for in the spirit world simplifies the process considerably. Boris and Svetlana's case was not serious. No one had a calling to become a shaman. Instead, they simply needed to re-establish a relationship with their ancestors by holding a clan ceremony to offer them a sheep every year. I asked whether they had to travel to their ancestral land, as clan offerings are supposed to be made in the place that a family is from. "No," Boris explained. "We don't know exactly where that is, so we do the ceremonies here at the Tengeri offices."

The organization had built their shamanic center on a stretch of land in a suburb precisely so that they would have space for this kind of ritual. Other people, who were skeptical of Tengeri's project, had told me that a clan ritual held in the wrong place would not be effective, but Boris and Svetlana seemed satisfied. This was the third year that they had made offerings. Their daughter was now married, and their son had a girlfriend, so they were hopeful. The ritual seemed to be working.

Boris and Svetlana's story is completely prosaic. I heard similar stories (and far more dramatic ones), but their story encapsulates the themes that will fill the coming pages. As a result of the socio-economic and political changes of the Soviet period, Boris and Svetlana do not know very much about their past. They describe themselves as having been disconnected from what they see as traditional Buryat forms of knowledge: genealogies, ancestral clan territories, and shamanic rituals. In the post-Soviet period, concerned about whether their family will have a future, they turn to religious practice to reconnect to their past. To fill the gaps in their historical knowledge, they combine archival research and oral history with information gleaned from spirits channeled through a shaman. They measure the success of this endeavor in the physical condition of their and their children's bodies: in this case, the birth of grandchildren.

Like Boris and Svetlana, many Buryats share a strong feeling that if you want to have a future, you have to have a good relationship to your past. After a century of Soviet modernity, however, achieving a relationship with your past requires effort and creativity. This book describes how people in Buryatia produce and reproduce knowledge about their past through rituals in the present. It is based on eighteen months of fieldwork, spread over a decade, in Ulan-Ude.

Ulan-Ude, now the capital city of the Republic of Buryatia, was founded as a Cossack trading post on the tea road connecting China to Europe. Contemporary Buryats are the descendants of Mongolian-speaking pastoral nomads whose ancestors were allied with Chinghis Khan, and who ended up on the Russian side of the border with Mongolia and China when it was drawn on a map in the 17th century. Although they are culturally similar to Mongolians, through incorporation into the Russian empire Buryats became a distinct and separate ethnic group, and the various dialects that make up the Buryat language are not mutually intelligible with Khalkh Mongol. Stretching south along the eastern shore of Lake Baikal to the border, Buryatia stands at the intersection of indigenous Siberia, European Russia, and the Tibetan Buddhist world; its people have been missionized by Tibetan Buddhists, Russian Orthodox Christians, and Soviet atheists. A highly educated, formerly Soviet, indigenous population, Buryats are trying to establish a new relationship to their past, and in the process, they are reviving shamanic and Buddhist practices after a century of state-sponsored atheism.

Like Buryatia itself, this book stands at the intersection between post-Soviet studies, indigenous studies, and the anthropology of religion. By combining these disciplinary perspectives, I hope to contribute to the anthropology of history, which is the anthropological study of how people produce knowledge about the past. As in other post-Soviet places, the post-Soviet moment in Buryatia (from 1991 through today's Putin era) is a window of imaginative potential in which people question received knowledge and imagine new futures.[2] The collapse of Soviet versions of history and nationality politics prompted Buryats to re-evaluate what it meant to be Buryat.[3] In search of national traditions, they turned, in large part, to Buddhist and shamanic religious practices and ended up finding new histories.

By engaging in Buddhist and shamanic religious practices, everyday Buryats not only learned and produced new information about the past, they were reintroduced to older, indigenous Buryat conceptions of time. Drawing on Mikhail Bakhtin, I call these conceptions of time chronotopes. These chronotopes, generated by ritual practice, offer new perspectives from which to make the present meaningful by offering different ways to connect the present to the past.

In this sense, Buryatia is part of a broader post-Soviet experience in which ethnic minorities within the former Soviet Union revived previously suppressed religious practices. For Buryats, as for most post-Soviet nationalities, religious and ethnic revival went hand-in-hand. However, much of the existing literature has tended to view these processes through the lens of Soviet nationality policy. There is great merit to this approach; interlocutors in the field insist that religious practice is about expressing national identity, and it makes sense to examine this expression of identity in relationship to the Soviet nationality policies that produced it. However, this approach views religious rituals as expressing underlying beliefs. In contrast, current perspectives see rituals as doing things, creating subjects and groups, and producing effects in the world. It is precisely this productive and creative aspect of ritual that makes it an appealing resource for post-Soviet subjects who are re-imagining who they were, are, and can become. Rituals produce identities, collectivities, chronologies, and cosmologies. What kinds of effects are produced by religious rituals conducted by former atheists in a multi-religious setting?

I revisit existing ideas about the post-Soviet religious revival by focusing both on ritual as a productive practice, by comparing across religious and civic settings, and on Buryats as an indigenous population (a category that, admittedly, not all Buryats accept). Viewing post-Soviet identity projects solely through the lens of nationality policy obscures similarities between the Soviet experience and other colonial projects. By reframing Buryatia through the lens of indigeneity, we can see how their religious practices contribute to a broader project of rediscovering and reclaiming the languages, arts, and knowledge of their ancestors, in ways comparable to similar efforts of indigenous peoples around the world. By viewing Buryatia through the lens of indigeneity, we are able to see that the production of history is both a post-Soviet and a decolonizing project.

As they produce new knowledge about the past in religious rituals, Buryats are discovering older, religious, and Buryat ways of being in time and space. The situation in Buryatia is particularly striking due to the multiplicity of genres in which they produce the past. Over the centuries, Buryatia has been subject to multiple waves of religious missionization. Older indigenous forms of religion that are now called "shamanism" were overlaid by Buddhist, Russian Orthodox, and finally Soviet conceptions of time, space, and subjectivity. Produced through material practices of ritual, these genres of knowing the past are resources that Buryats draw on as they negotiate the present.

As Michel-Rolph Trouillot has argued, both social groups and knowledge of the past are shaped by structures of power, and these two processes are co-constitutive: "the collective subjects who supposedly remember did not exist as such at the time of the events they claim to remember. Rather, their constitution as subjects goes hand in hand with the continuous creation of the past. As such, they do not succeed such a past: they are its contemporaries" (1995, 16). Shamanic practitioners such as Boris and Svetlana are constituted as indigenous subjects through the reconstruction of their family genealogies and reconnection with their ancestors (see Chapters 5 and 6). Through rituals where ancestor spirits enter the bodies of shamans and speak to their living descendants, people engaging in these rituals come to understand the past as existing continuously in relationship to the present.

In Buddhist contexts, pilgrims visiting the miraculously preserved body of Dashi-Dorzho Etigelov, a reincarnate pre-Soviet Buddhist monk, are presented with recursive time, in which Etigelov (who, as a bodhisattva, exists outside of time) reappears in the linear national timeline, fulfilling prophecy and re-ordering the meaning of the Soviet years that passed between his arrivals.[4] This Buddhist history produces the Buryat nation, a nation of scholars and intellectuals that has long been a bridge between the Russian empire and the Tibetan Buddhist community (see Chapters 1 and 4).

Both Buddhist and shamanic practices are generating new historical knowledge and new ways of thinking about space and time, but these religiously generated chronotopes have not erased or superseded Soviet ways of thinking about the past. Participating in civic rituals such as Victory Day (see Chapter 2) and City Day (see Chapter 3) continues to reproduce Buryats as Soviet citizens and residents of a multi-ethnic republic. These civic festivals reproduce both familiar historical knowledge and familiar linear Soviet chronotopes. Victory Day—commemorating the end of World War II—reproduces the Soviet view of history as the progressive inclusion of Buryats into modernity. However, the mismatch between Soviet ritual forms and contemporary post-Soviet lives offers an alternative perspective from which to re-evaluate the Soviet version of the past. The ritual of City Day—an annual holiday celebrating the anniversary of the city's founding—echoes the Soviet genre, but tweaks it into a sub-genre I call the "hospitality genre." The hospitality genre recounts the history of Buryatia as successive waves of immigration to a welcoming land, producing a local ethic of multi-ethnic tolerance and conviviality. This version of the past both mutes the history of Russian colonization and produces a local identity that stands in opposition to the Russian center.

Each of these ritual forms tells a history of Buryatia in a distinctive genre, and through this history, produces a collective subject in the present. These genres have different chronotopes: within each of these genres of the past, time flows differently. Soviet time is linear and progressive, moving ever forward toward the radiant future (Burawoy and Lukacs 1994). Buddhist time is recursive and cyclical, as reincarnate lamas return to infuse linear time with dharmic meaning. In shamanic genres, the past remains present, as ancestors continue to act on and interact with their descendants.

Theoretical and Other Groundings

I went to Ulan-Ude because I was interested in the intersection between identity politics and religion. I am not indigenous, but my previous work in museums repatriating Native American collections had sparked a deep interest in how political claims by indigenous actors are often interwoven with religious claims. Buryatia was particularly interesting to me because in most places indigenous religion stands in a binary contrast to Christianity (or occasionally Islam or Buddhism). In the existing literature on post-Soviet religious revival, religion and national identity are often equated, even if the relationship between them is, in practice, complicated, and it is difficult to parse religion from nationality when there is a one-to-one equation (Borowik, Babinski, and Babinski 1997; Balzer 1999, 2005, 2011; Lewis 2000; Agadjanian 2001; Goluboff 2002; Skrynnikova 2003; Wanner 2007, 2012; Rogers 2009; Hann and Pelkmans 2009; Hann 2006, 2010; Amogolonova 2014). In Buryatia, however, ethnic Buryats practice both Buddhism and shamanism. Buddhism is more visible in the public sphere, and more Buryats, especially urban Buryats, identify Buddhism as their "national religion" than they do shamanism.[5] That does not, however, mean that they do not engage in the practices of other traditions.

Most ethnic Russians will publicly identify as Russian Orthodox. However, since approximately a third of Buryatia's ethnic Russians were the descendants of Old Believer exiles—a schismatic and largely endogamous group of Russian Orthodox Christians—ethnic Russians in Buryatia looking for their national religion can turn to either official Russian Orthodoxy or Old Believer Orthodoxy.[6] This multiplicity of choices seemed to disrupt the easy binary pairing between identity and religion presumed in the literature, and allow the local contours of the category of religion and its Soviet legacy to stand out.

Once I got to Ulan-Ude, I found that although both Buryats and Russians occasionally argued about which religion was the true "national religion" of their respective ethnic group, these arguments were largely made in relationship to claims for state funding and carried little emotional investment. "Religion" in these contexts was a bureaucratic category. In other contexts, however, "our local tradition of tolerance," which enabled people to turn to all of these religions as resources, was lauded as a local form of multiculturalism, and the reason why, in contrast to the violent separatism in the

Caucasus, "everything here is calm, thank God." Rather than arguing over national religions, the people I met at the religious rituals seemed to be primarily interested in history. Nationality (or ethnic identity) mattered at these rituals not in terms of who did or did not belong at the ritual—they were all explicitly open to everyone—but rather in terms of whose history was being presented, and how.

When I started to write the requisite historical background for this project, I struggled to pick a position from which to view that history. The history of Buryatia as explained at a Buddhist ritual was completely different from the history of Buryatia I would be told at a shamanic ritual, and both were different from the history of Buryatia in a Soviet textbook. Moreover, the person telling me these three histories might be the same person, the only difference being that they told that history in a different ritual context.

This book is my attempt to make sense of these histories. It is an ethnography about how people in post-Soviet, Putin-era Buryatia produce knowledge about the past in religious and civic rituals, and how this knowledge of the past produces identities in the present. This book attempts what Stephan Palmié and Charles Stewart (2016) call an "anthropology of history" or what Rian Thum (2014) labels "global comparative historiography." The study of how people produce histories is important because, as Thum argues, "as both a practice and an imagination, history shapes communal and individual identities, enacts and provides justifications for political projects, and serves as a continually re-created general framework for understanding the present" (2014, 7). The anthropology of history, as Palmié and Stewart envision it, is the anthropological study of the knowledge-production practices of non-historians, an ethnographically situated study of historical poetics, grounded in two assertions: first, that producing knowledge about the past is not limited to professional historians, and second, that people produce knowledge about the past in order to make sense of the present. Although most of the events discussed in this book took place in the past, this is a story about the present that traces how knowledge of the past is produced in the present, and what kinds of identities are imagined in doing so.

I make two further assertions: first, the stakes of this knowledge production are higher and the engagement with them more intense in indigenous, post-colonial, and post-authoritarian societies where history has been highly politicized and state violence has silenced alternative voices.

Second, I assert that religion and ritual are particularly conducive media within which to imagine alternative histories. Religious practices are grounded in and produce cosmologies, teleologies, and anthropologies—claims about the shape of the world, how time works, and what it means to be human.

These are the parameters within which "history" happens. In its cosmological and teleological capacities, religious practices are especially conducive to making sense of the world and time, and thus to making history.

My endeavor is both old and new. It seems painfully obvious that people have conceptions of past events and that the value they endow these events with situates both people and events within culturally specific conceptions of time and space. Ethnographies of post-socialism, rife with dead body politics (Gal 1991; Verdery 1999) and ghosts (Mueggler 2001; Buyandelgeriyn 2007), frequently address transformations in perceptions of time and history (Burawoy and Lukacs 1994; Watson 1994; Verdery 1996; Wanner 1998; Platz 2000; Ten Dyke 2000). Many anthropological studies of religion examine rituals and religious practice as loci of history-making, but the emphasis of the analyses have been on the rituals, not on the historical narratives produced in them. Rituals bring past forms into the present. Spirit possession can give voice to ancestors and historical figures. In colonial and post-colonial contexts, ritual is often presented as a historical genre of the colonized, offering forms of memory that stand as an alternative, and in opposition to, the official history of the colonizer (Bloch 1986; Kelly and Kaplan 1990; Comaroff and Comaroff 1992; Palmié 2002; Lambek 2003; Buyandelger 2013). And yet, as Palmié and Stewart argue, the anthropology of history has not yet solidified into a recognized sub-discipline (2016).

The need for a sub-discipline of anthropology that studies how people produce knowledge about the past is located at the intersection between two strands of scholarship. The first is the self-critique of historians such as Reinhart Koselleck (1985) and Hayden White (1987), who drew attention to the fact that even historians are interested in the past from the perspective of the present, and that the form in which history is told, the emplotment of the events that a history narrates, indelibly defines its content. More recently, Jaume Aurell (2015) has focused on the idea of historical genres, broadening his view of what counts as history to include popular genres such as historical re-enactments and video games. On the other hand, we have, beginning with Maurice Halbwachs (1992) and Paul Connerton (1989), the assertion that regular people also think about the past, under the theoretical framework of collective memory.

However useful the idea of collective memory may have once been, it has become stretched beyond recognition (Berliner 2005). Collective memory is productive in relationship to the study of how particular groups of people remember events that they lived through. Collective memory, however, rides an uncertain boundary between history and psychology, as if personal memory and representations of events are somehow comparable forms of data. It sets up a false dichotomy between the knowledge of the past produced by historians, which is textual and objective, and the knowledge of the past produced by non-historians, which is oral and personal. In literate or semi-literate societies, which would include most people today, textual sources used and produced by historians are part of the resources that people use in producing popular knowledge about the past. Textual sources are read, argued about, and used to authorize the historical knowledge production of ordinary people (see, e.g., Rappaport 1993). In some cases, textual sources are experienced orally by non- or semi-literate audiences, through reading aloud or performance, often in religious contexts (see Thum 2014). In other cases, such as in Buryatia, a highly literate population that has survived a century of heavy state censorship and alphabet reforms may supplement textual sources with oral histories.[7] When I sat in the state archives in Ulan-Ude, the people around me included history students writing dissertations, journalists doing research for personal interest stories, and people researching census records in the hope of identifying shamanic ancestors who had been repressed. Textual and oral forms of history-making inform and implicate each other in complicated and locally specific ways that undermine distinctions between "history" as an academic enterprise and "collective memory" as a popular one.

Collective memory also loses its utility when we begin to study how people "remember" events that happened long before their birth, such as when Buryats born in the last years of socialism explain the violence of Stalin's purges (1936–37) by comparing Stalin to Chinghis Khan (1162–1227), or when people use archival sources, such as Soviet census records, to produce knowledge about events and people that have been erased by the state. One of the key characteristics of history-making following the end of authoritarian state violence is the conviction that local knowledge of the past has been silenced. The past is experienced as a palpable absence, and textual sources such as state archives can be combined with religious prophecy and divination (as we will see in Chapters 1 and 4) or the testimony of ancestors embodied in shamanic trance (as in Chapters 5 and 6) to fill in the gaps left in textual sources. Neither traditional forms of historiography nor the analytic framework of collective memory is sufficiently nuanced to grapple with these kinds of historical poesis.

From the disciplinary perspective of traditional history, this kind of history often lacks the appropriate evidentiary standards. As Trouillot (1995) has argued, however, the preserved evidence that meets appropriate historical evidentiary standards tends to favor the narratives of states and people in power. Structures of power have produced silences that are being filled by these alternative forms of knowledge production. Different cultural and religious communities have different evidentiary criteria for knowledge about the past, and these criteria are situated within a history of power structures. It is useless to open ourselves to the culturally situated nature of historical knowledge production if we do not also recognize the culturally situated nature of evidentiary standards and the power structures that enforce them. Thus the need, as argued by Palmié and Stewart (2016), and seen in a flurry of new work on historicity and history-making (Routon 2008; Hodges 2010; Wirtz 2011; 2016; Bacigalupo 2016; Handman 2016; Lambek 2016 to list a few), for an anthropology of history.

Defining Our Terms: Bakhtin's Chronotopes

Reading an anthropology of history that describes current practices of history-making is often confusing because the ethnographer is writing about the way in which people are talking about the past. We are writing about past events, but instead of interrogating the truth of these past events (which would be a historian's job), we focus on the way in which people endow these past events with significance in the present. I suggest some terminology that I hope will help to make this distinction clearer.

J. L. Austin draws a distinction between the constative meaning of speech and the performative aspect of speech (1962). He does, in fact, note, that most speech acts exist on a continuum between these two poles, and contain both constative and performative meaning. Constative meaning is about the content of speech, and can be evaluated as true or false (e.g., "this is a table"—whatever you are pointing to either is a table or is not). In contrast, performative speech does something. The prototypical example is "I hereby pronounce you husband and wife," in which "I am not reporting on a marriage: I am indulging in it" (Austin 1962, 6). As Austin notes, these two speech acts are extremes that illustrate the concepts. In practice, most speech acts are both constative and performative at the same time.

I propose that this linguistic distinction, between constative and performative speech, can be mapped onto history-making as an activity, and in doing so provides us with a terminology that will allow us to parse the content from the performative value of stating that fact in a particular context. So for example, the historical fact that Buryat troops were at the battle of Stalingrad might be recounted in order to argue that "we have been proud members of the Soviet brotherhood of nations since the sacrificial moment that consecrated our union." Conversely, the same historical event (Buryat soldiers at Stalingrad) might be used to justify the claim "see how the Soviet Union was willing to exploit our soldiers in battles that had no bearing on our lives." The historical event occurred, but the rhetorical effect of referencing that event can change dramatically depending on the context in which it is evoked. The event occurred in the past, but the rhetorical, performative effect of producing knowledge about it, is very much about the present.

I therefore propose the following terminology, adapted from a combination of Austin (1962) and Bakhtin (1981). A historical genre is a mode of history-making. Like a literary genre, a genre of history-making has certain recognizable conventions, although these vary significantly across genres. A historical genre will have recognizable forms and its own evidentiary standards. These genres are made up of constative content (historical events), and the performative aspect of producing knowledge about these events, which I shall call, following Bakhtin, a "chronotope" (see also Bender and Wellbery 1991; Lemon 2009; Handman 2016; Wirtz 2016).

Bakhtin's idea of the chronotope, drawn from literary analysis, is particularly useful because a chronotope is a relationship between modes of time and space that act upon the characters within them. Does the particular historical time matter to the story, or is it merely a neutral backdrop against which the action takes place? Does one event in a story produce the next, or is the novel simply a series of random events? Does the hero remain the same throughout the story, or is her character transformed or revealed? Does a particular chronotope posit a Golden Age in the past, from which we have fallen, or is it working toward a utopian future? Or does everything take place at exactly the same moment, even if the reader encounters the information sequentially? Just as time can flow differently in a literary text, so our understanding of how time flows can vary across genres of historical-knowledge production.

Bakhtin's idea of the chronotope focuses not merely on the different ways time flows (linear, recursive, or concurrent) and how this time intersects with a landscape (national, local, universal, or animate), but also how the hero moves through these times and spaces and is shaped by them. The hero, in the instances I describe in this book, is the community imagined and produced through these rituals. While I am taking the descriptive terminology from Bakhtin, the contours of the chronotopes themselves—the relationship formed between subject, time, and space—are produced by the civic, shamanic, and Buddhist rituals I witnessed in Buryatia and will describe in the following chapters. These civic, Buddhist, and shamanic rituals all posit a community with profoundly different contours from one ritual context, one chronotope, to the next. Since none of these rituals produces a stable and bounded imagined community, no one conception of the Buryat nation emerges as dominant. Rather, each is experienced as uniquely realistic through the ritual, but fades into one of several imaginative possibilities as soon as the ritual ends. This is why the same person can recount one history of Buryatia at the Buddhist Maidari festival (see Chapter 4), and a completely different history to explain Victory Day festivities (see Chapter 2). Drawing further on my linguistic analogy, I refer to this as code-switching.

Applying the idea of the chronotope to practices of historical knowledge production allows us to examine the performative effects of producing knowledge about the past. In discussions of alternative historicities, indigenous chronotopes are usually placed in contrast to Western academic historicism, which is predicated on a linear concept of time, and "linear uniform causality" (Palmié and Stewart 2016, 212). However, as Palmié and Stewart point out, even in the West there are alternative popular forms of historicism that co-exist alongside academic historicism. This co-existence is also the case in Ulan-Ude.

Unlike the rural Buryat herders whom Ippei Shimamura (2011), Katherine Swancutt (2012), and Manduhai Buyandelger (2013) worked with, urban Buryats in Ulan-Ude live like contemporary residents of other big cities across the world. Many hold higher education degrees and work in educational, scientific, cultural, and medical fields. Western historicism (in its Marxist variant), with its linear uniform causality and a commitment to a teleology of progress, is their default historical genre. They learned this way of knowing the past in Soviet-era schools and universities, and use this genre in popular media. However, as they engage with religious rituals in a search for "cultural heritage," they encounter not merely new historical information, but older ways of experiencing time, which are both personally "new" and culturally "traditional." These rituals evoke, perform, and embody time in profoundly different ways, producing not only new historical knowledge but different chronotopes.

Why Ritual?

The idea that rituals form social conceptions of time and space, at least from within social scientific theory, goes back to Emile Durkheim, who posited that religious practice is the source of collective representations (1995, 10–11). The claim that ritual brings time and space into being clearly predates Durkheim within religious contexts. The idea that a being, human or otherwise, sang or danced the world into existence, and that certain rituals maintain the continued existence of the universe are extremely common. Durkheim, however, is, to my knowledge, the first to stake this claim as the basis of scientific theory. Durkheim's argument is that ritual brings society into being, and society is the origin of collective representations of time and space.

Very little seems to happen with this insight for quite a long time in anthropological theories of ritual as a result of the way in which ritual was conceptualized. From a functionalist perspective, ritual reaffirmed society's conceptions of time and space, while from a structuralist perspective, ritual represented it. Anthropologists from E. E. Evans-Pritchard (1940) to Roy Rappaport (1992) argued that ritual structured time, but this remained a relatively uninteresting insight so long as ritual was theorized to be primarily a representation. As interpretations of ritual move toward seeing ritual as producing bodies, subjectivities and social relations (see, e.g., Asad 1993b; Daniel 2002; Mahmood 2011), Durkheim's claim that ritual produces collective representations of time and space begins to become epistemologically and ontologically complicated. Does ritual produce a cultural representation of the underlying universal reality of time, or, since time is in the eye of the observer, does ritual actually produce time?

Frederique Apffel-Marglin pushes this theoretical ambiguity to its furthest conclusion when she claims, "I understand the performativity of rituals in terms of an alternative to the modernist epistemology of representationalism, where a pre-given reality is 'represented' by the human mind" (2011, 15). She argues that representationalism enables a western modernist discourse of science (which she is careful to distinguish from actual scientific theories of time) to lay claim to the exclusive ability to define the underlying reality, thereby disenfranchising other ways of knowing (see also Rifkin 2017). Ritual, for Apffel-Marglin, brings time and space into being. I must, however, confess, that as an anthropologist trained to think about discourse, I am not sure what it means to abandon the idea of representation. Bracketing questions about the underlying reality of time, I turn back to linguistically grounded analogies, specifically, Webb Keane's claim that "language is one medium by which the presence and activity of beings that are otherwise unavailable to the senses can be made presupposable, even compelling, in ways that are publically yet also subjectively available to people as members of social groups" (1997, 49). Language can make these beings presupposable through indexicality, by "pointing" to their presence. In a similar way I see ritual as making chronotopes presupposable by indexing them.

What I mean is similar to Erving Goffman's idea of "footing"—an underlying understanding of how time and space are organized that distinguish one genre from another (1979). This chronotopic footing may or may not be explicitly produced through the ritual or liturgical system, but it becomes visible through comparison. To say that rituals "do things," whether it is serving a social function, representing something, producing collectivities, transforming individuals or disciplining subjectivities, cannot always be usefully generalized. Any particular ritual may "do" any number of things, but being a form of human creative activity, rituals necessarily take place within particular conceptions of time, space, and subjectivity, and any ritual may index such conceptions to greater or lesser degrees, in different ways, and to different effect. In the particular post-Soviet context that I am examining, the performative value of the past is particularly powerful, the way in which rituals index their chronotopes takes center stage because the past is under construction.

Michael Silverstein argues that "the presumptively shared knowledge and beliefs of a group are accessed in a society's rituals under dynamic gestural (indexical) figuration. Ritual works in a kind of pictorial or iconic (specifically, diagrammatic) mode. Ritual as enacted traces a moving structure of indexical gestures toward the knowledge presupposed to be necessary to its own effectiveness in accomplishing something" (2004, 626; see also Tomlinson 2014). The rituals I describe here relate to their chronotopes in this way: Ritual actions, ritual speech, and speech around the rituals pointed to a particular chronotope. However, unlike in Silverstein's characterization, the chronotope to which participants pointed could not be presumed to be shared by everyone present. Sometimes speakers would invoke the chronotope and the historical events that characterized it explicitly in response to my questions, but I was not the only one asking questions. At both Buddhist and shamanic rituals participants asked about the proper way to do things, about what elements of the ritual meant, and why we were to do these things. They asked other participants, shamans or lamas or other professionals, and even from time to time, they asked me. The answers to these questions made the indexed chronotope explicit, producing it as shared cultural knowledge, instead of merely pointing to an already shared understanding. It is in this sense that I use the term "produced." Chronotopic presumptions inherent in the ritual form (e.g., that ancestors are co-present, or that a bodhisattva can exist and then return) become shared cultural conceptions through participation in the ritual, but the practice is always contingent and in dialog with other chronotopes.

Durkheim wrote from a context that presumed that a society ought to have a stable and unified sense of time and space. He diagnosed turn-of-the-century European society as sick because it did not, and fetishized Australian aboriginals because he presumed they retained a unified sense of time and space, when in fact the reverse is more likely to be true. Colonizing Europeans seem to have been singularly unimaginative in their conceptions of time and space, whereas populations subjected to colonial regimes were forced to confront multiple conceptions of time. As Apffel-Marglin's Peruvian interlocutors, like mine in Buryatia, demonstrate, an indigenous population that has been subject to state-sponsored acculturation and educational projects is understandably quite self-conscious about the conceptions of time and space that the state desires them to inhabit in contrast to the ones that their grandparents did. Re-introducing rituals as projects of cultural revitalization can be seen as reversing the ethnographic process. If the ethnographer takes habitus and turns it into symbolic representation, ritual revitalization projects seek to take symbolic representations and turn them into habitus.

While this might, at first glance, appear to be "invented tradition," I do not find this label particularly useful (Hobsbawm and Ranger 1983). As Ronald Grimes argues, all traditions are to some degree invented and "improvisation and revision are essential parts of many, if not most, ritual traditions" (1992, 33; see also Lindquist 2005). Civic rituals such as Victory Day and City Day are explicitly and self-consciously designed by their organizers, and the Buddhist and shamanic rituals I describe are not invented so much as redesigned versions drawn from ethnographic materials and ritual manuals. They are old rituals self-consciously adapted to new contexts. Furthermore, my analysis does not focus on how they are re-imagined by their participants, but rather on the chronotopes they index.

Using the term "genre" to describe ways of speaking and thinking about the past opens up an analogy with the way people code-switch between speech genres. Chapter 1 describes the way people can code-switch between historical genres within a single ritual. Rather than thinking of history-making as a search for a single truth about the past, examining historical genres enables us to see the ways in which the past becomes a resource for understanding the present. Just as speech genres enable people to mark different modes of sociality, code-switching between historical genres enables different relationships to the past. Since each historical genre has a unique chronotope, each genre enables an alternative perspective from which to render events meaningful, enabling different methods of explaining a present that had become increasingly inexplicable. Contemporary social problems that make no sense from a linear, causative reading of history can be re-interpreted as the karmic legacy of past violence, the wrath of forgotten ancestors, or the fulfillment of prophecy.

For example, I argue that history-making around the miraculously preserved body of Etigelov can occur in several different genres.[8] One of these genres I call a Buddhist genre, and it is primarily produced by official representatives of the Traditional Buddhist Sangha, the oldest Buddhist institution in Buryatia. Within this genre, time has a recursive, double-layered quality. One layer is the chronological linear time of the Russian imperial state, and the second is recursive, in which Etigelov repeatedly returns to the first timeline through reincarnation. As a reincarnate lama, Etigelov appeared in Buryatia as Zaiaev, the very first leader of Buryat Buddhists, in the 18th century; returned as himself in the early 20th century; and then returned in the 21st as his miraculously preserved body, folding time into cyclical returns, in which the present and the past fulfill each other. This perspective endows Russian national linear time with a Buddhist theological interpretation that produces the Buryat landscape and the Buryat nation as an intersection between Russia and Asia. New meaning is revealed that has already always been there. Buddhist memorializing practices, such as building stupas and rebuilding temples, reveal the hidden Buddhist histories of a landscape that only appears to have been secular.

This stands in stark contrast to a Soviet historical genre, within which time is linear and progressive, moving toward greater modernity manifested in scientific understanding, which can be measured in material, observable phenomenon. Soviet histories are histories told through graphs of grain production quotas and photographs of war heroes, and grounded in the social constructs of Soviet life: the collective farm, the nationality, the state. The "hero" of this genre is also the Buryat nation, but unlike its Buddhist counterpart, this Buryat nation is a "backward" Siberian nationality that entered "modernity" by participating in the Soviet brotherhood of nations. The reality of this genre is reinforced through the contours of a daily life lived in the institutional structures, buildings, and streets produced by the Soviet century and the memory of World War II as the sacrificial moment in which the violence of the Stalinist state was redeemed. However, even though it is a familiar genre, some of the people who told me this history endowed the historical events with a sharp criticism, using the Soviet genre to produce the Buryat nation as a colonized people whose history had been stolen from them. Linear, utopian, and familiar, this historical genre produces silences that the other genres seek to fill.

The shamanic genre stands in contrast to both Buddhist and Soviet genres. The past is constantly co-present in the form of ancestors in the spirit world who are coexisting social actors, whose will and intentions continue to act on the bodies of the living, and who must be taken into account when the living make plans. The shamanic past is both past and an unseen dimension of the present. The Buryat nation imagined through shamanic rituals is connected through genealogical and genetic ties that include ethnic Russians and other nationalities. The Buryat nation that is the "hero" of this story is a Central Asian nomadic indigenous people whose heritage reaches back to Chinghis Khan.

Although I discuss these genres separately, in order to make them clear to the reader, the boundaries between them are fuzzy. These chronotopes are, following my linguistic analogy, produced performatively and indexically through ritual and other types of human interaction. They do not exist as webs of signification floating above actor's heads. Therefore, as I show in Chapter 1, they can and do coexist side by side, intertwining and in dialog with each other.

The dead are present in all three genres (Buddhist, Soviet, and shamanic). Most obviously, the *ongons* who enter the bodies of shamans are their dead shamanic ancestors. Etigelov, as a bodhisattva, may not in fact be dead, but he is not exactly alive either, and it is this ontological uncertainty that makes him compelling. The dead are less vocal in the civic rituals of Victory Day and City Day, grounded as these are in Soviet modernist material discourse, but an awareness of ancestors and the causes they died for is nonetheless central to these celebrations. As Verdery (1999) has argued, dead body politics are an effective medium for debating questions of who and what a community is.

Recent ontological approaches encourage anthropologists to consider the agency of nonhuman actors, but these are, in all three historical genres, human actors, so attributing agency to them hardly seems radical, and has a long tradition in anthropological analysis (Hallowell 1940). It must also be remembered that the living do not simply do the will of the dead; they attempt to discern the agency of the dead through signs, argue about these signs, and then decide what to think about them. Debates rage within anthropology about the utility of taking interactions with spirits "at face value" or seeing them as expressive of underlying political and economic concerns (White 2013; Graeber 2015). I have tried here to walk the uneasy tightrope of middle ground in that these interactions with spirits and bodies occur in a sociocultural context that constantly argues about what taking them at face value might mean. I have seen my task as describing the debates that Buryats and other residents of Buryatia have about these encounters and the histories they produce, not in order to fix Buryat ontological claims about spirits but rather to understand the post-Soviet secular sociocultural and political context within which these claims are made and debated.

Ritual Materiality and Secular Embodiment

The underlying question that drives Buryat engagement with the past in these rituals is the question, "who are we?" That question is not unique to religious contexts and is rooted in the particular and profoundly unstable socioeconomic and political conditions of a post-Soviet national minority republic with a marginal economy. When I worked in Buryatia in the early 2000s, people were preoccupied with healing because they were sick and their access to healthcare was unstable. Although the economic situation had improved by a return trip in 2012, the underlying sense of social and economic instability continued. Their sense of instability was proven correct when the ruble collapsed again in 2014.

The transition from socialism to neo-liberal Russia was experienced as a transition from a world with limited but relatively stable possibilities, into one with vast theoretical possibilities, but few resources and unstable institutions. The economy, healthcare, the legal status of the republic within the Russian Federation, the social position of Buryats within a newly Russian nation-state, and the possibilities of knowing the past were all profoundly unstable, and this context is essential to the questions that Buryats are exploring through rituals. Religious institutions were similarly unstable, and religious practices were one of many of the relatively new possibilities available at the time.

"Who are we?"; "where did we come from?"; and "where are we going?" are classic cosmological questions. However, most people who were asking these questions in a religious context in Ulan-Ude were coming to these rituals from a Soviet secular background. As Buyandelger, (who has also published under Buyandelgeriyn, 2007, 2013) found with Buryat shamans in Mongolia, while socio-economic and political questions prompt people's engagements with ritual, these rituals do not always, or even often, resolve their questions. Instead they often raise new problems and produce logics that take on lives of their own. Buyandelger argues that rural Buryats in Mongolia turn to shamans to resolve economic problems and inadvertently produce histories. Among urban Buryats within the Russian Federation, I argue that people turn to rituals to find solutions to quotidian problems, out of curiosity or kinship obligation, and through these rituals produce different genres of history and different chronotopes. Producing multiple conceptions of time and history further destabilizes already unstable imaginary constructs, but also offers creative resources for rethinking the questions of who they are and where they are going.

There are threads of continuity, however, which weave through these different genres, despite the code-switching. These threads are a secular discourse of proof and doubt, grounded in a rhetoric of materiality. Conversations with spirits as they inhabit the bodies of shamans; medical tests performed on the preserved body of Etigelov; and the physical symptoms of illness are read as evidence of the veracity of truth claims made in these genres, providing subjects with a sense of stability within shifting chronotopes. Grounded in the embodied sensory and material experience of ritual, stories of the past are anchored in the embodied materiality of the present, lending them a pre-discursive, materialist, and scientific "aura of factuality" (Geertz 1973). As Asad (1993) points out, however, auras of factuality are produced through power, and the aura of factuality produced by materiality plays on and with secular conceptions of scientific evidence.

By focusing on rituals, I engage with contemporary concerns about the role of materiality and matter in the world. Rituals, especially the kinds of rituals I describe, are above all else, embodied sensory experiences. Bodies move through space; hear chanting, singing, and drumming; speak to spirits, recite mantras, smell incense, and taste the vodka that is offered to other-than-human beings. However, my subjects engage with materiality in much the same way as some ontologically focused anthropologists, by providing the possibility of connecting to a reality that transcends discourse, that will give them "knowledge" rather than "belief." However, as David Graeber argues in his critique of the ontological turn, "reality is that which can never be fully encompassed in our imaginative constructs" (Graber 2015, 28). Just as "reality" for Graeber is characterized by the "stubborn . . . immediate unpredictability, ultimate unknowability of the physical environment that surrounds us" (Graeber 2015, 28), so too, for my Buryat interlocutors, proof that something was "real" was generally constituted by the fact that it could be experienced but not explained. One could observe that Etigelov's body was not decaying. One could (and in fact people did) prove that it was not decaying in a laboratory, but no one could explain it. The inability of scientific imaginative constructs to explain material evidence became proof that another imaginative construct (whether that be the theological arguments presented by members of the Traditional Buddhist Sangha or the idiosyncratic speculations of pilgrims, shamans, historians, and taxi drivers) might be true, and the possibility of the truth of these imaginative constructs became the justification for human actions, even as they all entertained and debated the possibility that these imaginative constructs might be just imaginary.

In a period of prolonged ideological, political, social, and economic inexplicability, rituals both conjure up multifaceted explanations of the world and allow people to act in the world without committing to one imaginative construct. Am I reviving the argument that post-Soviet subjects turned to religion to fill the ideological vacuum produced by the collapse of Soviet ideology? Yes and no. I do not believe we should dismiss the fact that our post-Soviet interlocutors consistently tell us that they turned to religion to fill the ideological vacuum, but I do not think we should read this statement at face value. If historians and anthropologists like Alexei Yurchak (2006) are to be believed, Soviet ideology had ceased to provide a comprehensive worldview to anyone long before the collapse of the USSR as a political entity. It is true, however, that as the political and economic institutions of the USSR became something else in the post-Soviet period, life became increasingly inexplicable. To many people living in that inexplicability, religion became a resource worth trying.

Indigeneity and the Stakes of History in Buryatia

Ethnographies usually offer a history of the place they are written about to help orient the reader. However, that can privilege the Western, academic, linear genre of history in contrast to alternative religious and indigenous chronotopes. It establishes the history in the introduction as the "real history" against which we will measure the histories that my interlocutors produce. I do not want to take sides.

The reader may find this disorienting; I intend it to be. Instead, I offer some information (in part historical, and I am aware of the irony) that may help explain what is at stake in Buryat history-making projects. Buryats are an indigenous population, and the survivors of Stalin's purges and decades of Soviet social engineering. For both indigenous populations and post-authoritarian societies—more so than for other populations—to write or speak a history is a political act.

Rubie Watson (1994, 1) argues that "[u]nder state socialism, Marxism-Leninism was not one ideology or political economy among many, but rather was the inevitable and glorious outcome of a discernable historical process. If one of the primary justifications of communist rule is its inevitability, then the production of history takes on tremendous significance—political, ideological, and moral." The communist project rested on a teleology that made the present merely a moment on the path toward a radiant utopian future. History, even academic history, was not merely an account of past events, but rather a meaningful structure that situated present citizens in relationship to a "backward" past and a "radiant" future. While historians such as White (1987) and Koselleck (1985) remind us that all history is a story written from a present perspective, the political consequences for historical narratives are heightened in political regimes such as communist or colonial ones, in which political interventions are justified through teleologies of progress. Teleologies of progress are effective tools of governance because people identify with them and aspire to their goals. When the Soviet Union was dissolved, people mourned the loss of the radiant future toward which their everyday was directed, more than they mourned the admittedly mediocre living conditions of late socialism (Burawoy and Lukacs 1994; see also Paxson 2005, 99; Shimamura 2011, 69).

The end of the Soviet Union produced an intense interest in history both among former Soviet citizens and ethnographers of the period. Early ethnographic accounts such as Watson's edited collection (1994) focused on oppositional histories produced when socialist states still retained the power to control, or at least aspire to control, public discourse. Other accounts focus on the new histories of successor states (Gal 1991; Wanner 1998; Verdery 1999; Platz 1996, 2000; Pelkmans 2006; Adams 2010; Buyandelgeriyn 2007, 2013). In many of these states the new government and native intellectuals were able to articulate national histories in opposition to the Soviet experience, which they saw as imposed from outside, or to excise the Soviet experience, as an anomaly, from the longer trajectory of national history (Verdery 1999, 116–17). In Russia, in contrast, the Russian Federation's relationship to the Soviet Union was far more ambiguous (Oushakine 2000, see also 2009; Boym 2001; Paxson 2005; Wertsch 2000, 2002). In many provincial areas, including most of Siberia, pre-Soviet life was so radically different from the present that even those who seek pre-Soviet continuity cannot excise the Soviet century from their narrative.

In Buryatia, as in other autonomous republics with non-ethnically-Russian titular nationalities, revising historical narratives became intertwined with questions of ethno-national identity. Here, Soviet nationality policies intersect with the colonizing projects of other western states; the theoretical lens of indigeneity reveals crucial similarities (as well as instructive differences) between colonial timelines that produce indigenous peoples as primitive, backward, and less-than-fully modern. Within the Soviet version of the Marxist teleology of progress, Siberian peoples were discursively marked as the most "backward" of all Russia's inhabitants. The Soviet Union's unique historical task was to bring modernity, progress, and enlightenment to all its citizens, but as the most "backward" the stakes of this modernization were especially high for Siberian indigenous peoples (Slezkine 1992, 1994; Grant 1995; Skrynnikova, Batomunkuev, and Varnavskii 2004; Chakars 2014).

On paper, Soviet nationality policies were ethnically neutral. Lenin and Stalin sought to distinguish Soviet nationality policy from its imperial predecessors by explicitly opposing what Lenin termed "great Russian chauvinism," the belief that Russian culture was superior to that of other nationalities (Lenin 1975a, 1975b, 1975c). Union republics, autonomous republics, and ethnic okrugs were established to allow nationalities self-determination. These territories were defined in relationship to their "titular" nationality, and the status of the territory depended on how developed that nationality was deemed to be.[9] In practice, however, since "Soviet progress" built on preexisting imperial discourses of backwardness and was usually delivered in the

Russian language by ethnic Russians, Soviet modernization must be examined within an ethnic context (Skrynnikova, Batomunkuev, and Varnavskii 2004, 2–5). In practice, just as assimilation meant culture loss for indigenous populations around the world, Soviet modernization meant becoming more like Russians.

In 1991, the Soviet Union became the Russian Federation, and Yeltsin famously declared that national republics should take all the autonomy they could swallow. While the Union republics became independent countries, autonomous republics, such as Buryatia, did not have the right to secede. Nonetheless, they retained a separate legislature, a president, and a limited amount of autonomy in internal affairs. Despite massive ideological, political, and economic changes, the state institutions that structured daily life remained relatively stable. As one Buryat friend cynically noted, the sign on the door changed, but the person behind the desk was usually the same. However, the ideological legitimacy of political, economic, and social structures was profoundly destabilized. Initially, perestroika appeared to offer the potential for national cultural revival, but projects to support and fund Buryat culture and language that were officially approved by the republic's legislature were subsequently underfunded and faltered. Religion re-entered the public sphere with enthusiasm, but no one—not scholars, priests, or laypeople—was quite sure what to make of the apparently sudden return of religion.

Like other autonomous republics within the Russian Federation, Buryatia has its own president, its own legislature, and limited autonomy. That autonomy has been even more limited since 2004, when President Vladimir Putin passed a law that regional governors and presidents were to be appointed, rather than elected. In the 2010 census, Buryats represented approximately 29.5 percent of the republic's 972,021 residents.[10] Like other native Siberian populations, they are a demographic minority within their own republic, where 62.16 percent of the population is ethnically Russian.

The Buryats with whom I worked and lived in Ulan-Ude in 2004–5, and again in 2012, are, for the most part, urban, secular, and educated post-Soviet subjects who are, at the same time, members of an indigenous minority nationality. A majority of Buryats, and many ethnic Russians in Buryatia, were deeply interested and invested in reviving and rediscovering their "traditional culture," their national language, and their "religious traditions," as well as their connections to a broader Mongolian culture area, but they often described themselves as interested precisely because these things had been "lost," reproducing and revaluing Soviet and Western tropes about indigeneity, even as they sought to inhabit the category.

I am staking a somewhat contradictory claim. I want to use the idea of indigeneity as a theoretical lens, without taking sides on whether or not Buryats are an indigenous people. Although I find it productive to think about Buryats as indigenous, not all Buryats identify as such. Some Buryats (including many shamans) see themselves as indigenous, and actively seek out connections and comparisons to other indigenous groups. The majority of Buryats accept Soviet state categories out of habit, thinking of themselves as a nationality, and by contrast think of what the Soviets called the "numerically small peoples of the north," such as the Evenki of northern Siberia, as indigenous. Others—often Buddhists and Buryat nationalists—are actively opposed to the category of indigeneity, and see themselves as a Mongolian diaspora population or an Asian nation.

Whether or not Buryats should be considered indigenous is a complicated question. In many cases, who should be considered indigenous appears fairly self-evident, obscuring the ways in which this category is constructed and contested in practice. The United Nations Permanent Forum for Indigenous Issues offers guidelines, but explicitly refuses to define who should count or not count as indigenous precisely because the stakes of being recognized as belonging to the category can be very high ("Indigenous Peoples, Indigenous Voices Factsheet," n.d.). Instead, the UN Forum encourages self-determination, which acknowledges that a group may consider themselves to be indigenous, even if they are not recognized as such by the state in which they live. However, the historical conditions under which Buryats and Buryat territories were colonized by and incorporated into the Russian empire complicate the ways in which Buryats might identify as indigenous.[11]

I consider Buryats to be indigenous in the sense that they are the long-standing occupants of lands that have since been brought under the political control of larger nation-states (Russia, Mongolia, and China) that are dominated by other ethnic groups. In addition, there is a strong relationship between land and Buryat identity, at the personal, family, regional, and national levels. Although it has been nearly a century since most Buryats in Russia practiced pastoral nomadism, land remains key to identity in symbolic ways, from annual clan offering rituals to an intense concern with the 1937 partition of the republic during Stalin's purges.[12]

However, although Buryat territories were incorporated into the Russian empire, they were not done so in a way that produced the Buryats as an autonomous political entity separate from the imperial state. Initially, Russian Cossacks entered into an existing system of Central Asian tributary relationships. The Russian tsar was simply another *khan* to whom payment was due in exchange for protection from other *khanates*. Individual

Buryat clans paid tribute to different khans. After the borders between the Romanov and Qing empires were set by the 1689 Treaty of Nerchinsk and the 1727 Treaty of Kiakhta, theoretically those clans on the Russian side were subjects of the Russian tsar and owed him tribute, but movement across the border continued. Mikhail Speransky's 1822 reforms established a form of indirect rule, codifying local clan leaders as official members of the "steppe duma," thereby incorporating the Buryats into the existing structures of the imperial government (Hundley 1984). As Buryats and Buryat territories were increasingly brought under the control of the Russian empire, they were incorporated under a system modeled on the Ottoman empire, in which religious affiliation stood for ethnic identity and determined the legal status of individuals. Religious conversion produced a change in legal status (Kappeler 1992; Slezkine 1994; Brower and Lazzerini 1997; Schorkowitz 2001a, 2001b; Khodarkovsky 2002; Werth 2002, 2016; Murray 2012). Therefore, Buryats who converted to Christianity became "peasants" (*krest'iane*) rather than "internal foreigners" (*inorodtsy*).[13] Unlike a treaty system, which negotiates the relationship between two sovereign entities, Buryats were incorporated into the empire as clan groups or as individuals, and were incorporated into legal systems that applied across the empire. Buryat was produced as a nationality through intellectual and bureaucratic categories of race and religion, but not as an independent political entity. The Buryat republic itself was not a territorial entity until the fledgling Bolshevik government established it in 1923.

At present, Buryats are too numerous to be considered "indigenous" under Russian law, as that status is reserved for the numerically small peoples of the North. Under Soviet law, as the titular nationality of a republic, Buryats had a special status, but only in relationship to their territory (Martin 2001; Hirsch 2005). This produced an ambiguity, in that each republic's government is supposed to represent "its" titular nationality, as well as its non-titular residents. Within this system, there was no legal difference between Siberian peoples, who were numerical minorities within their republics, and other nationalities (such as Chechens, Tatars, or Tuvans), who are numerical majorities within their republics. As Soviet-era forms of affirmative action within national republics were dismantled, the demographic differences between those republics where the titular nationality is in the majority and those where it is in the minority became starkly evident. Representative democracy sharply disadvantages Siberian populations. Since much of the literature on Soviet nationalities focuses on policy, it uses the categories of "national minority," which apply across these populations, obscuring the sharp differences between their historical experiences under both imperial and Soviet rule.

However, as a consequence of Soviet nationality policies, most Buryats think of themselves as a "nationality" and associate the term "indigenous" with the "numerically small nationalities of the North," such as the Evenki or Soyot, who also live in the Republic of Buryatia. Since the United Nations Working Group on Indigenous Affairs stresses self-identification as a central feature of indigeneity, the fact that Buryats do not consistently self-identify as indigenous fundamentally undermines the claim that they are. Due to the particular history of political incorporation, there is no political leadership, such as a tribal government, that would have the authority to make such a claim on behalf of the whole population.[14]

Given this ambiguity, I wish to use the idea of indigeneity as a theoretical lens without staking a claim. Whether or not Buryats should be considered indigenous is up to Buryats. However, seeing them as indigenous highlights their political situation, and their ability to draw on indigenous subject positions, even though at other times they refuse this identity. I use the lens of indigeneity to highlight the way in which, as a people living on "their" territory controlled by the political and institutional structures of a nation-state that is not "theirs," Buryat forms of historical knowledge production are always subject to the forces of the state. Authoritative, state-sponsored versions of history are formulated from a Russian perspective. As we shall see, this does not mean that all histories are Russian histories. They most emphatically are not. But this power structure shapes the possibilities of historical knowledge production and emphasizes the political nature and the stakes of history-making.

Furthermore, I suggest that the uncomfortable fit of Buryats within the category of indigenous suggests that this category is more constructed than we usually perceive it to be, and therefore Buryatia can offer an instructive comparison. Often, popular perspectives (and sometimes academic literature) present indigenous and Western groups in opposition, reifying the West (modernity) vs. the Rest (tradition), even though these are more properly seen as discursive subject positions that in turn limit and enable the projects of the people who inhabit them. Indigenous peoples are no less modern, but they occupy different subject positions within modernity. The study of historical knowledge production in post-Soviet Ulan-Ude breaks down these oppositions and shows how they are implicated within and entangled with each other.

As post-Soviet residents of Buryatia re-examined and re-imagined the Soviet teleology of progress, they necessarily also re-examined existing ideas about ethnicity and national identity. Local ethnographers Amogolonova, Elaeva, and Skrynnikova (2005, 7) argue:

> In post-Soviet identificatory discourse Buryat history is re-examined as that of a Siberian aboriginal people (*narod*) and as a Soviet socialist nation (*natsiia*): negative motifs of colonization, humiliation of national dignity and cultural assimilation, and at the same time the tendency to construct new identities is strengthened, the resources and basis therefore are provided by the glorious pages of history and within which one can notice the place taken by the mythologization of the historical past (before the unification with Russia in the 17th century) and its personages.

While local ethnographers and historians both re-examine the past and study the ways in which their colleagues do so, most local scholarship takes the category of "Buryat" for granted. As Yuri Slezkine (1996) and Ronald Suny (1993) have argued, Soviet bureaucratic practices and the "ethnos theory" that dominated late Soviet social sciences (Bromley 1975, 1980; Gellner et al. 1975, 1980; Dragadze 1975) reified nationality categories.[15] However, as I encountered these categories in the field, it became evident that they are much more fluid. "Buryat" and "Russian" are labels that people in Buryatia assign easily to individuals, but it rapidly became clear to me that these were place markers. The collectivities these labels referenced shifted depending on context. It was not merely that the state no longer authorized the official Soviet historical narrative or that people were no longer convinced by Soviet narratives. In fact, people continued to rely on these narratives. Rather, the referent of these histories had been destabilized.

Are new histories to be the history of the multi-ethnic and multi-religious republic? The Republic of Buryatia is the successor state to the Buryat Soviet Socialist Autonomous Republic (BASSR), and as a national republic, Buryatia is nominally the political entity that represents the Buryat nation. As a political entity, however, the BASSR had no pre-Soviet existence. Of the nearly 60 percent of the population that identify as ethnic Russians, many are descendants of Old Believer Orthodox exiles who consider Buryatia their homeland (Russ.—*rodina*), while others were brought to Buryatia to "build socialism" during the Soviet period and do not share this sense of belonging. Therefore, there is no self-evident identity around which to construct a history of the Republic of Buryatia, and any history that reached past 1937 would have to include territories that no longer belong to the republic.

In addition, by 2005 many Buryats felt that the boundaries of their republic were under threat. There was widespread debate about the continued existence of the republic (Graber and Long 2009; Peers 2009; Murray 2012, ix–xiv). Under proposed administrative reforms, several national okrugs (administrative units smaller than a republic) were to be dissolved into the surrounding non-national oblasts (administrative units larger than a republic), including the Ust-Orda Buryat okrug, which was dissolved into Irkutsk oblast in 2008. In 2005 the dissolution of Ust-Orda was already planned, but most people considered Aga's status to be safe. Referendums were held to determine the fate of both okrugs, but since national minority populations are by definition minorities, the results of each referendum were a foregone conclusion (Graber and Long 2009). Although as of 2005 there was no concrete plan to dissolve the Buryat republic, fears that autonomous status would be lost, and debates over what that would mean, were widespread. In addition, the president, Leonid Potapov, was planning to retire. Although many Buryat intellectuals were sharply critical of Potapov, others told me that because Potapov was an ethnic Russian who was raised by a Buryat family, he was widely perceived as a "compromise candidate" who avoided polarizing Russians and Buryats. He was also a familiar figure, who had overseen Buryatia's transition from Autonomous Soviet Socialist Republic into post-Soviet republic. In 2005 newspapers were speculating that the administrator of the Aga okrug, a Buryat, was favored to replace Potapov. In 2006, however, Putin appointed Viacheslav Vladimirovich Nagovitsyn, an ethnic Russian from outside Buryatia, to the position. Two years later, the Aga Buryat Autonomous Okrug was dissolved into Chita oblast, further confirming fears that the Republic of Buryatia would be next. Within this context of institutional instability, to tell a history of Buryatia meant to take a stand on who Buryats were, whom the republic represented, and whether it should continue to exist. To tell a history meant to take a stand in the present from which to imagine a future. The result is a shifting field of arguments about the past that refer to different imaginaries of "Buryatness." The "us" referenced in religious and civic rituals were imagined communities that people invoked to make particular arguments, but which were undermined or re-imagined in different contexts. As a result, they did not produce stable communities or identities.

This fluidity may be a good thing. From the perspective of a nation-state, stable identities sound positive, but I suspect that fluid identities have contributed to the absence of explicit inter-ethnic conflict in Buryatia in the Putin era. It is difficult, if not impossible, to make an explicit argument about absence, nor do I want to presume that inter-ethnic conflict is a norm from which Buryatia deviates. At the same time, both Russian and Buryat residents of the republic often contrasted Buryatia to the Caucasus, by saying "here, thank God, everything is quiet" (Russ.—*zdes, slava Bogu, vce spokoino*). As further discussed in Chapter 3, residents of Buryatia are very aware of inter-ethnic conflict in other areas of the Soviet Union and offer various local explanations, including the calming effect of Lake Baikal's sacred energy or a long history of inter-ethnic coexistence. Luehrmann, discussing similar ethics in the multi-religious republic of Mari-El, refers to these habits as "neighborliness" (2011, 27). I suspect that people's abilities to identify with histories that include their neighbors of different ethnic affiliations may contribute to this ethic of neighborliness.

Methodology: Rituals, Historical Genres, and the Nature of the Data

Each of the following chapters presents a ritual, and describes the history produced and referenced by that ritual. Although I use the rituals to explain and illustrate the historical genres that are produced, these histories are not produced only through these rituals. The rituals do not perform a particular event from the past, as, for example, Easter Passion processions or the Shia Muslim ritual of Muharram. History is not that explicit in Buryatia. Rather, the rituals both presume and produce knowledge about past events, thereby indexing, enacting, producing, and reaffirming different chronotopes. I use the rituals as a lens to refract these chronotopes, but in doing so, I draw on stories about the past that I was told during the rituals as well as in other contexts. In part, these histories were produced through the ethnographic encounter, in that I kept asking my interlocutors to explain what was happening and they would answer me by offering an historical explanation. Etigelov is important, they would say, because he was a pre-Soviet leader of the Buddhist community. Shamans would tell me that they must speak to their client's ancestors because the ancestors are angry that their descendants stopped worshiping them during the Soviet times. My analysis is discursive—I focus on the descriptions and narratives of my interlocutors. I aim to show how particular stories about groups, times, and places are indexed within these rituals.

The knowledge about the past produced by these rituals is fragmentary (see also Winter 1995; Cole 2001). None of the rituals that I discuss recounts a history of Buryatia from beginning to end. The purpose of these rituals is always different: to honor a deity, initiate a shaman, inaugurate an office. From a methodological perspective, however, I use these rituals as lenses to focus our attention on different historical genres. Rituals, as discussed above, index historical events, thereby evoking and producing the chronotopes within which these events are made meaningful. These indexes are often material as well as verbal. Images of the past are evoked in the ceremonies, such as wartime photographs during Victory Day or chronologies of Pandito Khambo

Lamas at the Ivolginsky *datsan*, and through their materiality, give weight to the narrative presented around them. Ancestral spirits manifest in bodies to ask why they have been forgotten. The ancestors do not narrate the past, but the living understand the question within the context of a history of state socialism where rituals were not observed and ancestral obligations forgotten. In Buryatia, ritual indexes and plays with the past; it does not always narrate it.

This presents a methodological dilemma. How do I write about this form of poesis for an audience that does not know these histories? As will become clear in the following chapters, the answer varies depending on the context, just as the past varies depending on the ritual being observed. My data also varies; I went to Buryatia to study Buddhist and shamanic rituals. I attended Victory Day and City Day festivities merely out of curiosity. It was only later that I realized I could not tell the versions of history that are presented in Buddhist and shamanic rituals without telling the secular and Soviet histories that the religious histories speak against. The civic rituals present the "common knowledge" version of history in Buryatia; they are important because they remind us why these versions of history remain compelling. However, because they were not the initial focus of my research, the nature of my field data was somewhat different for the Buddhist and shamanic rituals.

For each chapter I have relied on the classic Geertzian paradigm of thick description (Geertz 1973). I have tried to limit my data, and my descriptions, to the way in which the past is evoked by people in Buryatia in the present. However, there are places where what people do and say only makes sense within the context of greater background knowledge, and in these places I have filled in gaps from secondary sources. I have tried, in each instance, to make the distinctions and the sources as clear as possible.

My training is in post-Soviet ethnography, the anthropology of religion, and Soviet nationality policies, not Mongolian studies. This training offers a particular theoretical slant, one that emphasizes the Soviet context and de-emphasizes continuities with Mongolian cultural forms, such as Mongolian kinship structures and religious practices.[16] In part, my own training points to the way in which Cold War institutions shaped area studies, dividing Russian and Eastern European studies from East Asian studies, focusing on the political centers and relegating Mongolia and Central Asia to a theoretical periphery. The theoretical lens developed through my training was amplified by my interlocutors, whose daily frames of reference were primarily Soviet. Although the methods varied over time, beginning in the 1930s, when Buriyat cultural leaders were executed for harboring pan-Mongolian sympathies, to the 1950s when the term "Mongolian" was dropped from the name of the Republic, the Soviet state worked to de-emphasize the previously intimate connections between Buryatia and the wider Mongolian world. For most urban Buryats in Ulan-Ude, Mongolian cultural forms are an object of desire, the cultural heritage they are working to recover. The rituals I document are one of many ways in which they are reconnecting themselves to this wider Mongolian world.

This book is based on field research conducted in Ulan-Ude and a few surrounding areas, in the summer of 2003; twelve months in 2004–5; and a three-month return trip in 2012. Much of my data is from observing rituals and from discussing rituals with people during and after they took place. All but one of the rituals described in the following chapters were public events, open to anyone. Although in the shamanic and one of the Buddhist cases I knew the organizers and in all cases I had permission to be there, these were not the kind of rituals that you had to be a member of a community to attend. Only the shamanic initiation ritual, described in Chapter 6, is a private ritual. In this case Yuri, the initiate, and his family invited me and knew that I would be writing about the event.

Some of my data is from formal interviews, but for various reasons, formal interviews were difficult to conduct. A great deal of my data is from careful notes on conversations held on the margins of rituals, circumstances where recording was impossible and with people whom I did not manage to meet again. I spent many hours at the Tengeri shamans' offices talking to whoever was around. Given the ambient noise from ceremonies and consultations around me, I soon abandoned attempts to record these as well, but took copious notes.

Informed consent is easy to obtain when conducting formal interviews. Conversations with strangers at rituals are harder to evaluate, and so I use pseudonyms for anyone from whom I did not get explicit, written permission to use their real name. That said, everyone I spoke to knew who I was and what I was doing there. In 2001, 2003, and 2004–5 there were still relatively few foreigners in Ulan-Ude, and very few who stayed as long as I did. After a few months, many people I had never met seemed to know who I was and what I was doing. In addition, urban Buryats are, on average, very well educated. Many of the people I spoke with had college or graduate degrees or had a relative who was completing a thesis of their own. I therefore considered that a minimum level of informed consent had been met, even when I was not able to read a formal statement about my intentions. Many people I spoke to were very explicit: "write this down" they would say, pointing to my notebook, "this is important."

I was lucky enough to be in the field with my husband, who is a photographer. His photographs illustrate this text and also provided the opportunity to discuss the rituals in detail afterward with some of the participants. In the case of both Buddhist and shamanic rituals, I knew (at least some of) the organizers, and obtained explicit permission to attend and for my husband to photograph the rituals. We gave copies of the photographs my husband took to the Tengeri shamans' organization and to representatives of the Etigelov Institute, and they explicitly allowed all the photographs included here. In general, photographing Etigelov and inside the temples at Ivolginsky monastery is not allowed. The one photograph of Etigelov included in this book was explicitly approved for publication in the *Moscow Times* and in my future publications by the then head of the Traditional Sangha, Pandito Khambo Lama Damba Badmaevich Aiusheev.

Prior to attending graduate school, I worked for a museum, inventorying and consulting with representatives of Native American nations to identify and repatriate collections that were subject to the 1991 law on Native American Graves Protection and Repatriation. As a result, I went to the field with the presumption that ritual behavior would be subject to secrecy, and that much of it I would not be allowed to witness, share, or represent. I was very careful to ask permission to see, record, and photograph the rituals I attended. Most of my interlocutors in Buryatia thought my concerns were funny. After a few pointed conversations, I realized that this difference was due to the divergent histories of state suppression in the United States and the Soviet Union.

In many colonial contexts, indigenous ritual practitioners were forced to perform on demand for their colonizers. Those who forced them to perform then claimed exclusive rights to represent what they saw. In this context, a demand for secrecy is a demand for respect and indicates the desire to control knowledge production. In Russia under the Soviet regime, religious practices were pushed underground. At some points during 1920s and 30s, openly practicing religion courted repression, exile, imprisonment, and death. Thousands of lamas and shamans died; those who survived were forced to hide their practices. Thus, for present-day practitioners, practicing openly is an assertion of power. In the face of the historical silence of their ancestors, some of whom died practicing their religion, they were eager to have their rituals documented and shared with the public.

Furthermore, the production of cultural knowledge has a different valence for Buryats than for many indigenous populations. Buryats have been integrated into Russian educational systems, and Buryat scholars have been producing ethnographic knowledge about themselves since Dorzhi Banzarov wrote his dissertation at Kazan University on "Shamanism or the Black Faith among the Mongols" in 1846 (Banzarov 1997; Ulymzhiev 1993). In part due to the Soviet institutions that fostered national culture, Buryatia has a vibrant cultural scene, including literature, local news media, museums, music, dance, fashion, theater, and history. However, most Buryats are aware that precious little of these self-representations travel as far as Moscow, much less beyond Russian borders. Most of the Buryats with whom I spoke were not concerned about how they were represented by others; rather, they were more concerned that they were not represented at all. As one person explained, "Stalin was able to kill 20,000 lamas without anyone noticing, because no one knew we were here." Given this history, most of the Buryats with whom I spoke were happy that Western researchers were interested in representing Buryatia at all. I am, however, deeply cognizant of the trust they placed in me and have tried my best to represent the lives they shared with me truthfully and with respect.

Road Map

The following chapters focus on individual rituals and the chronotopes produced at them. I begin with the inauguration of a Buddhist monument in honor of Etigelov. This ritual allows us to see how three different historical genres coexist in the same context: a Buddhist institutional genre produced by the Buddhist Sangha; a local shamanic genre that focuses on state violence and draws on shamanic ideas about "place spirits"; and a Soviet genre that tells the history of the village as a collective farm. This chapter presents an example of the overall argument of the book: that multiple historical genres can and do coexist for the same people, depending on the context in which "us" is invoked.

The second and third chapters present the chronotopes produced by civic rituals. Chapter 2 presents the Soviet chronotope indexed by Victory Day celebrations. Victory Day is grounded in the familiar Soviet genre of history, in which the Soviet Union brought civilization to Buryatia, and Buryats achieved full citizenship in the Soviet utopian dream through their collective sacrifice during the war. Although not everyone in Buryatia agrees on how to evaluate this history, it is the backdrop against which religious practitioners define their own histories.

City Day is also a civic ritual, a celebration of the anniversary of Ulan-Ude's founding. The festival is similar in form to Victory Day, including a public holiday and a parade. The genre of history produced at City Day looks initially like the Soviet genre, but it differs enough to merit its own designation, the hospitality genre. This sub-genre tells the history of Buryatia as a series of arrivals, beginning with the Buryats, who were followed by the Cossacks, and then the Old Believer Orthodox Christians (*Semeiskie*). Both Cossacks and Old Believer Orthodox are Russian and yet not Russian, viewed as local ethnic groups, thereby transforming what might be a story of Russian colonization into a history of successive migrations. This genre produces a local history of multi-ethnic coexistence and tolerance that contrasts a local identity with a national one, and produces Buryatia as a place where many ethnicities have always, and will continue, to live together in peace and neighborly conviviality.

Chapter 4 returns to Etigelov, but this time at the summer festival of Maidari, the festival for the Maitreya Buddha. Both Etigelov and Maitreya are bodhisattvas who return, bringing enlightenment. While Maitreya will return in the future, Etigelov has already returned, bringing healing by producing a recursive chronotope, in which the Soviet experience is encompassed by a Buddhist history within which science and scholarship were always already Buddhist and Buryat.

Chapter 5 looks at the inauguration of the new center for the shamans' organization, Tengeri. Tengeri contests the history and the Buryat identity produced by both the Soviet and Buddhist genres. The shamans of Tengeri consider contemporary social problems to be the karmic debt from the Soviet period's violence, and see Buddhism as just another foreign colonizing power. Instead, Tengeri reaches further into the past, to produce Buryats as just one of many Central Asian indigenous peoples. By reaching back to the court of Chinghis Khan, when shamanism was a state religion, the shamans at Tengeri seek to recover the true and universal religion of all humanity, restore positive relationships with ancestor spirits, and, in the process, seek to solve some of the social problems faced by contemporary Buryats.

The sixth and final chapter moves to a smaller scale, looking at a family history produced through a shamanic initiation. Yuri's initiation shows the stakes of adhering to one historical genre or another. For Yuri, whose father is Buryat and mother is Russian, whether or not he accepts a shamanic genealogical genre of the past is a matter of life or death for him and his family. All these rituals produce different forms of knowledge about the past, different chronotopes, and thereby evoke different versions of "us" in the present. Through these rituals and these histories, post-Soviet Buryats are repeatedly producing the past.

I

An Inauguration for Etigelov

MULTIPLE GENRES OF HISTORY IN BURYATIA

ON SEPTEMBER 5, 2005, the leaders of the Traditional Buddhist Sangha consecrated a stupa outside the village of Orongoi, to commemorate the birthplace of Dashi-Dorzho Etigelov. Widespread throughout the Tibetan Buddhist world, a stupa (also known as a *suburgan*) is a monument that marks holy places or commemorates people.[1] However, in Buryatia the Soviets had destroyed most pre-revolutionary stupas during their regime, so the consecration of a new one was a notable occasion.

Dashi-Dorzho Etigelov was the 12th Pandito Khambo Lama of Eastern Siberia, who served as the spiritual leader of Russian Buddhists from 1911–17. Elected from the ranks of the leaders of all the monasteries in Buryatia, the Pandito Khambo Lama is the spiritual leader of Buryat Buddhists during his tenure, a position invested with considerable power and charisma. The first Pandito Khambo Lama, Damba Dorzha Zaiaev (1711–76), was elected to the position in 1764, after Buddhism was recognized as an official religion of the Russian Empire by Empress Elizabeth in 1741 (Chimitdorzhin 2004, 17).

Etigelov stepped down in 1917, at the time of the Bolshevik Revolution. According to a popular story, told to me by both lamas and laypeople, in 1927, he advised his students to flee to Mongolia. When his students asked him to come along, he replied, "they won't get me," and settled into a prolonged meditation. The students refused his request to read the prayers for the dead for him, so he did it himself. Seated in the lotus position, he "left" (Russ.—*ushël*). When members of the Sangha speak about Etigelov, they use the verb "left," which is a regular verb of motion. Although the verb can be used as a metaphor for death in other contexts, it is still striking that I never heard anyone at the Sangha use the verb for "died." Etigelov left behind a body so purified by his spiritual exercises that it never decayed. He was buried according to his instructions: in a cemetery in the countryside near Orongoi, in a wooden box, still seated in the lotus position.

In 2002, a lama at the Ivolginsky monastery, the seat of the current Pandito Khambo Lama, had a dream in which Etigelov appeared and stated that the time had come for his return. Etigelov was exhumed later that year and since then, his body—still seated in the lotus position—has been housed at the Ivolginsky monastery, where the public can view it seven times a year on Buddhist holidays.[2] Hundreds, and sometimes even the thousands, of visitors come to see him, for reasons ranging from simple curiosity to deep faith in his healing powers. It is often rumored that Richard Gere and Robert Thurman, famous practitioners of Tibetan Buddhism from the West, will come to visit, but while Putin visited in 2013, they are still waiting for Richard Gere.[3]

Etigelov's remains have been a point of fascination since his exhumation. The current head of the Traditional Buddhist Sangha of Buryatia, Damba Badmaevich Aiusheev, established the Etigelov Institute, led by Ianzhima Dabaevna Vasil'eva, to manage his legacy and sponsor translations of his scholarship.[4] In 2005, it seemed as if everyone in Buryatia was talking about Etigelov, but no one could agree. Some argued that when he "left" he entered a state of meditation so deep that it resembled death, and he persisted in that condition, neither alive nor dead, ever since.[5] Others argued that he left his body but remained attached to the earth either as a bodhisattva or as a place spirit, serving as a kind of patron saint of Buryatia, looking down on his fellow countrymen and waiting for a time when his miraculously imperishable (Russ.—*netlennyi*) body should be revealed to astound and amaze the people and bring them back to faith. The current head of the Traditional Sangha, Damba Aiusheev, argues that Etigelov left his body in this condition because he presciently knew that post-Soviet subjects would need scientific proof in order to believe.[6] Or perhaps—as most atheists and several of the shamans I spoke with argued—he just died and the preservation of his body is a freak of nature, an effect of being buried in ground that, while not permafrost, is very cold for much of the year.

The Etigelov phenomenon illustrates what Katherine Verdery has called "dead body politics" (1999; see also Gal 1991; Bernstein 2013). She argues that during political transformations, dead bodies—both those of famous individuals and the nameless dead (e.g., the unknown soldier)—can become focal points through which people redefine their communities. Bodies are particularly effective tools for this purpose, particularly because the dead produce a community of mourners who claim the deceased as "ours." Human, and yet unable to speak for themselves, the dead are powerfully multivalent, enabling the living to make claims through them and on their behalf.

Etigelov's body became such a focal point. His multiple lives, deaths, and returns constitute a perfect example of how religious practices produce new historical knowledge, and how this new historical knowledge produces new chronotopes that re-situate the living in relationship to both landscapes and time-scapes. Very few people, other than Buddhist lamas and a few local historians, had heard of Etigelov before his exhumation. The texts he wrote, as well as many of the records of his life, were written in the classical Mongolian script, which most contemporary Buryats cannot read. For most lay people encountering Etigelov, the events of his life are new information. However, people encounter the events of Etigelov's life not merely as new information, but as events embedded in Buddhist chronotopes that change the way the past becomes meaningful to the present.

In this chapter I describe the inauguration of the stupa in his honor. During this ritual, Etigelov's life and its meaning become embedded in three different genres of history. Each genre evokes a different (but overlapping) community and locates these communities within time and space in three different chronotopes.

The first genre is Buddhist history, within which Etigelov is a representative of the Traditional Buddhist Sangha who positions this institution in relationship to the Russian imperial state. Time in this chronotope is recursive: by repeatedly returning through reincarnation, Etigelov renders time and space meaningful.[7]

I call the second genre shamanic history, even though it is evoked in a Buddhist context, because it draws on the shamanic concept of a "spirit place-master," an other-than-human being (sometimes an ancestor) that watches over a particular territory. As an ancestor spirit, the past (as Etigelov) remains contemporaneous and exists in an ongoing social relationship to particular communities in the present.

The third genre is Soviet history, which incorporates the history of Orongoi, Etigelov's birthplace, as a Soviet collective farm. The Soviet genre's chronotope is linear and modernist. However, in this particular ritual context, it is uncoupled from the other timelines. It begins with collectivization and bears no explicit relationship to either the pre-Soviet past or the post-Soviet present.

These chronotopes were not produced by three different groups arguing over who gets to claim Etigelov as "their own." Rather, they were all used by participants at the same ritual, at slightly different points within the ritual. These historical genres overlapped, intertwined, complemented, and sometimes contradicted each other. I separate the genres so that the reader can recognize their differences and the work they do, but in practice the genres are much less defined. Ritual participants code-switch between them throughout, and no one seemed to find the genres to be in conflict, or explicitly sought to exclude or argue against one in favor of another. The genres simply coexisted and were drawn on by the participants in different contexts.

The Inauguration

Although Etigelov was born in Orongoi, he was orphaned at a young age and the exact location of his birth is unknown. Several participants told me that lamas from the Ivolginsky temple divined the location of his birthplace, although they did not know the exact method. The lamas discovered a spring on the site, which was seen by everyone to confirm the accuracy of the divination process.[8] Under the leadership of Buda Lama, a lama from Orongoi who had studied with the Dalai Lama and had become the head of the temple at Verkhnei Beriozovke, the villagers of Orongoi built the stupa and the surrounding complex over the course of a few months in preparation for the third anniversary of Etigelov's exhumation (see Figure 1.1).[9] The villagers came after work and on weekends to clear the site and build the structure with

FIGURE 1.1 The Etigelov stupa at Orongoi after the consecration. The fence encloses the stupa (*suburgan*) itself, a one-room wooden museum in what was once Etigelov's cabin, and a spring. Orongoi, September 5, 2005.

construction materials donated by local merchants. Everyone involved—as reported in the press and in communications with me—stressed that this was a grassroots effort by the village residents.

The consecration on September 5, 2005, was not widely publicized, but several reporters interviewed the organizers and the foreigners in attendance, including me. Naj Wikoff, an American and Fulbright scholar who was working in Ulan-Ude, reported on the event for National Public Radio, and I helped translate for him, speaking to many of the key participants (see Wikoff 2005). As foreigners, we were also one of the attractions. Our presence, several participants noted, lent an air of international importance to the event. Most of the other attendees were village residents, relatives of residents, or relatives of the lamas blessing the structure. People arrived throughout the day, greeting friends and relatives and streaming into the flow of people circumambulating the stupa, stepping out again to eat, view the museum, and, finally, attend the traditional Buryat games that concluded the day.

By the time I arrived, seats for the lamas who would be conducting the consecration had been set up facing the stupa (see Figure 1.2). Outside the little museum, display panels told the history of the village and its collective farm. The Etigelov Institute and the Verkhnei Beriozovke *datsan* offered pamphlets, books, and DVDs for sale. People from the Etigelov Institute handed out flyers and slips of paper with a mantra that participants were

FIGURE 1.2 Members of the Traditional Buddhist Sangha conducting the consecration, Orongoi, September 5, 2005. Pandito Khambo Lama Damba Aiusheev is seated at the far left.

FIGURE 1.3 Participants circumambulating the stupa. Orongoi, September 5, 2005.

supposed to read as they circumambulated the structure (see Figure 1.3). As is common at ritual events in Buryatia, people brought bags of cookies and candies, packets of milk and bottles of vodka, and placed them on tables surrounding the stupa. These would be blessed during the ceremony, and then consumed at home.

For the participants, the ritual was a mix of the familiar (circumambulating in a clockwise direction and blessing food at a sacred site) and the unfamiliar (chanting a mantra). People in Buryatia regularly bring food to religious ceremonies of all kinds for blessings, and then bring this food home, charged with spiritual power, to be eaten by family members who were unable to attend. At Buryat rituals, both shamanic and Buddhist, "white" foods (milk products, vodka, candy, and cookies) are considered to be traditional and appropriate for these blessings.[10] Although this practice is not as common or as explicit in Christian contexts, I have seen people bring bread to Russian Orthodox ceremonies to be blessed, and many people take home holy water to consume. At the inauguration in Orongoi, as at most ceremonies I attended, most people brought bags of this food with them, and those who did not were able to buy some from enterprising vendors who set up kiosks selling milk, cookies, and *buuza* (Bur.)/*pozy* (Russ.), which are soup dumplings that are considered the "national dish" of Buryatia. Attendees set the bags of food on tables around the stupa, or on the ground, rolling down the edges of the

FIGURE 1.4 Lamas circumambulating the stupa. Note the food in the foreground. These items were blessed during the ceremony and then taken home by participants to share with their families. Orongoi, September 5, 2005.

plastic bag they brought it in to make a placemat (see Figure 1.4). After the blessing, in a somewhat chaotic scene, people collect the food they brought and pack it back up again.

In contrast to blessing the food, the mantra was unfamiliar and unusual. In Buryatia, people regularly circumambulate Buddhist temples and ritual bonfires at both Buddhist and shamanic events, usually clockwise and in multiples of three. Russian Orthodox processions also routinely circumambulate churches or neighborhoods. However, this was the only time I observed anyone reciting a mantra. The slips of paper—with the mantra itself phonetically transliterated from Sanskrit into Cyrillic—contained this message:

> Mantra for recitation while circumambulating a suburgan
>
> We worship the Buddha Shakyamuni, the fully realized, he who has achieved victory over the ultimate nature of reality (*pobeditel'iu tatkhagate*). *Om namo dasha dika dirkala sarva ratna drayaya, mamabra daksha subra daksha, sarva babam bishodkhani sukha*[11]—with one

repetition of this mantra we worship the Buddha of ten directions and three eras. One cleanses oneself of all collected pollution from primordial times. To achieve the condition of the enlightened Buddha. We free ourselves from illness and negative influences.

Although mantras are unusual, other kinds of instructions are not. Several Buddhist temples have small instructional posters on the door, explaining to visitors—both local residents and the handful of tourists that visit each year—that they should move through the space in a clockwise direction and that hats should be removed. At the inauguration, some of the participants dutifully tried to recite the mantra phonetically, but most gave up and simply circled it three times (or in multiples of three), arm in arm with friends and relatives.

The current Pandito Khambo Lama, Damba Aiusheev, arrived in a white car, flanked by riders on horseback in Buryat national costume. Laypeople, predominantly village residents and their relatives, continued to circumambulate the stupa as the lamas got settled in their seats. Suddenly, the lamas began chanting the consecration, which was in either Sanskrit or Tibetan. The lamas probably understood the words, but the lay participants did not, and there was no attempt to translate. When the proper people (the lamas) performed the proper prayers, the structure was rendered sacred; it was not important that anyone understood the words.

As the chanting concluded, people gathered the food they had brought. Then we all knelt, covering our heads, while the Khambo Lama called down blessings into the food. This ritual and the incantation, in Buryat, are the same in both shamanic and Buddhist ceremonies.[12]

The food blessing ended the consecration. The villagers had prepared a meal for the lamas, served at long picnic tables in the open, while everyone else ate picnic lunches or purchased food from vendors. After lunch, most of the participants migrated to a nearby tent for a small *surkharban*, a competition of the three national sports. The village dance ensemble performed in Buryat national costume, followed by wrestling, archery, and horse-racing, all judged by the attending lamas. Prize money, probably donated by local merchants, ranged from 3,000 to 15,000 rubles (U.S. $100 to $500 at the time).[13] The organized events closed with the *surkharban*, but people continued to circle the stupa and lingered for several hours. Just as there was no formal beginning to the ceremony, there was no formal end, and eventually we accepted a ride back to the city, rather than risk being stranded in Orongoi for the night.

The ritual that consecrated the stupa was not explicitly about history. The consecration mantras were purely performative; the constative content of the mantras was unintelligible to the participants. Nor were there any opening speeches by anyone with authority framing or defining the "meaning" of the ritual for the audience during the consecration.

However, almost all the speech acts surrounding the ritual were about history. The museum displays and interviews given by organizers to members of the press were explicitly instructional, explaining the historical significance of the ritual and the history of Etigelov and the site. These accounts of the past were echoed by the laypeople and lamas I spoke to directly, who explained the ritual and its value as a practice of commemorating and teaching a forgotten history. Everyone spoke about the same historical events (Etigelov's birth, his reincarnation, his life, his service to the imperial Russian state, his evasion of Soviet power, the erasure and preservation of his legacy in the village, and his exhumation). However, they did so in three recognizably different genres of history: Buddhist, shamanic, and Soviet.

The Buddhist Genre of History: A Buddhist Buryatia, as argued by the Traditional Sangha of Russia

The first genre—a Buddhist history—is produced by the Traditional Buddhist Sangha and the Etigelov Institute and emphasizes Etigelov's lineage, biography, and status as a reincarnate lama. This genre produces a recursive chronotope, with two timelines. The first is the linear timeline of the Russian nation-state, which is made meaningful by the second timeline: the recursive re-appearance of Etigelov's reincarnations. When Etigelov was elected Pandito Khambo Lama in 1911, he was recognized as the reincarnation of the first Pandito Khambo Lama. Etigelov thus appears three times: first as Zaiaev, then as himself, and then in the form of his miraculously preserved body. As a bodhisattva, he sits outside time, periodically re-appearing to infuse the linear Russian national timeline with Buddhist religious meaning.

This chronotope also marks Russian national space as Buddhist. By constructing physical monuments that commemorate important Buddhist historical events, the historical genre reveals a landscape that is already Buddhist, and simply needs its Buddhist nature to be uncovered and marked. In the 1930s, during the height of Russia's Cultural Revolution, all the Buddhist temples and monasteries in Buryatia were closed, destroyed, or repurposed. The Soviet government invested considerable energy into removing Buddhist and other religious sites, and often repurposed religious sites as Soviet cultural sites. In Ulan-Ude, for example, the Russian Orthodox Odigitrievskii (Hodegetria) Cathedral served as a museum of atheism in the 1930s and the

Sviato-Troitskii (Holy Trinity) Orthodox cemetery was turned into an amusement park (see also Luehrmann 2005).

Since the 1995 election of Aiusheev as the Pandito Khambo Lama, the Traditional Sangha has worked very hard to rebuild temples, monasteries, and stupas, and add new ones. Etigelov's stupa is part of this extensive effort to re-establish Buddhist landmarks throughout Buryatia, which in effect re-inscribe Buddhism in the landscape. Since these construction projects mark historical sites, such as Etigelov's birthplace, or reconstruct temples that were destroyed, this new construction is rhetorically restorative: it reveals the Buddhist history that was already there.

A few days before the inauguration of the stupa at Orongoi, a smaller stupa in honor of Zaiaev was consecrated near the Mongolian border.[14] This private event was attended only by the lamas and members of the Etigelov Institute, but members of both groups mentioned it several times in Orongoi, framing the two as related events. In addition, at every event held in honor of Etigelov in 2004 and 2005, the full lineage of all 24 Pandito Khambo Lamas was on display, noting that the 12th (Etigelov) was the reincarnation of the first (Zaiaev) and that the 12th (Etigelov) was exhumed during the administrative tenure of the 24th (Aiusheev). No one endowed the numbers with any explicit symbolic significance, but the numbers were repeated over and over, linking the current Pandito Khambo Lama to these venerable ancestors.[15]

The one-room museum on the site contained a biography of Etigelov as well as the display of the lineage of Pandito Khambo Lamas. Ianzhima Dabaevna Vasil'eva, director of the Etigelov Institute, referenced these materials in her press interviews and stressed that the inauguration was "a significant event for Russia," since Etigelov was the reincarnation of Zaiaev, the first Russian Pandito Khambo Lama and the founding figure of Russian Buddhism.[16] In doing so, Ianzhima Dabaevna and the museum displays were retelling the history of an autonomous Russian Buddhist community, the Traditional Sangha of Buryatia. I have collated the following historical account of the Traditional Sangha from the museum, public speeches, displays at multiple rituals, and other materials produced by the Etigelov Institute (Blinnikov 2005; Chimitdorzhin 2004; Namzhilon 2005).[17]

Etigelov's Biography as told by the Traditional Sangha

Tibetan Buddhism began spreading into the Baikal area of Siberia at the end of the 17th century. Although Gelug monastic Buddhism was originally brought to Buryatia by Tibetans and Mongolians, it quickly found resonance among the native Buryat population, who embraced the dharma. In 1741, Empress Elizabeth I officially recognized Buddhism and legally limited Russian Orthodoxy to the western part of the region: Orthodox missionaries could proselytize on the western side of the lake, and Buddhists could proselytize on its eastern shores. The official reason for recognizing Buddhism was that it was more civilized, and hence more beneficial, than shamanism, but most historians agree it was also an attempt to assert control over the growing religion and limit the influx of foreign missionaries into Russian territory (Bernstein 2013; Schorkowitz 2001a, 2001b; Tsyrempilov 2010, 2012, 2014a, 2014b).

In 1764 Catherine the Great recognized Zaiaev as the first Pandito Khambo Lama of Russia and from this time on, the rulers of Russia were often referred to by Buryat Buddhists as incarnations of the goddess White Tara (Tsyrempilov 2010, 2014a). In publications such as Chimitdorzhin's compendium of the lives of the Pandito Khambo Lamas (2004), the Traditional Buddhist Sangha presents itself as representing an unbroken line of authority from Zaiaev to the current Pandito Khambo Lama Aiusheev.[18] Furthermore, by linking the beginning of institutional Buddhism to imperial recognition, the Sangha represents itself as representing all Russian Buryats, a claim which is contested by Buryat, Kalmyk, Tuvan, and ethnic Russian Buddhists.

Within the Buddhist genre of history, as articulated by representatives of the traditional Sangha (and often repeated by Etigelov's lay visitors), Russian imperial recognition of Zaiaev is the beginning of a specifically Buryat form of Buddhism on Russian territory. With the establishment of an imperially recognized Sangha in Russia, Buryatia is transformed from merely the northern borderlands of Mongolian Buddhism to an independent center of a distinct Buryat Buddhist culture that is an equal participant in a wider Tibetan Buddhist world. Following in Zaiaev's footsteps, Buryats began to travel to Tibet to study, and brought the teachings learned there back home. Buryats respected the learning of Buddhist lamas and supported the growing monastic institutions. Buryat lamas traveled back and forth to Tibet, connecting Buryatia to a wider pan-Tibetan Buddhist world, rising to positions of power and respect in Lhasa, the center of Tibetan Buddhism. Monastic Buddhism provided the basis for a nascent Buryat intelligentsia. These scholars wrote in classical Mongolian script, connecting Buddhist scholars in Buryatia to their colleagues in Mongolia (Montgomery 2005). Although they were only a small portion of the population, these Buryat intellectuals occupied positions of influence in Lhasa as well as St. Petersburg because they were able to provide a bridge between Tibet and Russian Orientalist scholars (see Bernstein 2013; Rupen 1956; Tsyrempilov 2010, 2012).

Etigelov was born in 1852 near the village of Orongoi and orphaned at a young age. He entered a monastic school as a young child, where he excelled in theology. He wrote several important exegeses of sutras on the subject of nothingness or emptiness (Russ.—*pustota*) and its relationship to enlightenment. Although he studied in various monasteries throughout Buryatia, in 1904, he was elected the head of the Iangazhinskii monastery, which was located a few kilometers to the northeast of his birthplace in Orongoi. During his tenure there he supervised extensive construction. In 1911 he was elected Khambo Lama of Pribaikalia and Siberia. In the film produced by the Etigelov Institute, the current Khambo Lama, Aiusheev, states that when Etigelov was elected to this position he was also recognized as the reincarnation of Zaiaev. As such he was recognized as a *tulku* (Bur.—*khutukhtu* or *khubilgan*), a person powerful and enlightened enough to choose when and where they will reincarnate.[19] The Traditional Sangha currently states that Etigelov was his 12th incarnation—he incarnated five times in India, five in Tibet, and twice in Buryatia.

As a *tulku*, Etigelov stands apart from the rest of the lineage of Pandito Khambo Lamas, who are elected by and from the ranks of directors of monasteries. At the same time, he possesses a powerful spiritual charisma, evoking popular devotion, like other, more famous *tulkus*, such as the Dalai Lama or the Panchen Lama. Although no one claims that Aiusheev is a reincarnation of the first and 12th, the numbers in the lineage (1st, 12th, and 24th) are often repeated. In addition, the Traditional Sangha has produced devotional postcards, available for purchase at every event, that visually, if not explicitly, draw a parallel between the three figures. Zaiaev is portrayed in the typical iconographic form of a *thangka* painting, while Etigelov and Aiusheev are photographed in similar robes and positions (see Figure 1.5). The numerology and the visual images subtly link the three lamas together, endowing Aiusheev with some of the charisma of Zaiaev and Etigelov, but without making any explicit claims. Etigelov, as a reincarnation, is able to provide a bridge between Zaiaev, the founder of the Buddhist Sangha in Buryatia, and Aiusheev, who is re-founding the institution in the post-Soviet period.

Etigelov was part of a delegation of Buryat elites invited to represent the Buryat nation at the celebration of the 300th anniversary of the Romanov Dynasty in 1913, where he also led the inaugural *khural* at the St. Petersburg *datsan*. During his tenure as Khambo Lama he organized efforts to have Tibetan medical experts (Bur.—*emchi lamas*) treat wounded soldiers during World War I. In 1917 he stepped down from the position of Khambo Lama to concentrate on theology and meditation. To Buryat intellectuals today, the period just before the Bolshevik Revolution represents a golden age—and as a

FIGURE I.5A, B, C Devotional postcards produced and sold by the Traditional Buddhist Sangha. The cards show: (a) the first Pandito Khambo Lama of Buryatia, Damba Dorzha Zaiaev (1764–76); (b) the 12th Pandito Khambo Lama, Dashi-Dorzho Etigelov (1911–1917), who is recognized as Zaiaev's reincarnation; and (c) the 24th Pandito Khambo Lama, Damba Aiusheev (1995–present). The postcards create a visual parallel between the three figures. These cards are sold at kiosks at Buddhist temples. They are often placed on home altars or taped to dashboards in cars. The image of Etigelov is by far the most popular.

scholar, philanthropist, and religious leader, Etigelov was a key figure in this golden age.

Etigelov's official biography, published by the institute, states only that he foresaw the coming Soviet repression, leaving the reader to decide if he was gifted with visions of the future or merely politically savvy (Chimitdorzhin 2004). As described above, in 1927 after advising his students to flee to Mongolia, he chanted the mantra for the dead, and, seated in the lotus position, passed into nirvana, leaving behind a body that never decayed.

According to the documents produced by the Traditional Sangha, Etigelov's body was exhumed in 1955 and 1973, determined to be in good condition, and reburied, as it was not yet time for his return. In the late 1990s, Etigelov appeared to a lama at the Ivolginsky monastery in dreams, informing him that it was time for his return. This lama spearheaded the efforts to exhume him. Etigelov was exhumed in September 2002 and his body brought to the Ivolginsky monastery, where he has remained, a focus of popular devotion and an authorizing figure for the Traditional Buddhist Sangha of Russia.

The Post-Soviet Context

Aiusheev usually explains that Etigelov returned to inspire post-Soviet subjects who, after decades of atheism, are skeptical of religion (see Chapter 4). What the current Khambo Lama does not say is that Etigelov returned at a time when the Traditional Buddhist Sangha of Russia, as an institution, needed to inspire the faithful. After 1989, when restrictions on religion and travel were lifted, missionaries began to swarm into Russia, and although most of these were Christian missionaries from the west, they also included Tibetan missionaries from India and Tibet. To the local population, most of whom had never met a foreigner, all of them were fascinatingly interesting. To Buryats seeking to learn more about Buddhism, monks trained in Dharamsala and Tibet were seen as vastly better educated and more knowledgeable, as well as untainted by Soviet politics, as compared to the local lamas. In the Soviet era, local Buddhist lamas had been allowed to practice Buddhism if they cooperated with the government, and their education was limited to the degrees they could earn in Mongolia, as travel outside the Soviet sphere of influence was not allowed. In response to this flood of missionaries, the Russian Orthodox church, with support from other religious organizations within Russia, including the Traditional Sangha, lobbied for legal restrictions on missionaries, resulting in the 1997 law titled "On Freedom of Conscience and Religious Associations."

The 1997 law recognizes Buddhism as a traditional religion of Russia. As such, Buddhist organizations, especially in Buryatia and Kalmykia, are afforded simpler registration and a legitimacy that makes their interactions with the state easier.[20] The Traditional Buddhist Sangha as an organization, however, is not specifically privileged under the law, and as the religious marketplace spread it was increasingly competing with other Buddhist organizations (see also Bernstein 2013). Buddhism in Buryatia is divided between temples that recognize the authority of the Traditional Sangha, temples founded by Tibetan émigrés, and several independent local organizations, such as the Green Tara Society. In this context, the Traditional Sangha is trying to boost its authority by re-grounding the history of Russian Buddhism as embodied in the reincarnated self of Etigelov.[21]

In the museum display at Orongoi, and in interviews with television reporters that day, representatives of the Buddhist Sangha stressed both his reincarnation lineage, as well as Etigelov's service to the Russian imperial state during World War I. In this genre of history Buryat Buddhism is native to Russia and a key part of the pre-revolutionary Russian world, which stood in opposition to the Soviet regime. Unlike Tibetan Buddhist lamas from Tibet and India who have come to Ulan-Ude in the post-Soviet era, the Traditional Sangha was loyal to and authorized by the pre-Soviet Russian imperial government. It is a native Russian form of Buddhism, not a foreign missionary faith.

The Buddhist Chronotope

Grounded in arguments about lineage and reincarnation, this genre of history is a Buddhist genre, but in order for it to authorize the Traditional Sangha of Buryatia as a Russian religious institution, and as an autocephalous Sangha within the broader Tibetan Buddhist community, Buryatia must be figured as Russian space. This is why representatives of the Sangha repeatedly emphasized that the inauguration was an important event "for Russia" and that these Buddhist monuments were built on "Russian soil" rather than Buryat lands. Although this genre of history emphasizes ties to the broader Tibetan Buddhist world, if Buryatia is only Tibetan Buddhist, then Buryat Buddhism is merely the northern periphery of a tradition located elsewhere. Buryatia must be both Buddhist and Russian if the Traditional Sangha is to represent a unique and therefore locally valuable form of Buddhism. Through Etigelov's reincarnations, the linear national time of Russia is infused with the recursive presence of Etigelov, who sustained a uniquely Russian form of Buddhism. First, as Zaiaev, he founded the autocephalous Russian Buddhist Sangha. As Etigelov, he reinforced the Russian nature of Buryat Buddhism through his support and cooperation with the Russian imperial state and his resistance against the Bolsheviks. Through his miraculously imperishable body, he returns to ensure that the Russian branch of Buddhism revives and thrives in the post-Soviet period as an independent organization and a unique form of Buddhism.

The stupas for Zaiaev and Etigelov, constructed on Russian soil, reveal a landscape that is already Buddhist. By marking the birthplaces of historical figures, these new monuments mark a history that is discursively figured as already there, but forgotten. It is important to remember that Etigelov "left" in 1927; by 1937, every single Buddhist building or monument in Buryatia had been destroyed or repurposed, leaving very little actual memory of Buddhism in the landscape or in popular practice. By reminding the audience of Soviet repression, the Buddhist chronotope establishes the Traditional Sangha as anti-Soviet. It also reminds everyone why these monuments that mark "old" places are so very new—they are restorations of what had been erased—thereby distinguishing them from the unequivocally new temples opened by recent Tibetan émigrés. The stupa, museum, and spring are the material proof of the discovery of a true but erased Buryat Buddhist past in Russia.

The historical events referred to in this genre—Zaiaev founding the Buryat Traditional Sangha as an institution, Etigelov's leadership as a pre-Soviet Buddhist intellectual and political figure, the ties between Buryat Buddhism and the Russian imperial state—are new pieces of historical information for most of the laypeople. These facts are drawn from pre-revolutionary Buddhist documents and archival work by local historians, which are then supplemented by revelations in dreams and divination. Historians and Buddhist scholars discovered that Etigelov was from Orongoi, but the exact site is verified by the discovery of a spring through divination. Moreover, this new historical information is not merely a collection of random facts; these events are embedded in a Buddhist chronotope that produces the linear Russian national history as the ground through which Etigelov worked to spread Buddhist dharma in Russia. It produces Buryat land and the Buryat people as a crucial link between Russia and the wider Tibetan Buddhist world, a link grounded in the past and continuing in the present.

The Shamanic Genre: The Village Khoziain and the Violence of Collectivization

The consecration may have been performed by the leadership of the Sangha and may have been an "important day for Russia," but the construction was, by all accounts, a grassroots effort by the villagers of Orongoi. This effort was reflected in the rest of the museum displays and the way that residents of the village spoke about the event and its significance. These sources thus presented new historical information, informing both younger residents of the village and outsiders about Etigelov's relationship to this place. However, they did so in a genre very different than the genre used by the Traditional Buddhist Sangha. Although Etigelov is a Buddhist leader, I call this genre shamanic, because it produces a shamanic chronotope, one that establishes a relationship between a revered ancestor spirit, a place, and the residents of that place.

One wall of the museum was devoted to the lineage of the Pandito Khambo Lama, while another side was devoted to the history of the museum itself, a cabin that had occasionally been used by Etigelov and other lamas at the nearby monastery as a meditation retreat. The heading on this display reads "In the people's memory" (Russ.—*v pamiati naroda*), and features quotations from three villagers who remembered Etigelov and his residence in Orongoi. Each memory includes the name and photograph of the person whose memory is recorded, followed by a quote from them about the cabin and Etigelov.

After Etigelov's death, the Soviet government destroyed the monastery and collectivized the village. After the cabin was relocated by the collective farm manager, a distant cousin of Etigelov's moved in to keep it from being destroyed, impressing upon his children the importance of remembering that this had once been Etigelov's house. Two of these children, now elderly women wrapped in sweaters and headscarves, attended the consecration, testifying that without oral history, preserved by their family during the Soviet era, no one would have known that this was Etigelov's birthplace or that this had been his house. The younger daughter noted that although she was not born in the cabin, her earliest memories were of living in it, and that her elder sister had been very strict about keeping it clean.

The cabin was maintained, and the knowledge that it had once belonged to a great lama, was preserved orally by the villagers, so that when the time came for Etigelov to return, they would know where to locate his stupa and could restore his house to him. In this example, the institutional history of the Traditional Sangha intersects with local oral history, each validating the other.

This history produces a chronotope that embeds the stupa in local time and space, connecting the larger narrative of the Sangha and Russia to the residents of the village. But the genre in which the villagers speak is different than that of the Sangha. They speak of Etigelov not only as a great religious leader, but also as if he were a local place spirit.

I asked one elderly Buryat woman, who was in charge of the museum, what Etigelov meant to her; she answered, "Oh, he means so much—he was a great teacher and he watches over us, over our village, he helps us. When I have problems I pray to him and he really helps. Going to see him is much better and even more effective."

"How does he help?" I asked, "do you mean healing?" (which was a common answer for pilgrims at Ivolginsky).

"Well, of course healing, but mostly I pray to him and my soul is lighter."

Unlike most of the pilgrims I spoke to at Ivolginsky, for her, Etigelov's appeal lay not in the imperishable status of his body (which will be discussed in Chapter 4), but in his status as "ours"—as belonging to the village. Most of the people I spoke to at the ceremony referred to him as "ours" (Russ.—*nash*) or as "our countryman" (Russ.—*nash zemliak*). Several villagers told me that they could feel his presence, watching over the village. The practice of commemorating a powerful local being, such as a place spirit (Russ.—*khoziain mesta*/Bur.—*ejin*/*ezen*) or the soul of a deceased shaman, by marking a site in the landscape, often near a spring, is a practice that predates Buddhism, and is observed by local residents regardless of whether or not they identify as shamanist. These shrines are often located by roadsides, where travelers diligently mark them by making offerings of coins, vodka, or milk and leaving strips of fabric tied to branches. By leaving an offering, they acknowledge that the territory is under the control of this being and ask for its protection. These observances are not limited to ethnic Buryats but are observed by all long-term residents of the area regardless of ethnicity, including many ethnic Russians who otherwise identify as Russian Orthodox Christians.[22] This shamanic genre of commemoration establishes a relationship between a living population, their ancestors, and the animate landscape in which they reside, ties that supersede ethnic and religious identification. Instead, these ties are based on geographical residence.

One woman I spoke to at the ceremony illustrated this relationship. She approached me while circumambulating the stupa to see if I, recognizably a foreigner, knew a group of American missionaries who had visited the village the year before. (I did not, as missionaries in Buryatia tended to avoid anthropologists like the plague). A resident of the village, her blonde hair and blue eyes indicated she was not Buryat. I asked if she had helped build the stupa. "Of course," she answered. I asked if she was a Buddhist, and she shrugged. She explained that her ancestors were Polish and had been exiled to the area before the revolution, so she is Christian and Buddhist.[23] "This and that, God is the same" (Russ.—*i tak i tak, Bog Odin*), she explained. She wanted to help build the stupa because "it helps, it brings merit, and is good for your health too." It was only appropriate for her to help build it, as Etigelov, she said, was "ours."

Her claim to Etigelov was based on her residence in the village, rather than in her religious affiliation, which was based on her ethnic identity. Etigelov, both monks and laypeople told me, was "a model of what a human being can accomplish," all the more inspiring because he was "our countryman" (Russ.—*nash zemliak*). One person told me that "he sees what we are doing for him and is pleased."

Since Etigelov is Buddhist and is worshiped by people who identify primarily as Buddhist, I did not immediately make the connection between his status as "our countryman" and shamanic place spirits. Instead, it was made for me by a very savvy taxi driver, on one of my many trips to Ivolginsky to see Etigelov. The driver, a Buryat man in his 30s, told me that Etigelov was becoming a *khoziain*. Although he had lived in Ulan-Ude his whole life, the driver explained that his family was from Barnaul in the north and his wife was Evenki, so he was more familiar with shamanism than Buddhism. He had never seen Etigelov, but like everyone, he had heard about him. I asked him what he thought about the relationship between Buddhism and shamanism, and whether he thought the spirits of particular places would be angry at all the Buddhist temples now being built, and he answered:

> Etigelov is becoming one of them. You have to make offerings to him, just like a place spirit. Buddhism and shamanism are not in conflict, not now anyway. It's all the same. Me, for example, I believe in one God, there's one God and everyone worships the same one, just it has different names, and different ones are right for different people. When you go out to the *datsan* there are lots of different pictures and it depends what you need them for.

Like many people in Buryatia, he equated all religions as versions of the same thing. He also equated a specific Buddhist bodhisattva—Etigelov—with a shamanic place spirit. The Russian term which I am translating as "place spirit" is *khoziain mesta*, which translates literally as "master of a place." There are several terms in Buryat for various kinds of deity. The most common is *burkhan*, which shamans have told me is a Buddhist term. The Buryat term for a place master is *ezhin*, although as Mikhailov notes, *ezhin* is a descriptive term, and a deity is more likely to be addressed with an honorific, such as "*khan*" or "*noion*" (Mikhailov 2004, 352–54). *Noion* is an honorific title that was also used for clan leaders and powerful men in the 19th century, a direct parallel to the Russian usage of *khoziain*.

However, few Buryats use the Buryat terms. Even shamans, when speaking to me in Russian, used the term Russian term for master of a place. Within the Russian folk traditions described by Paxson (2005) *khoziain* translates as "master" or "landlord" and can refer to the head of a household that has invited you to dinner, to the director of a factory, or to the spirit that controls a place.[24] What unites all of these definitions is that a *khoziain* is in a position of power—a *khoziain* can be appealed to (Russ.—*obratit'sia k*) for help, and he is far more likely to help those to whom he has a moral obligation. Those seeking help, from a raise at work to protection from a forest spirit, evoke a possessive relationship in order to elicit assistance. I found that the term *khoziain* was used similarly in Buryatia.

For both Russians and Buryats, place spirits usually fall under the purview of shamans and folk healers, although Buddhist lamas can make offerings to them as well. The shamans at the Tengeri Association explained to me their view of the origin of place spirits.[25] Some are deities (Bur.—*burkhan* or *ezhin*) who are responsible for or have control over a region. The more powerful the deity, the wider the region they control. The place where people go to make offerings is described as the place where the deity lives. These are generally unusual landscape features or rock cairns on hillsides. Some place spirits are powerful shamans, who died and remained linked to the places of their deaths. Both *burkhans* and these less powerful place spirits can be either generous or vengeful, depending on how they are treated by humans, and so it is important to maintain good relationships with them through regular offerings.

Just like with human *khoziain*, spirit *khoziain* are more likely to help their "own." As the shamans at Tengeri explained it, and as discussed in later chapters, a primary part of any interaction with any kind of spirit is establishing a relationship between the spirit and those who are addressing it. If the spirit is too distant, a shaman will ask his or her own clan spirits (*ongons*) to mediate the intervention because spirits are more likely to be able and to want to help their own.

Although I only rarely heard Etigelov referred to as a *khoziain*, when people claim Etigelov as "ours" (*nash*), which they often did, they are drawing on this type of relationship. The term "*zemliak*," which they also used, implies a similar mutual aid relationship. The claim that he is "ours" is not, however, limited to the residents of Orongoi. An ethnic Russian couple from Ivolga village told me they came to see him because "he is, after all, ours" (as residents of Ivolga, where the body is now in residence). Buryat students at the monastery, when explaining Etigelov to me, often merged the idea of a bodhisattva with the folk concept of a *khoziain*, stressing that because he is local, because he is "ours," he is a more powerful role model for them. He will be more likely, they said, to "help his own" to achieve enlightenment.

"Our Etigelov" indexes a collectivity that includes the speaker. For representatives of the Traditional Sangha, "ours" indexes a Russian Buddhist "us." For the residents of Orongoi and Ivolga, "ours" references the village, including non-Buddhists and non-Buryats, who nonetheless live on Buryat land. Claiming Etigelov as "ours" initiates a patronage relationship, in which Etigelov is more likely to help those whom he recognizes as "his own."

This village-level shamanic chronotope, which identifies Etigelov as "ours," ties him to the local residents of this multi-ethnic borderland, through quotidian shamanic genres of interaction that turn Etigelov into a local place spirit who watches over his descendants. The hero of this chronotope is not the Buddhist Sangha of Russia, but the residents of the village. Since many residents identify as Buddhist, and some are lamas, these two groups overlap. The Etigelov of this chronotope is very different from the statesman and intellectual reincarnate Buddhist leader of the Sangha's history.

Time in this chronotope also flows differently. As an ancestor, Etigelov is from the past, but his continuing presence in the village renders him eternally present. His status as the incarnation of Zaiaev becomes irrelevant; it is not mentioned by the local residents I spoke to. He is not going to return through reincarnation because he is already always there. Within this chronotope, the successful future of the village and its residents is dependent on an ongoing relationship to this ever-present past.

At the same time, because the historical events referenced by these two genres are the same, the oral history documented by the museum contextualizes and complements the chronotope offered by the Traditional Sangha's Buddhist genre. Both genres stand in opposition to the Soviet version of the past from different perspectives. Each genre draws on different sources of knowledge and different modes of authorizing that knowledge. While the Buddhist genre emphasizes the pre-Soviet ties between Buddhist institutions and the Russian state, the shamanic village genre emphasizes the resistance of the local population, who may not have understood the Buddhist texts that Etigelov interpreted, but valued him and the Buddhist institutions that he represented.

The source of historical information is oral, and it is verified by the residents' feeling that "he is watching over us." They explicitly identify their oral history of how the cabin was preserved when the village was collectivized as a site of resistance, a way of filling an absence in the written records. In the process they remind the audience why Buddhism must be re-inscribed in the landscape, further solidifying the Sangha's claim that this place is a Buddhist place. Through shared references to historical events, the institutional

Buddhist genre and the local village shamanic genre produce complementary versions of the past, even though their histories are told in opposing genres.

The Soviet Genre of History: The Collective Farm "Culture"

Alongside the "official" explanations given by members of the Buddhist Sangha and the Etigelov Institute, and the popular oral history documented in the museum, the villagers erected posters outside the museum building that were probably originally produced for the village's 2005 Victory Day celebration marking the 60th anniversary of the end of World War II.[26] These posters outline the history of Orongoi's collective farm, Soël, which means "culture" in Buryat. The history the posters document was not the history of the village, but of the collective farm (which, geographically, was contiguous with the village), subsuming the village's identity into that of the collective farm. The posters emphasize the collective farm's contribution to the great nation-building and nation-legitimizing event of the 20th century, the "Great Patriotic War" against Hitler and fascism (World War II). These posters, although recently produced, clearly re-produce a familiar Soviet genre: not only do they cite familiar Soviet topics of production quotas and labor heroes, but the form in which the history is presented is also Soviet: filled with dates, lists, and figures, and presented with very little narrative frame or interpretation, as their meaning should be self-evident to the audience.

The posters chronicle the history of the collective farm from its founding in 1928 through World War II and the "post-war years." The posters begin with a typewritten account of the founding of the collective farm itself:

> Massive collectivization of village agriculture in our country unfolded on the basis of fulfilling the decision of the 15th Party Congress at the end of 1927. At this period in the village of Orongoi there was no party organization. All mass-political work in our *ulus* was led by the *Komsomol* cell, founded in the fall of 1925, ratified by the *Verkhneudinsk uezdnym* (administrative center town) Komsomol committee on the 5th of January 1925, consisting of 11 people. [The names of leading village communists were listed here.]
>
> The Party cell in the village of Orongoi was established later, 2nd of November 1928 by decision of the bureau of the *Selenginskogo Raikoma* (district committee).

> In the fall of 1928, in a meeting of the active villagers, communists, Komsomol members, and those without party affiliation, it was decided to organize an agricultural collective. In this meeting a list of those wishing to join the commune was established. [The names of those who signed are included.] This meeting took place in the Baruun-Orongoiskoi elementary school. This building is still preserved, and can be found in our village on Railroad Street (*po ulitse zheleznodorozhnoi*). The organizational meeting of commune-members took place somewhat later, 23 January 1929, . . . At this meeting they already elected the Commune Soviet administration, established regulations and took the name "Soël" Kolkhoz-sel'khoz.

Unlike the oral history accounts in the museum, which are explicitly presented as the personal recollections of identified individuals, this text confines itself to a list of events, noting obscure details, such as the house in which the meeting took place, thus locating the founding of the collective farm in the landscape, in the same way as the construction of the stupa marks the landscape. There is no mention of why the name Soël was chosen, but we can presume it pointed to the goals of *korenizatsiia*, a Soviet nationality policy that was intended to "develop" native culture. Through Soël, the Soviet Union intended to bring "culture" to illiterate villagers in the Transbaikal steppe, in their native language (see Figure 1.6).

The Great Patriotic War is represented by two posters: the first includes 12 portraits of the "Soldiers of Orongoi—Cavaliers of the Order of Glory," whose names, birth years, and military honors are listed beneath each photo (see Figure 1.7).[27] The first soldier is described as "Participant in battles for Moscow, Leningrad, the liberation of the Baltics and among troops that reached Berlin. Was wounded. Cavalier of the Order of Glory second and third class. 'Order of the Patriotic War' second class." Ten of the twelve faces and names are clearly Buryat; the other two are most likely ethnically Russian. The facing poster identifies 16 "Veterans of the Home Front" (Russ.—*veterany tyla*) only by name. All 16—11 of them women—appear to have Buryat names and faces. Just as with the posters about the collective, there is no framing narrative to tell the audience how to understand or relate to these faces. However, the lists of battles, particularly the inclusion of Berlin, echoed stories told to me in several other contexts, which marked World War II as the moment in which Buryats became part of the greater Soviet project, standing beside other Soviet nationalities as they liberated Berlin from fascism. We will revisit this historical genre in Chapter 2.

FIGURE 1.6 Display board explaining the "Formation of the Commune 'Soël.'" Soël means "culture" in Buryat. Orongoi, September 5, 2005.

The posters continue to chronicle the post-war years with pictures of local collective members who won awards for labor, distinguished brigade leaders, and "meritorious toilers" (Russ.—*zasluzhennye truzheniki*). The post-war years are not dated, but another poster includes a "diagram of harvests" from 1935 to 2002, bringing the collective farm's history into the present.

Told in a Soviet "just the facts" style, this historical genre does not explicitly contradict the oral histories of the villagers or the institutional history produced by the Buddhist Sangha. The posters represent the Soviet history of the village, without any meta-discursive markers that indicate how it should be read. This is a story of a village that identified with Soviet goals, that chose the name "Culture" in accordance with state policies, and whose residents fought bravely on the Soviet battlefield and home front. Time in this chronotope is linear, a progression of ever-growing harvest production figures, taken, presumably, from the records of the collective farm.

Implicitly, however, the faces of military and home front veterans—likely relatives of contemporary villagers—appear to stare out at their descendants, demanding acknowledgement, if not identification. This historical genre implicitly opposes the story of Soviet repression that was emphasized by both

FIGURE 1.7 Display board showing portraits of the "Soldiers of Orongoi—Cavaliers of the Order of Glory." Orongoi, September 5, 2005.

the Buddhist and shamanic village genres. In this genre, the Soviet state is taken for granted as the worthy object of military sacrifice. There are no claims made about the significance of the events on these posters, and as a result, the viewer is free to interpret them as they wish. As a result, while this is also the history of Orongoi, the narrative on the posters does not orient this community toward a specific relationship to this past or to a future. No one involved in the consecration seemed to think it was inappropriate or disconcerting to include this history. This too, is the history of Orongoi, a narrative that takes pride in the villagers' achievements under socialism. Buddhism is not part of this narrative; neither Buddhism nor Etigelov is present in this past.

These three different historical genres coexisted at the ritual consecrating the stupa. In one sense, these genres are complementary, because each produces different kinds of knowledge about different time periods. The Buddhist genre produces new historical information about the pre-Soviet past. The oral histories documented by the shamanic village genre focus on the period of collectivization. That genre overlaps with the Soviet genre in the posters, which begin in collectivization and carry the viewer to the present. The Soviet genre may produce isolated new details about the past (most villagers probably did not know exactly how much grain was produced in any given year), but this genre does not produce a new perspective on the past. Instead, it verifies a familiar one.

The sources of knowledge and the legitimating authority of each of these genres is also different. The Buddhist genre is grounded in Buddhist manuscripts and legitimated through divination and the physical presence of the spring. The shamanic genre is grounded in oral history, legitimated through the personal authority of individual villagers. The Soviet genre is grounded in archival sources—the state farm archives—authorized by the Soviet state. In this sense, drawing on different sources for information, the three genres also complement each other.

However, as chronotopes, each produces time in profoundly different ways. In the Buddhist genre, time is recursive, endowing linear Russian history with Buddhist religious meaning through Etigelov's reincarnate returns, producing Buryat Buddhism as authentically Russian, and Buryat land as already Buddhist. In the shamanic genre, Etigelov is a spirit master, whose powerful presence from the past continuously watches over the multi-ethnic residents of his homeland, helping them live in the present. In the Soviet genre, time begins in collectivization, proceeds linearly, and continues into the present. Etigelov—and his reincarnations—are irrelevant to this chronotope.

The three genres exist side by side, each of them producing chronotopic frameworks within which those producing them can situate themselves. At the same time, each genre remains fragmentary, none of them able to produce a narrative that fully encompasses one community in the present in relationship to a single past. Subsequent chapters will focus on single rituals conducted in single genres, but as we encounter them we should not forget that, just as they do in Orongoi, these genres of history exist side by side with other genres for the residents of Buryatia.

2

Soviet Selves

VICTORY DAY

One loves in proportion to the sacrifices to which one has consented, and in proportion to the ills that one has suffered. . . . Where national memories are concerned, griefs are of more value than triumphs, for they impose duties, and require a common effort.

—RENAN 1996, 52–53

WHEN I LIVED in Ulan-Ude in 2004–5, I rented an apartment in the Prospekt Pobedy neighborhood. "Prospekt Pobedy" means Victory Avenue. The neighborhood, named for its central street, is a residential area near the city center, where employees of the city's cultural, medical, and educational institutions were given apartments by the Soviet state in the 1950s and '60s. Many of these now-retired cultural workers or their children still live in the neighborhood. While those residents who have made money in the post-Soviet period build individual houses on the outskirts of town, Prospekt Pobedy is still a desirable location because of its proximity to downtown.

At the center of the Prospekt stands a World War II monument: a Soviet tank on a pedestal, looming over a grand staircase, a plaque, metal bas-reliefs of soldiers, and an eternal flame. It is not a coincidence that the Buryat cultural elite of the late Soviet years were given apartments in a neighborhood distinguished by a World War II monument. The war is an integral part of the Soviet history of progress that produced that elite. The immense wartime losses of the Soviet victory in World War II are the foundational sacrifice of the Soviet Union.

The Soviet state no longer exists, but Victory Day continues to be celebrated every May 9. In 2005, the 60th anniversary celebration of the victory over Germany prompted more extensive festivities than usual, and thus more opportunities for the residents of Buryatia to revisit these historical events.

Norris (2011) argues that 2005 was the height of state-sponsored attempts to foster post-Soviet patriotism.

City preparations for the celebration began well before the actual holiday, and businesses throughout the city posted advertisements featuring World War II themes and tributes to veterans in the early spring. World War II was a common topic of discussion that year, and so this chapter is based not only on the actual holiday itself but also on the way in which Victory Day, and World War II veterans and memorials, were written about in local publications and discussed by residents of Ulan-Ude throughout the year.

By the time May 9 arrived, one might have thought that the Soviet Union had never dissolved. Victory Day recalled the Soviet Union through both the explicit use of Soviet imagery and the parade that formed the central activity of the day (Lane 1981; Petrone 2000; Rolf 2013). The public celebrations evoked the war through visual imagery: public spaces in the city were plastered with reproductions of wartime photographs and posters using 1940s fonts and images of military medals. This visual imagery, produced and displayed by the post-Soviet Russian state, evoked the war as an empty signifier, into which individuals could project their own significance. Local residents in Buryatia, from magazine editors to people on the street, reacted to this imagery by retelling the historical events of the war and re-evaluating what it meant for Buryats to participate in it. In doing so, they reproduced the (to them) familiar Soviet historical chronotope, in which time is linear, and the Soviet people are moving toward ever-greater modernity and progress. However, by re-valuing the wartime experience in various ways, they transformed the meaning of these events and produced a critical commentary on the role of Buryats in contemporary Russia.

As is the case with most of the rituals discussed in this book, no one explicitly narrated a history during the ritual. Rather, the ritual presumed and evoked a particular chronotope through its material forms, and people drew on this chronotope in their discussions of the ritual. Both the Soviet-style ritual forms and the Soviet version of Buryat history were familiar to most of the audience. However, rather than simply reinforcing the Soviet version of Buryat history, the ritual actually destabilized it. The mismatch between Soviet forms and the post-Soviet present opened up space for doubt and prompted reinterpretation.

Victory Day, 2005: The City as Backdrop

Contemporary civic rituals in Ulan-Ude take place in its central areas, in physical spaces that were constructed during the Soviet period. Like Barnaul, another Siberian city described by Oushakine (2009, 2–3), and unlike many cities in the European part of Russia, Ulan-Ude has not removed most of its Soviet-era monuments or renamed its main streets. As was typical for Soviet-style city planning, the heart of the city is Soviet Square, a large open space surrounded by administrative buildings. Parades, civic festivals, and political demonstrations take place in Soviet Square, which is flanked on two sides by government administrative buildings, on the third side by the Buryat State University, and on the fourth by cultural institutions including the Buryat State Philharmonic, the Baikal Hotel, and the Wedding Palace, where civil wedding ceremonies take place. Each side of Soviet Square is occupied by institutions (government, education, cultural) that represent the modernity that the Soviet Union brought to Buryatia.

The square is dominated by an enormous sculpture of Lenin's head, which sits atop a pedestal in front of the republic's administration building (see Figures 2.1, 2.2, 2.4). When I asked people why the head had not been removed, most people said this was their history, and so it should be preserved. Several also joked that it was too big to move. Post-Soviet countries in Eastern Europe can reach back to a pre-Soviet national past, excising the Soviet experience as something imposed from outside. In Siberia, however, that pre-Soviet past is so distant and so different from the present that excising the Soviet experience is unthinkable. Post-Soviet daily life is still lived within a physical world constructed by the Soviet Union.

Founded as a Cossack outpost in 1661, Ulan-Ude was known as Verkhneudinsk until 1934. Prior to the Bolshevik Revolution, Verkhneudinsk was a Russian trading post, a stopping place along the route that connected Beijing and Moscow, where tea and silk from China were brought to Russia in exchange for fur and honey from Russian forests. Wealthy merchants were exclusively ethnic Russians and Russian Jews, which meant Verkhneudinsk, like nearby Kiakhta and Irkutsk, were Russian cities surrounded by a predominantly Buryat semi-nomadic countryside.

After the Russian Civil War, Verkhneudinsk was designated the capital city of the newly created Buryat-Mongolian Autonomous Soviet Socialist Republic (BMASSR), formed in 1923. The BMASSR was one of many autonomous republics founded by the fledgling Bolshevik government to win the loyalty of national minority groups by assuring them territorial autonomy (Carr 1985; Suny 1993; Hirsch 2005). Soviet nationality policy was based on a Marxist teleology of historical development, arguing that each nationality must go through its own process of historical development. Autonomous territories and republics were created for nationalities so that they would have a territorial base for this historical development. The role of the state was to help foster individual national cultures so that nationalism would "wither away" and the

Soviet nationalities would be united into a "friendship of the peoples" (see also Chapter 3). Under *korenizatsiia* (nativization), as the nationality policy was called at the time, the Soviet government recruited Buryats to work in the cities to build a native intelligentsia and proletariat (Martin 2001; Chakars 2014).

In 1934, the city was renamed Ulan-Ude, which means "Red Uda," after one of the rivers that runs through the city, to mark its change from a Russian trading post to the capital city of an indigenous republic. The landscape of the city changed along with its demography, and the socio-economic position of Buryats within it. As a result of nearly a century of Soviet social planning, the city and the population that celebrated Victory Day in Ulan-Ude 2005 looked very little like Verkhneudinsk and its inhabitants in 1917. Although the Soviet Union's efforts at building a Buryat proletariat were not successful, their attempt to build a native intelligentsia succeeded beyond their wildest dreams. Cultural, government, educational, and medical professions in the republic were dominated by Buryats (Khalbaeva-Boronova 2005; Chakars 2014; Giuliano 2011). Although Russians remain the demographic majority throughout the republic, Ulan-Ude is, in terms of public monuments, cultural events, and tourism, very much a Buryat city.

In preparation for Victory Day, enormous banners were hung on all four sides of Soviet Square, reading "On the anniversary of the victory" (Russ.—*c iubileem pobedy*), "60 years of the Great Victory" (Russ.—*60 let velikoi pobedy*), "Glory to the Victorious People" (Russ.—*slava narodu pobediteliu*), and finally, on a banner featuring the Soviet Order of Victory medal and an image of Marshall Zhukov on a white horse at the original 1945 parade, "9 May, on the anniversary of the Great Victory" (Russ.—*9 Maia c prazdnikom velikoi pobedy*; see Figure 2.1). A small stage was built opposite Lenin's statue. It was decorated with a sculpture of five red metal stars, each bearing one year of the war, 1941 through 1945, and the words "five fiery years" (Russ.—*piat' ognennykh let*; see Figure 2.5).

For at least a week before the holiday, life went on as usual around these preparations, taxis parking in the square and skateboarders practicing under Lenin's head. The sculpture and stage were only set up for a short time, but the banners, in the center as well as the rest of the city, remained up for several months. People went about their daily lives surrounded by images of World War II.

Victory Day, 2005: The Event

On the morning of May 9, the square was filled with people watching the military parades. Politicians and dignitaries were seated directly under

FIGURE 2.1 Soviet square in Ulan-Ude, showing the Lenin monument. The government building behind it is decorated with banners for Victory Day reading "Celebrating the Great Victory" and "May 9th." The monument is a popular place for skateboarders to practice. Ulan-Ude, May 2005.

Lenin's head. A separate seating section was set aside, to the left of Lenin, for veterans and their families, who were almost exclusively home-front veterans (Russ.—*veterany tyla*): women and children who had filled in for the men away at the front during the war, producing record-breaking agricultural yields to feed the troops. Very few WWII combat veterans were still alive by 2005, because in the mid-2000s in Russia, male life expectancy was only 54 years, and anyone who had served at the front would have been in their 80's.[1]

Seated among these veterans was a middle-aged Buryat man, too young to be a veteran himself, holding a painted portrait of a young Stalin attached to a pole (see Figures 2.2, 2.3). The visual effect of the red banners with the Soviet Order of Victory behind Lenin's head and Stalin's portrait in the stands nearby was uncanny, as if we had all traveled back in time to the Soviet era.

A few politicians gave short speeches, but neither I nor the other audience members could hear a word of what was said. The speeches were quickly followed by a parade of military troops and a military band (see Figure 2.4), and then a dance performance by a group of young Buryat women dressed in bright red leotard dresses, who performed a modern dance around the metal sculpture of five stars (see Figure 2.5).

FIGURE 2.2 Stalin portrait under the Lenin monument before the parade, Soviet Square, Victory Day, Ulan-Ude, May 9, 2005.

After the parade, the crowd of spectators strolled down Lenin Street, the city's main thoroughfare. Locals call the street "our Arbat" in reference to the main pedestrian mall in Moscow, recognizing the way in which Soviet-built cities reproduce set patterns, and, at the same time, ironically marking their distance from the "original." Friends met us for the parade, but as one put it, "Well, you should go," (in reference to the fact that I was a foreigner and ethnographer, and therefore naturally interested in festivals and holidays) "but for most of us, it's just an excuse for a *gulianie*." Literally, *gulianie* means "stroll," but colloquially it means "to go out drinking with your friends." It seemed as if most of the city was strolling down Lenin Street or chatting and drinking on its benches.

Lenin Street leads down a hill, past the Buryat State Opera building, which is widely believed to have been built by World War II prisoners (although that is apparently untrue).[2] Lenin Street becomes a pedestrian mall, with a large monument bearing the symbol of the Buryat republic, and then leads into Revolution Square, the center of the pre-Soviet portion of the town,

FIGURE 2.3 Veterans and "heroes of the home front" sitting to the left of the Lenin head during the parade. Note the Stalin portrait, also visible prior to the parade in Figure 2.2. Victory Day Celebrations, Ulan-Ude, May 9, 2005.

FIGURE 2.4 Victory Day Parade, Ulan-Ude, May 9, 2005.

FIGURE 2.5 Sculpture and stage for Victory Day parade, Ulan-Ude, May 9, 2005. The sign reads "Five fiery years."

where pre-Soviet trading arches were turned into the State department store. A bouncy castle for children was set up in Revolution Square by an enterprising businessman. The strolling crowd then headed left at Revolution Square, across the tram tracks, to a small park at the foot of the Victory Monument on Prospekt Pobedy.

The park below the Victory Monument was filled with people, including many elderly men and women, both Buryat and Russian, all wearing medals, and often accompanied by younger family members who carefully shepherded them through the crowds. Anyone who owned a uniform of any sort seemed to be wearing it, but, unlike on religious holidays, no one I saw was wearing a Buryat national costume. Along the tram tracks across the street, huge posters showed historic World War II photographs of soldiers with small captions at the bottom: marching troops, a visibly Asian soldier "on the Central Front," troops "liberating Sevastopol," and an image of a troop transport labeled "77 km from Berlin." The series ended with the iconic photograph of the Red Army flag being raised over the Reichstag (see Figure 2.6).

The street in front of the Victory Monument was decorated with a large arch made from orange and black balloons (see Figure 2.7). Troops were lined

FIGURE 2.6 Historical photographs from World War II along the tram tracks across from Prospekt Pobedy, Ulan-Ude, May 9, 2005.

FIGURE 2.7 The World War II war memorial on Prospekt Pobedy on Victory Day, Ulan-Ude, May 9, 2005.

up alongside the stairs leading to the Victory Monument, keeping the public at bay. A Russian man and a Buryat woman stood at the base of the steps with a microphone, but again, no one could hear what they said. The then-president of the Republic of Buryatia, Leonid Potapov; Ulan-Ude's mayor at the time, Gennadii Aidaev; and a handful of other politicians climbed the steps and placed four enormous flower wreaths around the eternal flame at the base of the monument. After the politicians had paid their respects, the monument was opened for the public to leave flowers at the base. With this, the official celebration ended, and most of the city's residents spent the rest of the day strolling the streets and sitting with friends and families in cafes or at dinner at home.

Victory Day in the Russian National Imaginary

The extensive literature on the role of World War II and Victory Day in the popular Russian and Soviet imagination points out that it is a powerful holiday because the immense losses of World War II touched every family in the Soviet Union. Nina Tumarkin calls Victory Day "the only real, official holiday. It was both the tool of propagandists touting its triumphs and a memorial day for millions of relatives and friends of the war dead" (1994, 37). Personal emotion and family histories can be linked to the idea of the nation, precisely the way in which Victor Turner argues a symbol works, linking sensory and emotional significata to abstract and ideological meanings (1967, 28). Tumarkin and Lane (1981) both see Victory Day as one of the (if not the primary) state holidays during the Soviet period. After a brief lull immediately following the dissolution of the Soviet Union, Victory Day has continued to be the major state holiday for the post-Soviet Russian state. This continuity produces an anachronistic dissonance, in that a Soviet victory is being celebrated as a central state holiday by the Russian Federation, a government that both is and is not continuous with the Soviet Union.

Stephen Norris (2011) offers an excellent overview of the way in which Victory Day celebrations in Russia have changed since the end of World War II, focusing on the fraught relationship between Stalin's role as wartime leader and the potential incongruity of venerating a person responsible for millions of deaths in the 1937 purges. As Norris shows, both the role of the state in directing the commemoration and the role of Stalin in the celebrations have shifted dramatically over time. The 60th anniversary of Victory Day in 2005 was "the peak of ideological efforts to rehabilitate Soviet symbols and to consolidate the population of the Russian Federation—that nation in the making—on the basis of the Soviet, essentially Stalinist concept of the Great

Patriotic War" (Zolotov, cited in Norris, 2011, 228). By this account, then, the 2005 celebration that I describe here is not typical of Victory Day celebrations as a whole.

What matters here, however, is not whether the state's push toward reviving Stalinist imagery or glorifying the Soviet past is typical, but rather the way in which local residents in Buryatia responded to this national history by re-reading these historical events. Jonathan Brunstedt (2011) argues that although Victory Day is often considered by outside observers to be a Russian nationalist holiday, it is not the Russian people, in fact, but the multi-ethnic Soviet people (Russ.—*Sovetskii narod*) that is the referent of the holiday. By this reading, when a banner on a building in Ulan-Ude reads "glory to the victorious people" (Russ.—*slava narodu pobediteliu*), the *narod* evoked is the Soviet people. Brunstedt argues this is a multi-ethnic civic "us" that not only includes Buryats, but marks the historical moment when these nationalities became fully Soviet citizens through their participation in wartime sacrifice. The term "narod" was generally used in the context of Soviet nationality policies to define an ethnic group, such as "Russkii narod" or "Buriatskii narod." In contrast, "Sovetskii narod" is ambiguous, implying both multi-ethnic political unity, but also opening up a space for the audience to critically interrogate what it meant for Buryats to be part of the Soviet people. Furthermore, since the Soviet Union no longer exists, what does it mean for Buryats to have been one of the "Sovetskii narod" within the Russian Federation, which was increasingly identifying as an ethnically Russian nation-state?

A similar tension between Soviet unity and local difference pervaded the physical forms of the ritual. Part of the power of the ritual stemmed from its sameness across the Russian Federation. Citizens in cities throughout the Russian Federation did the same thing that day: watched military parades in Soviet Square, strolled down Lenin Street, and listened to a military salute in front of a war memorial on Victory Boulevard. Even the street names are the same from one city to the next.

However, each city also honored its own veterans, and its own population connected their personal narratives to this national form. Additionally, in Ulan-Ude, this form, like the phrase "Sovetskii narod," is open to interpretation. The majority of posters and banners bore very simple slogans, such as "*c prazdnikom*," which means merely "happy holiday," or "60 years of Victory" and the dates. Such simple slogans and visual images, like the picture of the raising of the Red Army flag over the Reichstag, act as empty signifiers, referencing the event without prescribing its meaning, prompting local residents to endow these empty signifiers with their own interpretations.

The Soviet Chronotope

There was not, during the Soviet or the post-Soviet period, a single official Buryat history. History was evoked in textbooks, ethnographies, and the media (all of which were vetted by state censors), and the state-produced version was not completely consistent. However, there is a fairly uniform Soviet historical genre, within which the incorporation of the Buryat people into the Soviet Union is recounted as a story of how the Soviet Union brought civilization to native Siberia, and unlike their tsarist predecessors, offered the possibility of full inclusion and citizenship. Within this genre, Buryats gratefully embraced this modernity and the union was sanctified by collective sacrifice in World War II. The chronotope of this genre is linear and modernist; the heroes are the Buryat nation and the Soviet state.

Claims to historical knowledge in this genre are grounded not only in state archives and published history books, but also in people's lived experience. By the 2000s, members of the oldest living generation were children during the height of Stalinist violence. The earliest memories and family stories of the vast majority of residents date to the post World War II period of political stability and steady economic development, corroborating the official version of history as a story of progress and modernity. As a result, for most Buryats, the Soviet genre is the most familiar, a taken-for-granted way of thinking about the past.

The Soviet Chronotope: Bringing Progress and Modernity to Buryatia

In the following section, I draw on historical sources to illustrate points. However, overall, I seek to recreate this historical genre as I encountered it in conversations, museum displays, and newspaper articles. As with the genres I discuss in other chapters, the historical events that are recounted in this genre happened. What is distinctive is how the genre presents these events, embeds them in a particular chronotope, thereby orienting time, actors, and meaning so that the events tell this particular story.

At the time of the revolution, most Buryats, like other Siberian nationalities, were illiterate, semi-nomadic herders. The tsars, concerned only with tribute payments, made no effort to spread civilization and enlightenment, and allowed Russian administrators, Buryat clan leaders, Buddhist lamas, and shamans to exploit the population, keeping them in ignorance and rife with disease. Buryats, however, had tremendous intellectual potential, as evidenced by the small but devout communist intelligentsia that had developed in Buryatia, initially fostered by the revolutionary Decembrists who had been exiled to the Baikal area in the 1830s. Young Buryat Bolsheviks spread support for Bolshevism among their fellow Buryats, and helped bring the enlightenment of communism to Mongolia.

In 1923, the new Bolshevik government granted the Buryat people their own Autonomous Soviet Socialist Republic so that they would be able to achieve their fullest potential among the Soviet brotherhood of nations. However, these efforts were hindered by the population's low levels of education and the malicious influences of both Buddhist lamas and shamans. Anti-religious propaganda in the 1920s and '30s denounced both shamans and lamas as corrupt and greedy, profiting from the ignorance of the population, working against socialist reforms and fostering disease. For example, a document produced by the Buryat branch of the League of the Militant Godless in 1930 states: "Lamaism in our republic is the most reactionary, most active opponent of Socialist construction and cultural revolution. The population's conservatism toward new habits, hospitals, schools, and *kolkhozes* is the result of corrupting work of many thousands of lamas" (NARB Fond R-245, Opis 1, Delo 450, List 21, also Aiusheeva et al. 2001,117). Articles in the atheist newspaper *Bezbozhnik* accused Buddhists of supporting the imperial government.[3] Anti-religious propaganda in the 1930s and 1940s assured readers that Soviet modernity was relegating religion to the past: "The old beliefs are collapsing, the datsans are declining, and the Buryat youth reach out for knowledge. The Buryat hunter brings sacrifices to the datsan, but in his heart, in his bag, next to the amulet the lamas gave him, lies the membership booklet of the Hunting Collective" (Okuneva 1930, 16). Socialism offered modernity and enlightenment.

Collectivization brought rationalized planning, scientific advances, and cultural development that rapidly improved the standard of living for most Buryats. Once isolated nomadic herding families were relocated to villages, both adults and children could attend school and could access medical services. Collectivization was also a key element in the fight against religious backwardness. In 1931, the height of collectivization in Buryatia, more than 200,000 hectares of land were "taken" from "kulaks, *noyons* [*sic*] and lamas" (Pomus 1943, 45–46).

Liberating the Buryat people from the influence of lamas and shamans was an essential part of this cultural transformation. In 1926, in a resolution by Mikhei Nikolaevich Erbanov, first Secretary of the Buryat Communist Party, Buddhism and shamanism were described as "certainly factors which strongly hamper national-cultural construction; the fight with these prejudices, without a doubt, is not only the task of the administration, but also of every Buryat-Mongol culture-worker" (NARB Fond P-1, Opis 1, Delo 864, List 76-77, also Aiusheeva et al. 2001, 83). By 1936 all three Russian Orthodox churches in Ulan-Ude and every Buddhist temple in Buryatia had been closed. Hans Braeker states that there were 6,900 lamas in Buryatia in 1929, but by 1936 that number had dropped to 900 (1989, 179). By 1936, Vyacheslav Mikhailovich Molotov, chairman of the Council of People's Commissars, was able to announce, "the Buryat Mongolians had forever put an end to the many-thousand-headed class of lamas, which had like leeches sucked the blood from the body of the people of Buryat Mongolia" (cited in Braeker 1989, 179; see also Snelling 1993, 243).

At the same time as it launched its anti-religious reforms, the regime pursued a policy of "nationalization," "nativization," or "indigenization" (*korenizatsiia*), which meant fostering the national culture of national minorities. In 1934, as noted, Verkhneudinsk was renamed Ulan-Ude, to mark its transformation from a Russian colonial outpost to an indigenous city. As one of the "backward" republics, *korenizatsiia* in Buryatia involved educating the Buryat population and integrating them into the working class and intelligentsia. As noted already, in 1930, a Latin alphabet was introduced for the Buryat language, which up until then was predominantly written in classical Mongolian script. Unlike the classical Mongolian script, which was difficult to learn, the new Latin alphabet would make it easier for the Buryat masses to learn to read and write in their own language. The Latin alphabet was described as more conducive to the Soviet state's scientific advances than Mongolian script, which "might have been alright for prayers to the Living Buddha but was not much good for agronomy, zoology, meteorology and sociology" (Phillips 1942, 155). The Latin alphabet was replaced by Cyrillic in 1938 to tie Buryats closer to Russian culture and language (Martin 2001; Montgomery 2005; Phillips 1942).[4]

By investing in education and cultural development, the Soviet state's official goal was to liberate oppressed minority nationalities from their backwardness, so that they could one day rule themselves as equal members of the Soviet Federation. Pomus cites the expenditure of 60 percent of the BMASSR's 1936 budget on social and cultural activities as "the steadfast application in Buriat-Mongolia of the Lenin-Stalin national policy which aims at liquidating the economic and cultural backwardness of the former colonial border regions of Tsarist Russia" (1943, 63). These policies were rhetorically important to the Communist Party in that they allowed the Soviet Union to occupy a moral high ground in comparison to both their imperial predecessors and Western colonial powers.

Collectivization and reform were so successful in Buryatia that it was sometimes used as an example of why Soviet nationality policies were superior to those of the Western democracies. Along with Pomus (1943), Phillips

(1942)—a British Soviet sympathizer—cites Soviet policies in Buryatia as an example of the benefits of socialism. In 1936, Erbanov, the Buryat party secretary cited above, who oversaw collectivization, was awarded the Order of Lenin "for his share in transforming the B.M.A.S.S.R. into 'one of the most advanced republics of the U.S.S.R.'" (cited in Kolarz 1954, 120).[5] Buryatia was a Soviet success story, an example of how benevolent Soviet educational policies could turn illiterate herders into scientists and scholars.

Although these sources are historical, these discourses had a lasting effect. Despite a great deal of discussion in the local popular media about pre-Soviet Buryat culture, the image of Buryats as primitive, illiterate herders was surprisingly resilient. For example, I asked a Russian taxi driver his opinion of the possible merger of Buryatia into Chita or Irkutsk oblasts. Like many Russians, he was in favor of it, as he thought it would improve the economy. Playing devil's advocate, I asked, "What do you think about the argument that Buryats will lose their culture?"

"What culture?" he scoffed. "Everything here the Soviets built. Buryats were just a bunch of dirty savages before we came." The efforts of Buryat intellectuals to dispute these claims testify to their continuing pervasiveness.

Victory Day, The Soviet Chronotope, and Its Permutations in 2005

Whenever World War II was mentioned—and in 2005 it was mentioned a lot—someone usually noted with pride that Buryats were there when Berlin was liberated. This may have been common knowledge, but it was also documented in detail in the magazine *Secrets of Buryatia* (Russ.—*Tainy Buriatii*), a locally produced magazine that emulates *National Geographic* and focuses on the history of the Baikal area. In 2005, the magazine ran a three-part article reproducing the journal and photographs of Semen Mitupovich Dugaron, chronicling the wartime exploits of the 321st Rifle Division (later renamed the 82nd Rifle Guards Division) in the battle for Stalingrad and the liberation of Berlin. The story of the 321st begins in July of 1942 as they are sent to fight for Stalingrad:

> Realizing that they were not moving forward toward the walls of Stalingrad in the stretch of territory guarded by our division, the enemy began distributing propaganda flyers from airplanes, calling our soldiers the "savage division." They promised a good life in prison. We were even proud of that name, "the Siberian savage division." . . . the

> 321st Rifle Division (later the 82nd Guards) was formed in March 1942 from conscripts from the Buryat-Mongolian ASSR and Chita oblast. In the division were about 4,000 soldiers of Buryat nationality. . . . Soldiers of the Division in Stalingrad showed themselves to be a miracle of bravery, courage and heroism . . . ." (Dugaron 2005a, 3)

The article lists individual names (although not all), including "the glorious daughter of the Buryat people, military doctor Margarita Andreeva, who, taking over for a slain machine-gunner, destroyed 45 fascists. She posthumously received the Order of the Red Banner" (Dugaron 2005a, 5). Photos around the articles show Buryat and Russian faces, often noting under the Russian faces that they are local, from Ulan-Ude or surrounding towns, whereas the Buryat faces are captioned only with names, self-evidently local and needing no explanation. The article about Stalingrad features a photograph of a Buryat soldier standing next to a captured German tank that had previously been used in North Africa under Rommel.

The final article focuses on the liberation of Berlin, which the 321st participated in. The last photograph in the four-page glossy spread is titled "Soldiers from Buryat-Mongolia at the Brandenburg Gate" and features four visibly Buryat soldiers and one Russian posing in front of the famous landmark. The conclusion notes that the 321st division "gave the country 18 Heroes of the Soviet Union and 32 Full Cavaliers of the Order of Glory" (Dugaron 2005b, 5).

Articles published to commemorate the 60th anniversary of Victory Day, such as this one showing Russians and Buryats fighting together, focus on the contributions of the Buryat people to the greater Soviet cause. A locally produced television documentary about the Buryat State Opera cited the fact that Buryat singers performed for the Red Army troops in World War II as evidence of "the high level of artistic skill and the high level of friendship between the Soviet peoples." These stories, told in 2005, emphasize the Buryat contribution to the Soviet narrative of progress, thereby reinforcing the Soviet genre of history, long after the Soviet Union ended.

World War II and the contributions of the Buryat people to the war effort were sometimes brought up in conversations that seemingly had very little to do with history. In 2004–5 the grocery stores were filled with European butter, which was quite expensive, while locally produced butter was difficult to find, despite the fact that Buryatia has traditionally been a dairy-producing area. Dairy products, as so-called "white foods," are appropriate ritual offerings, and Buddhist New Year is called Tsagaalgan, or White Month, after the dairy products that are eaten for this festival. Along with sour cream and milk, butter has a lot of symbolic weight in Buryatia, which made it the one product whose absence from grocery shelves provoked repeated comments. More than one elderly person stopped me in the grocery aisles or commented over tea that during World War II or the 1940s to '50s, Buryatia supplied the entire Soviet Union with butter and meat, and now there was only foreign butter in the stores. The current economic decline was critiqued by evoking a glorious past, when Buryatia fed the war-deprived Soviet Union and its troops.

After the war, returning veterans, whose perspectives had been broadened by the experience, continued building socialism in Buryatia. From the 1950s to 1989 Buryats became an urbanized, highly educated population that filled the ranks of Soviet cultural, administrative, academic, and medical institutions. In their experience, the collective sacrifice during World War II produced inclusion and prosperity after the war. For many of the Buryats I spoke with, especially members of the older generations, World War II and Victory Day represented that inclusive moment when Buryats became full participants in the glorious sacrifice of the Red Army and full participants in the Soviet project.

Critique Within the Soviet Genre

The accounts described above all offer a positive evaluation of the past. However, some people spoke about the past to critique the Soviet project. These speakers refer to the same historical events and engage with them through the same modernist, linear chronotope, but by including historical events and consequences that are usually left out, they evaluate the past very differently.

The historical events are not contested. Buryat herders were collectivized. Buryat soldiers fought in World War II. After World War II, large numbers of Buryats pursued higher education and professional jobs, while at the same time, large numbers of Buryats stopped speaking Buryat in daily life. From the perspective of Soviet state narratives, these were all good things because they brought "modernity" to a "backward" area of Russia. After the Soviet Union collapsed, many people began to doubt this version of history, arguing that the cost of modernity—namely, the loss of life and cultural traditions—was too high. Those who critiqued the Soviet version of the past often included other historical events that were not usually part of the Soviet genre, but they did so without disrupting the linear Soviet chronotope. For those who embraced the Soviet version, those who disagreed with it, and those who were not sure what to think, World War II remained a pivotal symbolic event.

A visit to a museum in Aga revealed the clear links between military victory in World War II and the preceding state violence. As we walked through the museum displays, the young Buryat tour guide recounted the history of the Baikal area. The museum followed a slightly different path than the standard Soviet historical narrative, beginning with the Huns, moving on to Chinghis Khan, the incorporation of Buryatia into the Russian Empire, and the late 19th-century Buryat intelligentsia. "There were such people among us in that generation," said the guide, commenting on such famous intellectuals as Tsybikov. Tsybikov, he noted, was lucky to have died in his own bed, unlike most of his contemporaries, who perished in the 1937 purges. "The generation of the Civil War were all equally cruel" (Russ.—*zhestokost' ne otlichaetsia*), he explained. We reached the museum panels on World War II. Of Stalin, the tour guide said:

> For all that he was cruel (Russ.—*zhestokii*), like Napoleon or Chinghis Khan, he was right in his own way (Russ.—*on byl prav po-svoemu*) because he understood that all the forces of the world were allied against Soviet power, that eventually there would be war, and Russia was weak. He had to protect Russia, and modernize it, so he had a three-pronged approach: collectivization, industrialization, and cultural revolution, so that the population would become educated (Russ.—*gramotnyi*). He understood that people are lazy, they need the knout, and although the cost was millions of lives, he was right, and did what he had to do to protect the government, and that's what Westerners don't understand.

Behind him, on the wall, were displays featuring local Buryats in the war effort, including a poster of female tractor drivers who brought in a 230 percent harvest (more than double the production target) while filling in for their men, who were away at the front.

I often heard variants of this explanation when I was in Buryatia: Stalin may have been cruel and brutal, but his brutality was justified because it prepared the people of the Soviet Union for their heroic victory against fascism. The state violence of the 1930s, while lamented, was redeemed by the victory over Hitler. By participating in this victory, Buryats became one with the greater Soviet people. By this account, Buryat suffering during collectivization and the purges is not particular to Buryats, nor a sign of the unique oppression of the Buryat people, but rather part of a greater collective suffering in the name of eventual victory. All the citizens of the Soviet Union suffered in the name of victory, and by suffering with them, Buryats became full citizens too. The tour guide's version of the past incorporates new historical events (the purges and state violence), but it does so in a way that reaffirms the just power of the state and the Soviet chronotope.

World War II and the celebrations of Victory Day were equally central to those who criticized the entire Soviet project. For example, Elena Mikhailovna, a Buryat intellectual who was nearing retirement, insisted on taking me to a spot in the forest outside the city, where she suspected people had been shot during the 1937 repressions.[6] The area we visited was littered with garbage, but we could see the remains of two larger houses with bullet holes in the walls, and a smaller house, set apart on a rise, that she suspected had been a guard house. Remnants of barbed wire rusted in the grass, but we were not able to tell when it had been left there. Most of the garbage was recent. She admitted that there was no concrete proof, but she had heard rumors of such a site, and concluded that these abandoned buildings were the most likely location of the old prison camp. There was no doubt that thousands had died in the Stalinist repressions in Buryatia, as throughout the Soviet Union, but no one seemed to know exactly where or how. Her suspicions were as good as any.

I asked her who was shot here. She answered:

"Buryats and Russians. The Buryats weren't enough, they also shot Russians. They would come and collect people in the middle of the night. My mother told me a story about someone who was arrested, and a friend then traveled home to warn family and neighbors, because there had been photos of them together with the person who had been arrested. They knew that Buryats tended to save money over several generations, and turn all their money into gold and hide it, so they assumed all Buryat families were hiding gold.[7] A lot of times people would turn in neighbors over greed."

"How many people do you think died here?" I asked.

"Who knows? If they could kill 50 lamas in a day when they closed a monastery, who knows how many they killed. There always had to be an enemy. They killed all those lamas, and then they said that we were an illiterate people. The first time I thought about the nationality question, I was 10, and where I lived there was a Russian *babushka* (grandmother/old lady), and I was enrolled in the music school, and the Russian lady, a nice lady, she took care of me. She asked 'where are you going to study?' and I said, 'at the music school' and the lady said 'that's good, we'll teach you well' (Russ.—*my tebe vyuchim*) and I resented it so, and it took me most of my life to get the words to express what I felt, that this ignorant babushka would say such a thing. . . ."

Elena Mikhailovna was unusual in her thoughtfulness about nationality relations and her refutation of the Soviet project. Her anger as a child arose from her perception that a village peasant grandmother assumed herself to be superior to a Buryat, in her declaration that "we Russians" will teach "you

Buryats," a moment when the abstract narrative of Soviet progress became a personally felt insult.

Quite a few people discussed the 1937 repressions with me. For some, the discussion in 2005 of dissolving the Aga and Ust-Orda Buryat okrugs called to mind similar events in 1937. In 1937 two smaller territories, the Ust-Orda and Aga okrugs, were split off from the republic, and the territories in between the okrugs and the republic were given to the neighboring Irkutsk and Chita oblasts. The territorial reform separated Buryat populations from each other and weakened Buryat political representation. These okrugs were now being dissolved, finalizing the territorial losses that had begun in 1937. For others, usually those who embraced a shamanic chronotope (see Chapters 1, 5, and 6), the violence of 1937 was described as a source of negative karma or bad energy, which was responsible for the present generation's problems. For everyone who spoke about the repressions and the violence of the 1930s, it was still present in contemporary life. No one, however, articulated the links between the Soviet narrative of national progress and the celebration of Victory Day as clearly as Elena Mikhailovna, and so I will cite her at length:

> My neighbor worked for the military hospital, and I asked him about this place [where we were walking in the forest]. He's a good person, but it was awful. He, of course, didn't say what it was, but I could see in his eyes, a shift, that the question made me an enemy in his eyes. I hate this attitude, this pagan patriotism (Russ.—*iazycheskii patriotizm*), for example, Victory Day. Yes, absolutely, freedom from fascism was bought with our flesh and blood. The Americans helped, but it was our blood that was poured out to save the world, but still, the Baltics have real complaints. It should be possible to celebrate without aggressively insulting them, but no, people like that have no fine-feeling (Russ.—*tonkoe chuvstvo*) . . . . The education system perpetuates this mentality, that smiles for outsiders and treats its own people badly, this Soviet mentality that they still have. I see the same mentality in the current leadership and so they can't change anything really . . . . I was in the hospital, and there was a Russian woman there and she had all sorts of problems. The four Buryat nurses had to do everything for her and she was bitter and cursed them all day, saying that they, Russians, had built everything for the Buryats, brought them everything, saying horrible things and I lost my temper and cursed at her. But then I felt bad. I talked to her later, and this woman, when you thought about her life, was a saint. You could tell, from the shine in her eyes, that she had turned in her friends when she was young, but later, she worked in a

factory, operating a crane, her entire life, and her husband was a drunk and beat her, and all that time in the hospital not a soul came to see her.

Through her story, Elena ties together the Soviet chronotope of progress and the sacrifices of World War II as a discursive structure that produces blind loyalty to an undeserving state. This loyalty corrupts otherwise sympathetic individuals: her good neighbor and the poor woman in the hospital. One sees her as an enemy for asking about the past. The other deals with her own helplessness by seeking power in the Soviet chronotope, which placed Russians in the position of the elder brother, first among equals, superior to the Buryat nurses on whom she is now dependent. For Elena Mikhailovna, this version of history masks state violence—not only the violence of the purges ("They killed all those lamas, and then they said that we were an illiterate people") but a regime that could bring a young girl to betray her friends, extract her labor, fail to protect her from her drunk husband, and then discard her. For Elena, the unwillingness of some contemporary Russians (and Buryats) to renounce the Soviet version of history, but who instead unthinkingly replicate that genre through holidays like Victory Day, stands in the way of any positive change.

Elena Mikhailovna is a Buryat intellectual with her own investment in Buryat nationhood. However, it is important to note that the critique of the Soviet narrative of the past is not determined by ethnicity. Just as there are Buryats who embrace the Soviet narrative, there are Russians in Buryatia who reject it. Another ethnic Russian taxi driver, about the same age as the one who declared Buryats had been savages, spoke about the fate of Etigelov and his contemporaries, saying "they killed the flower of an entire generation. Everyone cultured or smart was killed. We are the result of what was left. It's no wonder we have such problems." Even as he rejects and criticizes the actions of the Soviet government, he evokes a Soviet "we" that encompasses both Buryats and Russians, and all the other nationalities that suffered through the purges. He evaluates the historical events negatively, but accepts the Soviet identity that the chronotope evokes. These two taxi drivers—both ethnic Russians—speak from within the Soviet genre, using a linear, modernist chronotope. However, they highlight different events within that genre, and evaluate these events differently. As a result, although both speak from within a Soviet identity, the first refuses Buryats equal status within it, while the second incorporates them into a shared Soviet suffering.

Victory Day celebrated the iconic historical event, those five "burning" years, when through collective sacrifice Buryats became full members of the Soviet *narod*. Contemporary Buryats honored their elders through these celebrations, and read about the wartime exploits of their grandparents with a real sense of pride. Defeating Hitler and saving the world from fascism is no small thing, and love for the nation exists "in proportion to the sacrifices to which one has consented, and in proportion to the ills that one has suffered" (Renan 1996, 52). Victory Day remains a powerful holiday because it connects personal and familial sacrifice to the idea of the nation. The material forms of the holiday, the parade and strolls through Soviet streets, and the images and symbols of the war all reinforce the Soviet genre of the past.

However, the state currently celebrating that sacrifice is not the same state that won the war. Deploying Soviet imagery in the Russian Federation opens a space for reinterpretation of the past and its value in the present. Since perestroika, people in Buryatia have changed the way this pivotal moment of inclusion can be understood, bringing doubt into the genre. As the stories I have recounted show, people doubted whether the "modernity" brought by the Soviet regime was worth the price paid for it. People disagreed over the price: whether it was cultural traditions or the lives of their relatives. However, even for critics like Elena and the taxi driver, who bring new historical events into the genre and use these events to criticize the Soviet project, the collective Soviet identity and the linear mode of time evoked by the Soviet chronotope remains strong. Whether Buryat or Russian, the residents of Ulan-Ude live within the modernity built by the Soviet Union, so the story of progress told by the Soviet state is the familiar historical genre against which people produce new forms of historical knowledge.

3

City Day

HOSPITALITY, THE FRIENDSHIP OF THE PEOPLES, AND *MULTIKULTURALIZM*

"*MULTIKULTURALIZM*," A LOCAL colleague tells me, while drinking tea in her office, "is very popular these days." From discussions with intellectuals to public speeches and ritual toasts, I often heard local residents in Ulan-Ude invoke the Soviet phrase "friendship of the peoples" (Russ.—*druzhba narodov*) as a form or precursor of *multikulturalizm*. The "Friendship of the Peoples" was the Soviet government's metaphor for the nationality policy, which formally acknowledged national difference to render it politically powerless. In the early 2000s, in both Russia and Europe, multiculturalism was the buzzword for the politics of recognition, and appeared to offer a strategy for integrating minority groups into nation-states. Local residents in Ulan-Ude made arguments about what kind of polity Russia should be, and what their role in it should be, by laying claim to globally circulated discourses of multiculturalism, recognition, and tolerance. They grounded their claim to multiculturalism in a particular genre of local history, one I call a genre of hospitality.

The hospitality genre shares an elective affinity with the Soviet genre of history (see Luehrmann 2011). Versions of the past in this genre are linear and presume the Soviet definition of nationality, which views national identity as an inherent feature of both individuals and groups. The hospitality genre is expressed through Soviet performance forms, such as the parade and the national dance or singing troupe. Much like Soviet nationality performances, these performances celebrate coexistence and tolerance while at the same time reifying nationality categories.

However, the hospitality genre differs from the Soviet genre in certain key ways. The historical events that are narrated in this genre precede the

Soviet era by several centuries, reaching back to prehistoric and tsarist events. The hospitality genre tells the history of Buryatia as a history of successive waves of arrivals, in which many different ethnic groups make their home in a welcoming Buryatia. The chronotope produced through the hospitality genre allows local residents in Buryatia to produce a particularly local ethic of tolerance, hospitality, and national coexistence that positions a multicultural local identity against the Russian national center represented by Moscow. As Michel-Rolph Trouillot argues, however, any production of historical knowledge involves the production of silences: "As sources fill the historical landscape with their facts, they reduce the room available to other facts" (Trouillot 1995, 49). By producing a history of successive arrivals welcomed by Buryatia, this genre erases "Russian" as a nationality category, disrupting a binary opposition between the Russian state and Buryat land. The hospitality genre of history enables contemporary coexistence by reducing the room available for narratives of colonialism.

There were good reasons for local residents in Buryatia to be interested in the potential of multiculturalism. As noted previously, in 2005 the Ust-Orda Buryat autonomous okrug was merged into Irkutsk oblast, and a referendum was held on whether the Aga Buryat okrug would be merged into Chita oblast. The result of the referendum was a foregone conclusion, and rumors were rampant that the republic was next. As the nationally marked okrugs were dissolved into much larger ethnically un-marked (and therefore, by default, Russian) oblasts, the structure of Soviet nationality policies was literally being dissolved. Everyone I spoke to felt that the existence of their republic, the only political framework with the potential for sovereignty, was under threat.

Most of the people I worked with in Buryatia were skeptical about the practical value of that sovereignty. In the 1990s, the republic's legislature had initiated reforms to promote Buryat culture, such as recognizing Tsagaalgan (White Month/New Year) as an official holiday, requiring Buryat language instruction in the elementary school curriculum, and re-organizing the National Humanities Center at the Buryat State University to train Buryat language teachers for these teaching positions. Most of these initiatives had faltered due to lack of funding, and several people complained to me that the republic's administration did Moscow's bidding. That did not mean, however, that they were willing to renounce the symbolic sovereignty and perceived local sanctuary that the republic represented. They might criticize the republic's leadership and policies, but they did not want it gone.

Heightening their concerns, their nightly newscasts were filled with stories of ethnic conflict in other parts of the Russian Federation. In 2004, I arrived in Buryatia shortly after the tragedy in Beslan, where on September

1–3, 2004, Chechen terrorists held an elementary school hostage and approximately 334 people died, including 186 schoolchildren, in the attempt to liberate the school.[1]

One of the teachers who died protecting her students in Beslan was Buryat. Her death offered a local connection to this national tragedy.[2] Darima Batuevna Alikova had fallen in love with an Ossetian man in 1985 while they were both in college in Moscow. They married and moved back to his hometown of Beslan, where they both worked as schoolteachers and where Darima was welcomed and beloved by both her family and her new community. She had the opportunity to escape the occupied school, but sent her students out instead, choosing to stay with those who could not leave. Darima died heroically in the face of separatist ethnic terrorism, seemingly representing all that had been good about the Soviet "Friendship of the Peoples": education, true love between members of different ethnic groups, and service to the broader community. Her life embodied everything that was threatened by the Chechen terrorists' narrow vision of ethnic separatism, which was itself a response to the increasing Russianness of the Russian Federation.

In 2005, the threat of ethnic isolation and violence seemed to pervade the Russian Federation (see Shnirelman 2011). People spoke constantly about rumors of attacks in Moscow on people with "Asian faces" by Russian nationalist "hooligans." A Tatar man, married to a Buryat woman, told me he hoped his daughter would be accepted by a college in Mongolia, because he feared for her safety if she went to Moscow. "We used to go to Moscow all the time," my Buryat landlady complained, her voice filled with outrage and betrayal. "But the last time I was there, people thought I was Chinese, even though I have a Russian passport!" These attacks and the recent horror at Beslan were on everyone's mind when they insisted "Here, thank God everything is quiet" (Russ.—*zdes, slava Bogu, vce spokoino*). In doing so, they singled out Buryatia as a special and unique place, characterized by ethnic tolerance, and therefore different from the rest of the Russian Federation.[3]

Some residents attributed the "calm" in Buryatia to the powerful energy of Lake Baikal, which had always drawn people to its sacred center. Others attributed it to the nonviolent traditions of Buddhism or the value placed on hospitality in Mongolian culture. Their explanation for the causes of peace varied, but the evidence they offered was always the long history of ethnic coexistence, dating back to the 17th century, when the Russian Orthodox Church experienced a schism, and Old Believer Orthodox dissenters were exiled to Siberia. Whatever the specific reason they gave, residents—Buryat, Russian, and others—told me that Buryatia was and had always been a place where different nationalities could live together in peace, something that seemed increasingly difficult in the Russia outside the republic's borders.

Since everyone was talking about whether the republic might be dissolved, most people I spoke to doubted that this peaceful coexistence would continue if the territorial framework that protected it were gone (Graber and Long 2009; Peers 2009, 67; Murray 2012, ix–xiii). Although these fears have not materialized and the republic still exists, the anxiety expresses a deeper concern about what "national autonomy" means without the structure of Soviet nationality policy to support it. Buryats remain the "titular nationality" of the republic (i.e., the nationality for which the republic was named), but it is unclear what that means in the Russian Federation. From a legal perspective, the Russian Federation is a multinational federated state, but in the 2000s public discourse increasingly emphasized the ethnic Russian identity of the state. This moment of doubt hovered uneasily between "the friendship of the peoples" and a new discourse of "multiculturalism" that residents of Buryatia were absorbing from the internet and other popular media. The two concepts are not the same, and neither can be fully equated to the local ethic of hospitality that enables coexistence, but they bear enough of a family resemblance to offer the hope that multiculturalism might provide a framework for continued peaceful coexistence. This resemblance was on full display during the festivities for City Day.

Victory Day, discussed in the previous chapter, celebrated a moment of Buryat integration into a Soviet identity, an identity that to its critics masked a Russian identity. Both the Soviet and the Buddhist genres of history are predominantly concerned with Buryats and Russians. In contrast to these genres, and in common with the shamanic genre of history, City Day's hospitality genre presumed and produced a local multi-ethnic identity grounded in a history of migration and cooperation. It is not a narrative of colonialism, or of a "melting pot," or acculturation to a civic identity. Instead, the narrative of neighborly sociality and coexistence presumes and constructs separate ethnic identities. These identities were, of course, fostered by first imperial and then Soviet state policies that vested legal status in individuals based on their nationality and religion. However, these federal state–created identities then become the basis for a local discourse of harmonious coexistence that positions local sociality against the federal state. Through this genre of history, the uniqueness of local identity produced not a shared ethnicity but rather a shared neighborly ethic of conviviality, grounded in the recognition, performance, and respect for coexisting nationalities, and a history of coexistence.

City Day

City Day is a municipal holiday, celebrating the founding of the city in 1666. In 2005 there were two main events, a parade in the morning in Soviet Square, and an outdoor performance in the afternoon. Like Victory Day, the time in between was filled with a "mass stroll" (Rus.—*massovoe gulianie*) during which local residents strolled down Lenin Street. Even though most people had a holiday from work, the crowds were much smaller than at Victory Day.

In the morning a stage had been set up in the middle of Soviet Square, this time facing the administrative buildings. On the stage there were two masters of ceremonies, a Buryat man and a Russian woman, representing the two dominant nationalities of the republic. The ceremony began with Father Oleg Matveev, the most active local Russian Orthodox priest, blessing a loaf of bread by sprinkling it with holy water. The bread was then offered to the mayor of the city, who is Buryat. The announcers explained that it was Russian tradition to offer bread to show welcome and hospitality.

This struck me as odd. Russian Cossacks came to Buryatia and claimed the land for the Russian tsar. If this history were to be referenced in a ritual, it would make more sense (or at least so it seemed to me at the time) for Buryats to offer hospitality to Russians, not the other way around. In this ritual, however, Russians offered hospitality to Buryats.

The opening blessing was followed by a parade of cultural groups and clubs, some sponsored by businesses and others representing neighborhoods or cultural centers, which were continuations of cultural groups organized and sponsored by unions and factories during the Soviet Union. The marchers paraded down Victory Avenue and into Soviet Square. First were marchers representing the Teachers' Association, who were followed by several groups of children from different schools, carrying the flags of the Russian Federation and the Republic of Buryatia. The Russian Drama Theater was represented by a truck full of actors dressed in World War II costumes, promoting a play in honor of the 60th anniversary. They were followed by several groups from the October District, the most industrial area of the city, home to several factories and housing for their workers. Each of the factories was represented by its own cultural group, which marched in formation with banners. The marchers representing the Buryat Meat Processing Plant (Russ.—*Buriat Miaso Prom*) included a group of veterans carrying a large velvet flag with the faces of Lenin and Stalin on it.

The marchers were joined by the factory's dance troupe, *Bagul'nik* (the name of a local steppe flower). In contrast, the Buryat Milk Factory troupe was carrying a United Russia banner.[4] The announcers diligently provided information about each of the factories, including how many World War II veterans had worked there and any awards the factory had won. The parade—with groups of coworkers representing factories, unions, and schools, marching in rows—closely mirrors Soviet parade forms, and many of the banners looked as if they might have survived from the Soviet period (Petrone 2000; Lane 1981). Even the United Russia banner followed the Soviet form of a banner carried in a parade.

The factory workers were followed by dance troupes from cultural centers, representing the city's different nationalities. Along with Buryat dancers dressed in colorful (predominantly blue) satin *degels*, groups of female dancers from the Evenki, Azeri, and Armenian cultural centers, clothed in their national costumes, marched in a choreographed pattern. The Evenki dancers wore a stylized version of reindeer tunics over boots. Both the Azeri and Armenian dancers wore long red embroidered velvet dresses, the Armenians with gold belts and jaunty headbands, while the Azeri dancers wore red hats with long chiffon veils. National costume and national dance were quintessentially Soviet forms through which the Stalinist phrase "National in form, Socialist in content" was fostered and embodied (Slezkine 1996; Suny 1993; Hirsch 2005; Martin 2001). Like the parade, the national dance troupe has continued into the post-Soviet period.[5]

When the morning parade ended, the audience strolled away to spend the day in cafes or on benches in the park, chatting with friends and drinking. A string ensemble in Buryat national costume played near Revolution Square, and a special chess set was open to the public, where people could play chess using pieces that reached to their waists. Like Victory Day, enjoyment of a nice summer holiday from work did not necessarily indicate approval for the holiday itself. However, the ubiquity of the phrases and ideas embodied in the City Day celebration, which I experienced throughout the year, indicate that they are widespread discursive habits on which people rely, in most cases without actively thinking about them. Much of this habit is grounded in hospitality practices. For example, toasts to friendship (Rus.—*druzhba*) or friendship among peoples (Rus.—*druzhba narodov*) were a standard phrase repeated at every dinner, no matter how small. Often the presence of American guests like myself was included, my presence noted in toasts to the "friendship of the peoples."

Later in the afternoon, an open-air performance of "Dialogue of Cultures, Path of Peace" (Russ.—*dialog kul'tury, put' mir*) was held on the steps of the now-closed Soviet-era movie theater *Druzhba* (friendship). The stage was decorated to resemble the stylized hull of a ship with a steering wheel in front of the stage, and a banner behind the stage read "Full speed ahead!" Above

FIGURE 3.1 The mayor, Gennadii Aidaev, is at the microphone. The banner behind him, showing the city coat of arms, and the colors of the republic's flag, reads "Full speed ahead." The singing group in blue suits is sponsored by a factory, and the one on the right, in red dresses, is a Russian folk song group. Ulan-Ude, City Day, 2005.

the stage, a banner read, "I love you Ulan-Ude" (see Figure 3.1, 3.2). The city, then-mayor Gennadii Aidaev explained, was a ship, moving through time, and the passengers on the ship are the nationalities of the city, who have traveled together as the city-ship moves through time (see Figure 3.1). He also compared the city to a "living organism" and noted that, just as a person takes stock of their life and where they are going on their birthday, so too, should the city think about its future on its birthday. He thanked the republic's government for the money they had given the city, which the city had used to fix the roads and renovate public squares. Unlike Moscow, he claimed, where the city administration and the Russian Federation administration were at war, here there was no such conflict. He drew people's attention to two brand-new trams, parked across the street, and announced a new reform that would allow the municipal government to keep its own tax revenue, rather than pay them into a central fund that would later be re-disbursed. He argued that this would allow the city to solve its own problems: "Remember the 1990s. We lived through the hard years of the 1990s together. We know where we are going and we know for ourselves how to live (Rus.—*sami znaem kak zhit'*). We know that there is no uncle (Russ.—*diadia*) coming to save us, and we know

FIGURE 3.2 A Cossack dance troupe, with a ship's wheel in the foreground and the banner "I love you Ulan-Ude" above the stage. City Day, Ulan-Ude 2005.

that we can solve our own problems. We can help ourselves, and help those who need it, like our veterans." After urging the residents toward greater local independence, he urged them to "preserve a dignified, cultured life" (Russ.—*dostoinaia kul'turnaia zhizn' cokhranit'*), which could be understood as a reference to the cultural performances that followed the speech. But it also echoed a lament I had heard often, that in capitalist, post-Soviet Russia, it was no longer possible to live a dignified, cultured life. There was no explicit critique of the center, of Moscow, or the Russian Federation in his speech, but the metaphor of the ship and the idea of the "uncle" who was not coming to save them emphasized that the local situation was separate from the rest of Russia. The "we" in his speech are the (multi-national) residents of the city, who like the passengers on a boat, are alone and dependent on each other as they face the changing tides of the sea. Both the title of the performance and the mayor's speech presume separate and bounded but coexisting nationalities.

After the mayor's speech, the masters of ceremony took over. Reversing the pattern of that morning's presentation, a Buryat woman and a Russian man served as announcers, introducing each performance. They praised the "interesting and talented work" of the performers and the "high art that elevates our lives." Some of the dance and singing groups were, as in the

FIGURE 3.3 City Day in 2005. A Buryat singing group (back row, standing) and a Semeiskie (Old Believer Orthodox) singing group (front row—sitting), both in national costume, waiting to perform. City Day, Ulan-Ude, 2005.

parade earlier, sponsored by factories or unions. These groups were not explicitly marked by nationality, wore non-ethnic costumes, and were composed of members from mixed ethnic backgrounds. Other groups clearly represented a single ethnicity. A Cossack dance troupe of men and women performed Cossack dances. A Buryat troupe performed with *khadaks*, the white silk scarves presented on ritual occasions. The Evenki dance group performed a re-choreographed version of a round dance, forming a line on the theater steps rather than in a circle. The other national groups that had marched in the morning—Armenian, Azerbaijani, and Tartar—all performed stylized versions of national dances. The dances were interspersed with singing groups, including an Old Believer women's chorus, and a Buryat women's chorus, each dressed in a colorful array of national costumes (see Figure 3.3).

Finally, a professional dance group offered a special performance. It began with two dancers, one dressed in white, one in black, their faces covered by their hair (see Figure 3.4). They were beating drums, while in the background piercing flute music played in background, sounding more like the soundtrack of a Japanese film than any Buryat music I had ever heard. "What is that?" someone near me in the audience asked. "Shamans," her friend answered. The two "shamans" on stage beat their drums while two voices boomed over

FIGURE 3.4 From left to right, the spirit of Baikal, two Buddhist deities, a white shaman, a black shaman, and the White Old Man (Belyi Staretz). City Day Festival, Ulan-Ude, 2005.

the loudspeakers. The male shaman, dressed in black, spoke about his drum and his voice being heard far and wide, and the female voice called down blessings, which included strength (Russ.—*sila*), will (Russ.—*volia*), and truth (Russ.—*pravda*).

The two "shamans" then stepped to the back as two more dancers entered, wearing oversized masks, reminiscent of Tsam masks, while a recording of the mantra "Om mani padme hum" played behind them. Tsam (sometimes spelled Cham) is a Tibetan Buddhist ritual that was once practiced throughout Tibet, Mongolia, and Buryatia in which specially trained monks wear and dance in masks, embodying the power of the deities they represent.[6] These were followed by another dancer, in a female mask, surrounded by flowing blue and green chiffon fabric, representing either Mother Nature or Baikal—which was unclear, as the figure was clearly female, but the flowing chiffon evoked the image of water, and in Buryat folklore Baikal is usually referred to as male. Another dancer wore a mask of the Old White Man (Russ.—*Belyi Staretz*), whom the announcer described as a protector of the land. The Old White Man is a syncretic figure, who is found throughout Central and Inner Asia. He is widely considered to be a shamanic figure who is also venerated as a Buddhist deity (see Hummel and Vogliotti 1997).

Highly stylized, the performance seemed to represent the two "traditional" religions of the Buryat people: shamanism and Buddhism. Mirroring history, shamanism appeared first and was then followed by Buddhism. Both religions were presented as tied to the land of Buryatia, through the nature/water figure and the syncretic figure of the Old White Man. However, the audience around me seemed confused. Although the performance drew on folklore and religious imagery, it did not present a recognizable myth, nor was the genre as familiar as the national dance and singing groups that had preceded it. The blessings of strength, will, and truth that the white shaman had called down sounded more like communist slogans than shamanic ones.[7] The stylized representation of religious practice in the context of a civic festival did not fit into any recognizable genres. It did, however, represent the history of this land as a place of multi-religious harmony.

In the City Day celebration, history was explicitly evoked during the mayor's speech and through the simple fact that City Day celebrated the anniversary of the city's founding 339 years ago. Throughout the performance, there was tension between acknowledging the two dominant nationalities of the republic, Buryats and Russians and an emphasis on performing the city as multi-ethnic and multi-religious. The mayor's speech does not emphasize the civic identity of individuals, but rather the civic duty of coexistence between nationalities. The nationalities as groups, not individual ethnically diverse citizens, are on the boat of the city, traveling through time together.

Through the performance of cultural diversity, the holiday references a historical narrative of the city as a story of successive waves of immigration. This narrative stresses the multi-ethnic character of the republic and the city, complicating and undercutting the binary representation of Buryats and Russians as the two dominant ethnic groups. The binary relationship of Buryats and Russians was represented by the announcers at each event and the blessing at the beginning of the parade. The performances, however, represented national and ethnic diversity, and, most notably, "Russian" was not explicitly represented. The professional troupes representing factories were all multi-ethnic, featuring both Buryat and Russian performers. "Russian" was represented by Cossack and Old Believer performers. Both of these categories function as nationality categories, which are both "Russian" and yet not Russian at the same time. This seemingly contradictory claim will be explored further in my analysis of the historical narrative that City Day evokes. As with the other rituals, I have pieced this history together from multiple sources, including museum displays, written sources, and conversations over the course of my time in Buryatia.

The Peoples of Welcoming Buryatia

Museum displays in Buryatia start their historical narratives with the Huns, who occupied the area around present day Ulan-Ude sometime in the distant past. There are displays of pre-Buryat archeological settlements at the Khangalov History Museum in downtown Ulan-Ude and at the Open Air Ethnographic Museum outside the city, along with models of Evenki *chum* (tents) and Buryat *ger* (yurts). Recently, an archeological site identified as belonging to the Huns was located outside the city, prompting some locals to argue that Ulan-Ude should be declared the oldest continuously occupied city in Russia. When Cossacks began to explore the area in 1625, the countryside was occupied by semi-nomadic herders who spoke various dialects of Mongolian referred to in some of the early Russian records as "Bratskie" and which came to be called Buryat. To the north, within the boundaries of the present-day republic, lived Evenki. Some of the Buryat groups had tributary relationships with Mongolian and Manchu tribal leaders. Tibetan Buddhist missionaries from Mongolia began to bring Buddhism into the area via Mongolia around the same time that the Cossacks arrived.

Verkhneudinsk was founded as a Cossack outpost named Udinskoye in 1666.[8] Cossacks were the military representatives of the Russian Empire and are closely associated with Russian Orthodox Christianity. On the other hand, however, Cossacks are a multi-ethnic group that was traditionally endogamous and self-governing, which rendered military service to the empire, protecting its borders in exchange for autonomy. Although the Cossacks who founded the original Udinskoye fort were not local, Cossack groups stayed, guarding the border with Mongolia and China, and became local, in part by recruiting local residents and intermarrying with them. The Transbaikalian Cossack host eventually included both Evenki and Buryat divisions (Chakars 2014, 33–34). Although it was disbanded during the Soviet period, the Transbaikalian host has since been officially re-recognized by the federal government, with its seat in Chita, located in nearby Chita oblast.

I had the opportunity to meet the *ataman* (leader) of the Verkhneudinsk Cossack Host. This diminutive elderly man, with Asian features, in full military dress, dropped by the office of a friend whom I was hoping to interview. My friend, who loved to chat but did not particularly want to be interviewed, encouraged the interruption. The Cossack leader was excited, like most elderly people, by the prospect of new ears, and I was an American no less, so he solemnly instructed me in the code of the Cossack: "To protect the border, the Tsar, and the Church."

"Well, at least one of those isn't around any more," I pointed out. "Yes, but Border and Church are still here, and the Cossack still lives to protect them, and always will," he insisted. My friend, a Buryat intellectual, whom I had met at a shamanic ceremony, but whom I know had been baptized as a Russian Orthodox Christian (to the chagrin of his Buddhist mother), teased the elderly Cossack: "What church?"

"Buddhist, of course," he answered proudly. "I'm Buryat, after all."

"But isn't the national religion of Russia Orthodoxy?" my friend pushed, probably for my edification. I'm glad he asked, because I would not have dared interrogate the *ataman*, but I was confused. I had first seen the *ataman* at a Cossack dance troupe performance, where an icon of Christ was hung over the stage, with the slogan "*Bog s nami*" (God is with us) on a banner. The performers repeatedly referenced Orthodox Christian practices as part of the "traditions" they were performing. Orthodox Christianity seemed so central to the performance of Cossack identity it seemed absurd for a Cossack *ataman* to identify himself as Buddhist. When challenged on this, the old man frowned and insisted it didn't really matter.

Hoping to test my instincts, I suggested a phrase I had heard repeatedly in Buryatia. "*Bog Odin*?" I asked.

"Of course!" he agreed enthusiastically, "*Bog Odin*!" which can be translated alternatively as God is One, there is one God, or God is all the same.

While this example primarily illustrates the way in which local residents draw parallels between religious traditions, it also emphasizes the way in which "Cossack" both is and is not a nationality or ethnic identity. The *ataman* himself identified both as Cossack and as Buryat. At the dance performance, the *ataman* had praised the performers, who were all blonde and blue-eyed students, for a performance of the "heritage of the Transbaikalian Cossacks. These are *our* songs and *our* heritage and should not be forgotten . . . there are 42,000 Cossacks in Buryatia and we should remember our heritage. Tell your ancestors that you saw this performance and heard the songs and they are not forgotten." Both identities were presented in the language of kinship, cultural heritage, and ancestry, but were not mutually exclusive.

The language of ancestors and cultural heritage used by and for Cossacks is similar to that of other nationalities, but the Soviet concept of nationality fit awkwardly on what, in imperial times, was more properly a multi-ethnic social class or military estate.[9] The Cossacks advanced the interests of the Russian Empire, and guarded its borders, but are not entirely Russian. They have become local, and are performed and produced in the present as one of the many local groups that seeks to preserve and perform their traditions. However, performing Cossack identity this way has consequences for how the history of

Buryatia is understood. In the hospitality genre, Cossacks are one of many successive arrivals: first Huns, then Buryats and Evenki, then Cossacks, who came to reside in the welcoming lands of Buryatia, to be followed by Semeiskie, Ukrainians, Tatars, Azeris, and Armenians. By producing Cossacks as local, the hospitality genre de-emphasizes why they came, namely, to claim the territory on behalf of the tsar. This is a historical event that proves troublesome to contemporary understandings of Buryat history.

The Trouble Over "Voluntary Unification"

As I noted earlier, at the beginning of the City Day festival, Father Matveev of the Russian Orthodox Church blessed a loaf of bread and offered it to the mayor of the city, who is Buryat. The announcer explained the act as a recreation of a Russian tradition of hospitality and welcome. In this moment in the ritual, a representative of the Russian nation (an Orthodox priest) was welcoming the Buryat mayor.

The Buryat and Mongolian gesture of hospitality, offering white foods and a silk scarf (*khadak*) to a visitor, is a common element in public rituals in Buryatia, whether Buddhist, shamanic, or civic. The gesture is enshrined in a massive metal sculpture titled "Welcoming Buryatia," which depicts a Buryat woman in traditional costume, holding a bowl of white foods, and a *khadak*, ready to offer them to visitors (see Figure 3.5). The statue was first erected behind the Opera House, overlooking an open area meant to be a park. The renovations to the park were not completed, and by 2012 the statue had been moved to a bridge that connected the airport to the city. Anyone traveling from the airport into the city passed beneath her welcoming arms. The enormous figure of the young Buryat woman stands ready to welcome visitors to the Buryat city. Both Buryats and ethnic Russians often attributed the positive relations between nationalities in the republic to the Buryat, and by extension Mongolian, custom of offering anyone who arrives at a yurt food and shelter. Given the ubiquity of "Welcoming Buryatia" imagery, I had never seen the Russian equivalent at a public event.[10] Why would Russians be welcoming Buryats?

The answer lies in a particular debate over the "voluntary unification" (Russ.—*dobrovol'noe soedinenie*) of Buryatia with the Russian Empire. The territory on the eastern shore of Lake Baikal and around Ulan-Ude was brought under Russian control by Cossacks in the 1600s, and in 1689 the Treaty of Nerchinsk set the boundaries between China and Russia. Local history books and museum displays tell this history as a process by which individual Buryat clan leaders chose to request Russian protection

FIGURE 3.5 "Welcoming Buryatia" statue behind the Opera House near Soviet Square, Ulan-Ude, 2005.

from Chinese and Mongolian clan leaders, thereby voluntarily joining the Russian Empire. In 1959, the 300th anniversary of the "voluntary unification" of Buryats with the Russian Empire was commemorated (Boliachevets and Sablin 2016, 398). Although the phrase "voluntary unification" isn't always used, the historical events are commonly narrated in a way that supports this claim. For example, a bilingual English and Russian book published under the auspices of the City Administration, *Ulan-Ude: History and Modern Day*, explains:

> On March 12, 1689, the Russian ambassador Fyodor Golovin after long negotiations concluded a peace treaty with the Tabungut Sayt people. According to the treaty the Argun River flowing into the Amur River was recognized as the eastern Russian Chinese border. And already on the 18th of July the Tabungut taishas Irdinei and Tsiren Sokulai asked the authorities of the Udinski *ostrog* to let them join Russia and accept Russian citizenship (Imithenov and Egorov 2001, 53–54).[11]

This statement, in an official municipal publication, is a good example of the idea of voluntary unification, which naturalizes the Russian presence by noting that Buryat *taishas* (clan leaders) requested Russian "citizenship," using an anachronistic concept to describe tributary relationships with representatives of the tsar. These events are an excellent example of the impossibility of producing a text that presents history "as it really happened." The history of Cossack and Russian expansion into the Baikal area must be reconstructed from fragmentary archival documents referring to collectivities and concepts that bear little resemblance to contemporary ones. Neither Russia, China, nor the Buryats existed then in the forms they do now. It is virtually impossible to describe the event in such a way as to be recognizable to a contemporary audience without using words that imply a political stance toward these events.

There are other ways these events can and have been told.[12] Instead of arguing for or against a particular interpretation of them, I want to show how the particular way of narrating historical events in the present produces effects in the present. In contemporary public discourse in Buryatia, the idea of "voluntary unification" of Buryat clan leaders into the Russian Empire is a common trope. It is a discursive habit left over from the late Soviet genre of history, but its formulaic nature renders it unconvincing. It becomes a parody of itself.

The trouble with "voluntary unification" came to a head in 2003. Museum displays and books like the one cited above state that in 1703, 11 Khori Buryat clan leaders traveled to Petersburg to swear allegiance to Peter the Great. The event is commemorated in a painting by Solbon Rinchinov. Kolarz states that "a collector of Buryat folklore conveniently discovered a Buryat ballad paying tribute to the Russian Czar for assistance granted to the Buryat people. The ballad refers to the chiefs of eleven Buryat clans who, in 1703, sent a delegation to Peter asking him to protect them against unjust demands, levies and oppression on the part of Chinese officials" (Kolarz 1954, 127). The republic government attempted to plan a celebration in 2003 to commemorate the event, but it quickly became clear that any attempt to recruit the participation of local historians was going to produce a very critical reading of the history, a reading that would undermine any claims of "voluntary unification." Although plans to commemorate the events in 2003 were scrapped, in 2016 an exhibition was mounted at the History Museum. A newspaper article on the exhibit notes that the clan leaders traveled to Peter I to complain about the abuses of local colonial administrators; the online comments section of the article begins with a commenter insisting that Buryats "never voluntarily joined the Russian empire" (*Nomer Odin Ulan-Ude* 2017). In 2012 there was still a mural celebrating the dates 1703–2003 and the words "voluntary unification" on the side of a building in Ulan-Ude, but whenever I heard the phrase, it was used sarcastically.

Whether intended to reference it or not, having an Orthodox priest bless bread and offer it to a Buryat politician as a sign of hospitality must be read within the discourse of "voluntary unification." It performs the idea that Russians welcomed Buryats into their empire, and reverses the popular Buryat idea that Buryats welcomed Russian internal exiles, such as the Old Believers and Decembrists. The hospitality genre of history may offer a convincing and familiar story of successive waves of ethnic groups being "welcomed" to Buryatia, but the controversy over "voluntary unification" shows that this historical genre is riven with fault lines.

More Arrivals in "Welcoming Buryatia"

Udinskoye, the fort and trading post established in 1666, remained a Cossack stronghold and grew steadily as a trading point on the route that brought Chinese tea into Russia. The Russian imperial government established tribute relations with Buryat and Evenki groups, who paid taxes to the tsar in fur (Russ.—*iasak*). The next group of arrivals to be welcomed to Buryatia were the Old Believer Orthodox.

In 1652 Patriarch Nikon instituted reforms to bring Russian Orthodox Christian practice in line with Greek Orthodox standards. These reforms led to a schism in the Russian Orthodox church: those who rejected the reforms—the Old Believers—were either exiled to Siberia or fled on their own, settling in large numbers in the area between Lake Baikal and Chita. Although there are doctrinal differences between schismatic groups, they are all called Old Believer Orthodox or Semeiskie, meaning "ones with families," because unlike political exiles and common criminals, they were sent to Siberia with their families. Like people in Buryatia, I use both terms interchangeably.

Until the Soviet period, most Semeiskie lived in relatively isolated and endogamous communities, purposefully separating themselves from the world for religious reasons. Due to this cultural and religious separation, the Semeiskie are widely seen as more authentically "Russian" than other Russians since they preserve pre-reform traditions. Although originally ethnically Russian, they are in many ways treated as a separate ethnic group, which is both separate from "regular" Russians, but which has preserved a more authentic "Russianness." As Rogers notes, "Many [Russian scholars] came to argue that Russian national traditions were preserved—perhaps uniquely preserved—by Old Believer elders seeking the separation of the worlds. . . ." (Rogers 2009, 172). Since the Old Believer identity originated from an act of opposition to imperial rule, and since as a religious group they were implicitly opposed to the Soviet state, they can position themselves as "local" in contrast to the Russianness of Moscow and European Russia. Within local discourse in Buryatia, Old Believers are one among many local ethnic groups that expresses its uniqueness through preserving and performing cultural traditions.

I had the pleasure of attending an Old Believer Easter celebration in a village outside of Ulan-Ude, held in the former House of Culture. In the main room, each of the village's farms set up a table, from which they "hosted" guests, offering home-brewed alcohol shots (Russ.—*samogon*) and boiled eggs, in a performance of "traditional" Easter hosting, where neighbors would visit each other's homes. Along with food and drink we were hosted with songs performed by a chorus of women, who sang Old Believer Russian folk songs and danced with infectious glee and exhausting vigor (see Figure 3.6).

Along with visiting foreign anthropologists (I was there with my husband and another couple, both American scholars), the "guests" included the village's Buryat government officials. As a visiting foreigner, I was, at one point, seated in a place of honor next to the representatives of the local government. I asked one member of the administration, a very distinguished older Buryat man, whether the village was half Buryat and half Old Believer. "Yes," he answered. "Has it always been?" I asked, meaning "as long as you can remember." I was well aware of the dates of the schism, but, in my defense,

FIGURE 3.6 Old Believer/Semeiskie Easter celebration at the House of Culture, Mukhorshibirskii Raion, Republic of Buryatia, 2005.

I had already had a lot of vodka and it was still not yet noon. His answer was very interesting.

"No." he answered. "It used to be pure Buryat (Russ.—*chistie Buriatskie*), but 250 years ago the Semeiskie came and we have lived together ever since." His sense of "always" was significantly longer than mine. "We" refers to the two separate and separable groups—Buryats and Semeiskie—who share the village, living together ever since. "We" is not a mestizo identity, although it is highly likely that there has been intermarriage in the last 250 years. In his statement, as in the performances of City Day, the 250 years of coexistence reify the separate nature of the two identities.

Every guest and every villager at the Easter celebration was asked to give a toast over the course of the morning and the banquet that followed. While each toast was a little different, there were three clear themes. The first was to wish all the participants health, happiness, and a happy Easter. The second theme was peaceful coexistence, usually expressed through "*Druzhba*" (Friendship) or "*Druzhba Narodov*" (Friendship of the Peoples). One notable toast, perhaps in response to our presence, noted that the village was international, the home of Buryats, Semeiskie, and Tatars. Finally, many of the toasts and speeches stressed the value of traditions and keeping them, and how performances such as this one are the means by which traditions are preserved. Several speeches compared *Tsagaalgan*, which is Buddhist New Year and the quintessential "Buryat" holiday, to Easter, the quintessential Old Believer holiday: both are "traditions" that must be maintained and performed.

At another event I attended in an Old Believer village, part of a conference funded by UNESCO, a local librarian offered a toast in which she compared culture to a trunk (Russ.—*sunduk*) which can be full, if you continue to perform your traditions, or empty, if you forget them. The speaker emphasized that "you want to bequeath a full trunk to your children." In these toasts, as in the mayor's speech, coexistence, continued cultural performance, and preservation of traditions would lead to a future of peaceful and respectful coexistence. Both of these events performed Semeiskie as a unique ethnic group that, like Buryats, have an identifiable culture, one that is performed through song, dance, cuisine, and costume. Performing these traditions acknowledges respect for both the practices and the ethnic group that performs them, and this respect enables coexistence. Like Cossacks, Semeiskie are both Russian and not Russian. As a persecuted and (until the 20th century) endogamous religious group, they can be both more authentically Russian than other Russians, and at the same time not Russian at all. They have become local.

In addition to a trading hub, Ulan-Ude was also a place of internal exile for the Russian Empire. One of the other largest groups are the descendants of Polish exiles. A Polish cultural center in Ulan-Ude, with staff sent from Poland, offers Polish language lessons. Someone told me that the Catholic Church that opened in Ulan-Ude in 2005 should not be considered a "new religion" to the city (although it was the first Catholic church in Russia to be built east of Lake Baikal) because it primarily served the Catholic descendants of Polish exiles. The opening of the church was documented in a short article in *Inform Polis*, a very popular Ulan-Ude newspaper. Its report on the Christmas mass at this newly opened Catholic church quotes Father Adam: "In Ulan-Ude there are few Catholics, but our doors are open to all. Members of other confessions often turn to me." The reporter continues:

> As he [Father Adam] explains it, in order to adopt the Catholic faith, one must understand and study it. This takes at least a year. No one is prohibited from just coming to the church for mass. Bair Baranzaev is a Buddhist, but he came to the sacred Christmas mass with pleasure. He helped to build the church, so he finds being in this beautiful building doubly pleasing (Badueva 2004).

The tone of the article implies that the average reader knows nothing about Catholicism and probably views it with suspicion. By emphasizing its openness to all, the journalist is bringing the Catholic church into the community of local neighborly conviviality, respect, and tolerance, and distinguishing it from popular assumptions about foreign religions, missionaries, and their "intolerance." The Catholics are presented as welcoming and therefore welcome in Buryatia.

The city is also home to sizeable populations of Tatars, Armenians, and Azerbaijanis, some of whom came to Ulan-Ude prior to the 1917 Revolution, and many who came later. Each of these groups, as evidenced by the dance troupes at the parade, are represented by a cultural center, national costumes, and performances, even if the populations are statistically quite small, and are not as often represented in public spaces and discourse. Although the arrivals of these groups are not as recognizable historical events as the arrival of Cossacks and Semeiskie, their existence as distinct nationalities, with performable traditions, who are part of the multi-ethnic "ship" that constitutes the city, brings their presence into the hospitality genre. They, too, are groups that have been welcomed to Buryatia.

The only exception I encountered was the complete erasure of the Jewish population from the history of the city. In 1901, the adult population of Verkhneudinsk included 772 Jews (Aiusheeva et al. 2001). It was the second largest confessional population in the town, second only to Russian Orthodoxy

(4,734 adults) and outnumbering by far the 90 Lutherans, 67 Muslims, and 58 "Lamaists" (aka Buddhists) who represented the next largest confessional groups. These figures highlight the extreme demographic changes that Verkhneudinsk/Ulan-Ude has undergone in the past century. Not only did it grow from a tiny village to a city, but it shifted from a Russian outpost in a predominantly Buryat countryside to a Buryat capital city. Its history as a trading post, and the concomitant role of Jewish traders in the city, were de-emphasized by Soviet histories of the city to the point that the presence of a significant Jewish community was almost completely erased.[13]

All the descendants of the aforementioned nationalities, in my experience, identified themselves as members of that nationality, regardless of how many generations their families had resided in Ulan-Ude. In some cases, people would note a mixed heritage, but long-standing residence in Buryatia made Russians, Tatars, and Poles "local" (Russ.—*mestnye*) without changing their nationality. They often said "I am local" or "Buryatia is my homeland" (Russ.—*rodina*) but also identified themselves as Polish, or Tatar, Georgian, or Azeri. In contrast, one man with a European appearance whom I met at a Buddhist ceremony said, "my ancestors were Jewish," but identified himself as an atheist. His interest in visiting Etigelov (see Chapter 1 and 4) was because as a resident of Ivolga village, he (Etigelov) was "ours."

The erasure of Judaism from the city's history is so complete that during a roundtable discussion with a group of college students they volunteered "Judaism" as an example of a "new religion." When their teacher and I objected that Judaism was hardly a new religion, one clarified "well, not a new religion, but new to Buryatia," and they were shocked to hear of the pre-revolutionary Jewish population. The absence of Jews from the hospitality genre version of Buryatia's history shows its Soviet roots. Jews fit uneasily within the Soviet Union's rhetoric of the Friendship of the Peoples, and they were never treated as simply one of many peacefully coexisting nationalities. Many Jews left the area and Russia as a whole. There is no visibly practicing Jewish community in Buryatia anymore, and the few descendants of Jewish residents do not identify themselves as Jewish, but merely as local. They are the exception that reveals the logic of the hospitality genre, a genre in which different nationalities come to Buryatia and maintain their separate identities through cultural performances, while also becoming local.

Local Practices of Coexistence

Despite its roots in Soviet nationality categories, the hospitality genre of history is performed through local practices. The nationality categories may have been produced by the imperial, Soviet, and then the federal state, but the nationalities and their history are evoked by local residents to produce a local multi-ethnic identity that is positioned very much against the central Russian state. As the 1901 census data cited above shows, the population of Ulan-Ude grew exponentially over the course of the Soviet century. Huge numbers of ethnic Russians and members of other nationalities emigrated to Buryatia, especially after World War II, as part of the Soviet Union's planned economy. Representatives of nationalities who came to Buryatia in the pre-revolutionary period are likely to call Buryatia their homeland (Russ.—*rodina*), or to refer to themselves as local (Russ.—*mestnye*) or as Siberians (Russ.—*sibiriaki*). Understandably, those who had emigrated during the Soviet period, or whose parents had, were less likely to use these terms when describing themselves.

One of the dividing lines between those who considered Buryatia their homeland and those who considered it their place of residence was whether or not they made offerings at roadside shrines. Roadside shrines are locations where, as discussed in Chapter 1, spirit masters of place (Russ.—*khoziain mesta*) reside, and most long-standing local residents consider it necessary to stop and acknowledge these entities, by offering a coin, a match, a strip of fabric, or a splash of alcohol. Failing to make an offering to the spirit master is a sign of disrespect that may have terrible consequences. Many people with whom I made these offerings told me they were not sure if they believed in spirits, but they had heard too many stories of people who failed to make an offering and subsequently suffered a terrible accident. It is most important to make an offering while on a journey; if you make the proper observances on the way to a place, on the return leg you can simply toss a coin out the window as you pass by.

I have traveled outside the city with drivers who are Buryat, Russian, Evenki, Tartar, Uzbek, and Georgian. To a man (and the drivers were always men), those whose ancestors had come to Buryatia before World War II stopped at or threw offerings out the window at roadside shrines, whereas those who had emigrated to the republic in the post-war period did not. Ethnic Russian and Tartar drivers who stopped and made offerings always justified the practice by explaining "that's what you do here" or "that's the local tradition." I also witnessed several heated arguments between irate Buryat passengers and recent émigré drivers about stopping at these shrines. For "locals," Buryat or otherwise, if you wished to travel through these lands you had to acknowledge the spirits who owned them, and whether or not you believed in spirits, the risk of an accident was worth the small effort of acknowledging the shrines. The unwillingness of recent émigré taxi drivers provoked anger in part because it was dangerous, but also because it was a violation of a local ethic of tolerance and respect for traditions.

One woman's life story also illustrates the hospitality genre. I met Elvira at a shamanic initiation (described in Chapter 6). Elvira was there to offer moral support to her Russian friend, whose half-Buryat son was being initiated as a shaman. Elvira explained to me that her father was Buryat and her mother was Semeiskie. In those days (the 1930s or '40s), Semeiskie girls were not supposed to marry outside the group, she explained, but her mother had married a Buryat and left the community. Tragically, Elvira and her sister's father died soon after their births. Her mother then married a Chuvash man, and they moved away from Buryatia. Before they left, her Semeiskie grandmother hand-sewed *degels*, Buryat national costumes, for each of her granddaughters so that they would not forget their homeland. "Can you imagine that?" she asked me, "Even though she didn't want her daughter to marry a Buryat, she still sewed us *degels*." As an adult, Elvira returned to Buryatia, fulfilling her grandmother's wish. The neighborly conviviality that enables peace and mutual respect was, for her, embodied in her grandmother's gesture, her attempt to ensure that her grandchildren knew and respected their father's tradition, even though she opposed the marriage.

Although Elvira did not say so, her mother was likely a member of the first generation to be raised in the Soviet Union, many of whom embraced the Soviet vision of modernity as a process of abandoning "traditions." Nor is it a coincidence that a national costume was the form in which her heritage was expressed, as costumes are one of the quintessential Soviet forms of national expression standardized through their use in museum displays and dance troupe performances. Her story is an example of how people lived in relationship to Soviet forms of national identity, both accepting the ethnic categories and their forms of performance and mobilizing them to produce a particular ethic of local coexistence and tolerance that is like, but more than, an abstract friendship of the peoples. The hospitality genre produces Buryatia as the product of a long history of coexistence and tolerance.

The Theoretical Consequences of False Equations

At the beginning of this chapter I argued that the popularity of *multikulturalizm* in the early 2000s was due to the hope that it might offer a new paradigm for the inclusion of minority groups into Putin's neoliberal Russia. While the Soviet Union's "Friendship of the Peoples" had once been the framework for inclusion, local residents hoped multiculturalism might be a new iteration of that framework, which would continue to support the neighborly tolerance and coexistence that allows them to claim, "Thank God all is quiet here."

For residents of the republic, faced with news reports of Chechen separatists and Russian neo-fascist "hooligans" in Moscow, both committing ethnically motivated violence, the history of peaceful coexistence implied by the "friendship of the peoples" was extremely valuable. Told through the hospitality genre, the history of Buryatia is a history of unique coexistence, one which allows locals to conceptualize the state violence that produced imperial expansion, internal exile, and the Soviet suppression of religion, culture, and native languages as coming from Moscow, and against which the local community defined itself. It is understandably tempting to see the local tradition of coexistence, performed at City Day and other venues, as a local precursor to "multiculturalism," which as a global value, Moscow might support.

However tempting this equation may be, the Soviet politics of difference and local forms of coexistence do not easily translate into Western forms of identity politics. By translating this local ethic into multiculturalism, a valuable grounding for peaceful coexistence may be lost.

As Spivak (1988), Appiah (1994), and Povinelli (2002) all argue, recognizing an identity, whether in Western liberal or in Soviet systems of difference, requires that the identity be recognizable, a demand that exerts force and constraint on the lived experience of individuals. Inherent in these arguments is the idea that these identities do not exist a priori. They are made real through the experience of power relations. Under different power relations, identity categories, and more importantly, the lived experience of inhabiting these categories, are different. The power relations that shaped Soviet identity categories are fundamentally different than the power relations in Western liberalism.

In Western liberal democracies, political approaches to difference are marked by a tension between universal rights vested in the individual, in contrast to group rights linked to particular identities (Kymlicka 1995, 2001; Taylor 1994; LaClau 1996). Modern models of Western multicultural politics from critics, such as Fanon (1991), are based on the argument that if oppression takes an ethnic/national/racial form, then politics designed to redress that oppression must take that form. As Appiah states, if one has been oppressed as a Black "one will end up asking to be respected as a Black" (1994, 161). Western multicultural politics are an attempt to recognize and redress inequalities vested in group identity that are rendered invisible in a legal system grounded in individual rights. The problem with multiculturalism as a structure of inclusion, however, is that "recognition" is granted by the unmarked group, thereby re-inscribing unequal power relations. The unmarked group "recognizes and tolerates" the marked group, rather than oppressing them, but the unmarked is still the symbolic possessor of state power.

Lenin, in fact, offered a similar critique of Western liberalism. In his writings on "the national question," Lenin argued that the fledgling Soviet government had to acknowledge national identity as a real phenomenon to win the support of the working classes of Russia's subject nations (Lenin 1975a, 1975b, 1975c, 1975d). He argued that as long as people feel that they are oppressed as a nation, they will not be able to see that they are really being oppressed as a class. Allow them national sovereignty, he argued, and national difference will "wither away." Lenin's argument underlay all future permutations of Soviet nationality politics, but it must also be understood in relationship to the imperial legacy that the Soviet Union inherited.

In imperial Russia, subjecthood (rather than citizenship) varied based on the status of the individual, which was determined by a mixture of social class, language, race, and religion. Religion and ethnicity were closely correlated; conversion to Orthodoxy could transform an "internal foreigner" (Russ.—*inorodets*), who had to pay tribute to the crown, into a peasant (Russ.—*krest'ianin*), a shift into a different legal category. It should also be remembered that Siberia, where semi-nomadic peoples were brought into tribute relationships and the land was settled by dissidents and exiles, was profoundly different from the western borderlands, such as Poland or the Baltics, where subject peoples had a sense of nationhood and were brought under Russian imperial control as nations.

Early Soviet nationality policies, first under Lenin and then Stalin, were aimed at allowing and encouraging nationalities to express their national culture to diffuse any sense of national oppression without relinquishing control over their territory.[14] Formalized versions of national culture (literature, dance, music, food, costume) were required from every nationality so that assimilation into Soviet social forms would not be experienced as the oppression of national minorities by the Russian majority. By the late Soviet period, what began under Lenin as a *realpolitik* nationality policy had been transformed into a Soviet politics of difference. The "Friendship of the Peoples" posited a community of nations, striving to achieve a vision of communist modernity. Gray states:

> The Soviet Union did have its own ideology of bringing together many groups into one society, with the goal of creating Soviet citizens. Yet at the same time, it was always clearly kept in mind that the Soviet citizenry was made up of many distinct nationalities, not merely minority segments, and this national (rather than ethnic) diversity was an

> official source of pride. . . . Thus, the concept of less-numerous peoples fits with a society that views itself not as a multi-ethnic "mixed salad" of many minorities, but as a family of many intact "peoples" joining together. . . . The Chukchi are not a minority interspersed within a Russian society, but rather a unit alongside other units within one overarching whole (Gray 2005, 60).

From a Soviet-Leninist perspective, this "family of intact peoples" appears to offer a non-coercive model for multi-ethnic coexistence. However, this "friendship of peoples" shared the Enlightenment legacy within which non-Western, non-white, non-European populations are discursively positioned in relation to a teleology of historical development, within which these populations are judged to be less developed than Europeans. The legitimacy of the Soviet regime was heavily invested in its ability to modernize these "backward" populations. Soviet nationality policy presumed that different ethnic groups (ethnoses) were in different stages of historical development. As a result, the way in which the mandate of "state-sponsored evolutionism" was implemented varied widely (Hirsch 2005). Policy-level decisions made in Moscow were based on the specific needs of that nationality, as determined by ethnographers and bureaucrats in Moscow and frequently changing to address the political concerns of the center.

During the early years of the Bolshevik regime, the Buryats were seen as a vanguard nation that would bring communism to Asia. Their similarity to other Mongolian and Asian peoples was seen as positive. By the 1930s, after Japan established Manchukuo to the east of Mongolia, Buryat ties to the Mongolian world began to be seen differently. Fears of "pan-Mongolism," the argument that all the Mongolian peoples should be united into a larger Mongolian nation, prompted the center to redefine the Buryats as dangerously nationalistic. The Soviet Union declared some ethnic groups, such as the Chechens and Kalmyk Mongols, to be enemy "nations" and deported them to Siberia and Central Asia. Numerically small groups throughout the Soviet Union were "dissolved" or "merged" into their larger neighbors.[15] In contrast, the Chukchis in the Arctic were praised as the primary example of a group making the "great leap forward" due to Soviet interventionism (Gray 2005). Willerslev argues that because the Yukaghir in eastern Siberia served as Engel's example of "primitive communism" they were exempted from Soviet social engineering efforts (Willerslev 2007, 122). Local differences in how policies were enacted mean that the Soviet experience plays a different role in locally produced histories. The Soviet emphasis on what Slezkine (1996) calls "ethnic particularism" also hinders the post-Soviet formation of the pan-indigenous or pan-ethnic movements that have been crucial to indigenous identity politics elsewhere.

This teleology of progress, combined with the assertion that each nation was flowering on its own terms, produced a reified and essentialized idea of national identity, which is illustrated by ethnos theory, a guiding principle of Soviet ethnography. Yuri Bromley, a leading Soviet ethnographer, describes an ethnos as a community with a shared ethnic/national character and consciousness, and notes that the "relative conservatism and a certain independence of strictly ethnic features that make it possible for one and the same ethnicos (in reference to its ethnic parameters) to continue its existence under several socio-economic formations" (Bromley 1980, 155). Although originally understood to be an illusion, by the end of the Soviet period, national identity—as defined in ethnos theory and in official Soviet documents—was a quality inherent in individuals that persisted no matter how their cultural practices changed.[16]

The Soviet political system acknowledged ethnic/national difference in order to dismiss it. Soviet nationality policies fostered representations of cultural difference. It is easy to mistake these performances of difference as a manifestation of Western multiculturalism, which also recognizes cultural difference in the form of food, dress, and holidays, among other "traditions." For post-Soviet Buryats confronted by massive shifts in politics, worried about their position within an increasingly "Russian" Russia, it was tempting to see "multiculturalism" as a return to the familiar. However, in Western forms of multiculturalism, the positions of recognizer and recognized are inhabited by members of different ethnic/national groups. The oppressed minority seeks recognition for its cultural otherness from the dominant ethnic group. In the Soviet Union, cultural forms of difference were required by the state. Expressions of cultural difference that did not fit state-recognized forms were classified as "bourgeois nationalism" and suppressed. Although Russians occupied the unmarked category and de facto dominated the government, unlike in Western colonial settler states, they did not hold power by virtue of that unmarked status.[17] Power was not negotiated (at least in theory) along ethnic/national lines. Power to recognize any social group resided in the Communist Party. Access to power was contingent on party membership and, in theory at least, open to all ethnic groups. Members of any ethnic group could occupy positions of both recognizer and recognized.

Unlike many other Siberian national groups, who were only slowly brought into the fold of Soviet culture, some Buryats were Bolsheviks from the very beginning of the 1917 revolution. The requirements of party membership (atheism, disregard of kinship obligations, etc.) may have required individual

Buryats to compromise their own sense of Buryat identity, but Buryats were not excluded from Party membership or from access to power by virtue of being Buryat. Not only were they not excluded, but members of Siberian nationalities who did achieve power within the Party were celebrated as examples of the equality possible within the Soviet system. The vectors of power within the Soviet politics of difference worked initially through class distinction and eventually through Party membership (which was supposed to represent class), rendering national difference merely tokens of a type, as representations of "tradition" like costumes, holidays, and cultural performances.

There is a difference, however, between the ideological vectors of power and how these vectors were experienced by those living within the system. Armstrong (1990), Khazanov (1995), and Amogolonova, Elaeva, and Skrynnikova (2005) all argue that when national difference "withered away," in practice this meant fading into an unmarked but ethnically Russian culture. Elena Mikhailovna's story (described in Chapter 2) supports this argument. Ideologically speaking, Sovietization was supposed to produce a universal Soviet culture, but for many non-Russian Soviet citizens, Sovietization felt like "Russification."

And then, in 1991, the Soviet Union became the Russian Federation. Initially, this moment was interpreted, by analysts and members of minority groups alike, as the opportunity to restore forms of national culture, most especially religious forms, that had been suppressed during the Soviet Union. However, this fluorescence of national revival movements destabilized the existing structures of political difference—because if Russia is no longer defined by ideology, the unmarked category of "ethnic Russian" becomes the obvious choice for state identification. Officially, however, the Russian Federation presents itself as a multi-ethnic state. To do otherwise is difficult, given that 20 percent of the population is not ethnically Russian, and the census recognizes 160 different nationalities. The result is an uneasy tension between multi-ethnicity and ethnic Russian dominance. In 2005, residents of Buryatia saw the increasing numbers of racially motivated crimes in Moscow as a sign that Russia was shifting into a very different regime of recognizing difference, where—instead of being one nation among many—Buryats would be merely a statistical minority within an ethnic Russian nation-state.

The rhetorical power of the Soviet promise of equality, represented through the metaphor of the "friendship of the peoples," was referenced repeatedly, in speeches, toasts, and newspaper articles I observed during my fieldwork. For post-Soviet Buryats who were faced with the possibility of being forever excluded from full citizenship in an ethnically defined Russian nation-state, the Soviet friendship of the peoples represented an ideal vision of inclusion against which people could judge the present. Nostalgia for a Soviet politics of inclusion was not nostalgia for the actual Soviet state repression of culture, religion, and historical information, which most Buryats criticized, but rather nostalgia for the possibility of full political inclusion into a civic Soviet identity, even if that possibility had remained unfulfilled in practice.

However, the ethic of coexistence expressed in the hospitality genre of history is not the same as the Soviet Friendship of the Peoples nor is it a Western form of multiculturalism. Both of those are top-down forms of political ideology. In contrast, the hospitality genre produces a local form of coexistence that refracts the Soviet concept of separate nationalities, but positions these local identities against the power of the central state.

The hospitality genre is not merely about the past, but rather about inhabiting and valuing a particular kind of sociality that can provide a foundation for a more stable form of local coexistence. In the ritual of City Day, Soviet performance forms are marshalled to represent and produce separate national groups who live in convivial tolerance. The history of Buryatia becomes a series of arrivals in a welcoming territory, rather than a story of the Russian conquest of Buryat land. Through speeches and performance, a version of the past is produced which tells the history of "Welcoming Buryatia," producing the city and the republic as a place of coexistence from which the residents can move forward into a peaceable future.

4

Etigelov at Maidari

THE ONCE AND FUTURE BUDDHIST

IN 2005 MAIDARI, the festival of the future Buddha (known as Maitreya), fell on a weekend, which accounted for the unusually large crowds that came out to see Etigelov at the Ivolginsky monastery. Maidari is not the only day when the public can view Etigelov, but as a midsummer holiday, it is one of the most popular. Maidari is also a particularly appropriate setting to discuss Etigelov, because both Maitreya and Etigelov are time-travelers of a particularly Buddhist sort. Both walked the earth, but became and are becoming bodhisattvas, who return to fulfill prophecies. The stories of their departure and return produce a recursive chronotope, within which the present and future become fulfillments of the past.

The historical Buddha, Sakyamuni, is the Buddha of the present age. Maitreya is the Buddha of the future. A being that may once have been incarnated as a disciple of the Gautama Buddha, Maitreya ascended to the Tusita Heaven, from which he is expected to return, bringing enlightenment in the future.[1] The Maidari festival celebrates and calls for the Maitreya Buddha's return. Worshiping the Maitreya Buddha in the present brings about his future return.

As discussed in Chapter 1, Etigelov is a pre-revolutionary Buryat Buddhist intellectual who left and returned in the form of a miraculously imperishable body that inspires faith in the post-Soviet population by offering scientific proof of his ability to transcend death. Etigelov's preserved body has been determined to be a miracle by various doctors and scientists—most notably, the Russian Academy of Forensic Science in Moscow, which verified that his condition "cannot be explained by science." By visiting, touching, and seeing Etigelov, by experiencing the unexplainable, unbelievers are inspired to belief and the sick are healed.

In the cases of both Maitreya and Etigelov, time is not linear, but merely an illusion. As bodhisattvas, enlightened beings who choose to remain incarnated in order to bring enlightenment to others, they are able to incarnate within linear time at will. Etigelov, however, is a particularly post-Soviet bodhisattva, whose biography produces a Buddhist chronotope through which Soviet scientific materialism becomes the foundation of belief in the dharma, and through which pre-Soviet Buddhist science returns to Buryatia.

Through their worship of Etigelov, visitors to the Ivolginsky *datsan* experience the Buddhist genre of history. Through the Buddhist genre, they learn new historical information about pre-Soviet Buddhist intellectual life and the purges of Buryat Buddhists in the early years of the Soviet Union. However, the Buddhist genre does not just produce new knowledge for participants. It also reframes preexisting historical knowledge of the Soviet period by offering a perspective that stands outside of linear time. Through Etigelov's returns, both new and old historical events are embedded into a Buddhist chronotope that subsumes the Soviet period into a larger recursive timeline of Buryat Buddhism and renders the entire Soviet experience merely a precondition for contemporary Buddhist faith. The truth of this chronotope is proven through contact with Etigelov's undecaying body and through the embodied sensation of a lightened soul. Lenin, the patron saint of Soviet science, becomes a precursive copy of Etigelov. Lenin's scientifically preserved corpse, on display in Red Square in Moscow, both prefigures Etigelov and reveals him to be a lesser copy of Etigelov, a perspective that is only possible from Etigelov's position outside of linear time. Reinterpreting Soviet history through this recursive chronotope, the healed bodies and souls of those worshiping Etigelov become proof that Buryats always had science and that post-Soviet subjects need Buddhist faith.

Maidari at the Ivolginsky Datsan

The Ivolginsky monastery is just outside the village of Ivolga, a 40-minute ride from Ulan-Ude. Built on a swamp, it has been the seat of the Pandito Khambo Lama of the Traditional Buddhist Sangha of Russia since its founding in 1946 and home to Etigelov's body since 2002. Minibuses run between the city and the monastery, bringing both locals and the occasional tourist. Locals come to attend services (*khurals*), visit the Tibetan medical specialists (*emchi* lamas), consult astrologists about auspicious dates, and, on holidays, they flock to see Etigelov. The biggest crowds come for Tsagaalgan (Buddhist New Year) in February, and Maidari in the summer.

The monastery complex has six temple buildings and some wooden houses where the lamas live, work, and study. In 2005, Etigelov was housed in one of the temple buildings and brought out for display in the main temple. At the time, the monastery was building a beautifully elaborate temple where Etigelov would be permanently housed, copied from old photographs of a pre-Soviet Buddhist temple that Etigelov had constructed during his tenure as the director of the Iangazhinskii monastery.[2] If the weather permits, pilgrims circumambulate the monastery grounds, leaving coins and cookies at prayer wheels, before coming to the main temple.

It was hot and dry in Ivolga in mid-July. Buryatia has what the locals call a "sharply continental climate," with temperatures ranging from minus 40–50 degrees Fahrenheit in the winter to the mid-90s in the short summers. The crowds who arrived in cars, buses, and *mikriks* (privately run vans that travel the bus routes) for the festival were sweaty. Cars parked on the road all the way to the main highway and spread into the pastureland that surrounds the temple complex. Thousands of people were there, most of them clustered in a crowded line, waiting to get into the main temple to see Etigelov (see Figure 4.1).

In the center of this crowd, on the flagstone courtyard in front of the main temple, was a palanquin, surrounded by young lamas, bearing a stuffed black fabric horse–Maitreya's horse, on which he will return to earth when the time comes (see Figure 4.2). People shoved their way through the crowd to touch it and to take photographs in front of it. Elderly people, who were either especially adept at pushing through crowds or were allowed to pass, draped silk scarves (*khadaks*) over the horse and petted it as though it were real. Outside the gates, people bought soup dumplings (*Russ.—pozy /Bur.—buuza*) or water from vendors.

Everyone was waiting for the procession to start. Most were Buryat, but at least a quarter of the visitors looked Russian. We could hear rhythmic chanting from inside the temple through loudspeakers on the porch. The chanting stopped briefly and everyone waited, expectantly, for something to happen. But the chanting resumed and people continued fanning themselves and chatting, jostling bystanders to get a better view. Children rode on shoulders to see over the crowd. A group of policemen, mostly Buryat but some Russian, and young student lamas formed a chain to hold back the crowd and keep the line in some semblance of order (see Figure 4.3).

The air was perfumed with incense from dragon-headed burners held by two young lamas wearing satin patchwork capes. Made from wild thyme that grows on the steppe (*Thymus serpyllum*, called *aia ganga* in Buryat and *bogoroditskaia trava* [god-born herb] in Russian [Metzo 2011, 41]), which is

FIGURE 4.1 Pilgrims lining up outside the temple where Etigelov was displayed, Maidari Festival, Ivolginsky *datsan*, July 2005.

also burnt at shamanic ceremonies. Normally a pleasant and familiar smell, I found it cloying in the heat. Two other lamas were pouring *aia ganga*–infused water into containers for people to take home in plastic water or soda bottles.

"What do you do with it?" I asked an elderly Buryat lady who was sitting in the shade, wearing a satin *degel*. Her face was creased from years of worry and work but she exuded a calm dignity that I found very appealing among the hot and pushy crowd. She had come by bus from Aga, a Buryat territory to the east of the republic, and as a special visitor she had been given a seat in the shade on the porch of the temple.

"You use it to bless things (Russ.—*osviatit'*)," she said. "Can you drink it?" I asked, somewhat concerned, because in the heat people were drinking it, and it was very yellow.

"We're used to it," she said, which didn't entirely reassure me. "Is it like the holy water you get at the Orthodox churches on Epiphany (Russ.—*Kreshchenie*)?" I asked. "Exactly (Russ.—*tochno*)," she assured me.[3]

FIGURE 4.2 Maitreya's horse, Maidari festival, Ivolginsky *datsan*, July 2005.

FIGURE 4.3 Lamas performing crowd control, Maidari festival, Ivolginsky *datsan*, July 2005.

Finally, the center door to the temple, which is only used on ritual occasions, opened. A parade of lamas playing conch shells and drums, carrying flags and chanting, exited the temple and surrounded the horse on the palanquin. Lifting it up, they led a procession out of the courtyard to circle the monastery grounds. The crowds parted; about half the people fell in line behind the lamas, the other half moving to the side so they could watch the procession on its return to the temple. The Maidari *khural* is chanted on three days, but the procession is held only once (see Figure 4.4).

A deity recognized throughout the Buddhist world, the details of Maitreya Buddha's role in the Buddhist universe vary over place and time, but generally speaking, Maitreya is the Buddha of the future; now reigning in the Tusita heaven, he will return when his time comes, fulfilling the dharma. About Maidari festivals in Mongolia, Caroline Humphrey and Hürelbaatar Ujeed write:

> The great attribute of Maidar Buddha is that he will appear during his eon at just this apex time of supreme possibilities . . . . By worshipping him now, people can somehow participate in this future blessed state, devoutly willing that their souls will be reborn at the time of Maidar and enlightenment become possible. In fact, Hürelbaatar continued,

FIGURE 4.4 The procession with Maitreya's horse, Maidari festival, Ivolginsky *datsan*, Maidari, July 2005.

> when you consider these matters more deeply as a Buddhist, the difference between past, present and future is annulled. What happened in the past is contained in the present, and what is being done right now determines the future (Humphrey and Ujeed 2013, 17).

Existing outside of linear time, Maitreya Buddha and other reincarnate beings offer a different perspective from which to understand historical events. Theological details about Maitreya were, however, lost on the vast majority of the lay participants, who were there to see Etigelov. Nevertheless, the stories of Maitreya and Etigelov share a sense of time that shapes the chronotope of the history encountered by the ritual's participants. A young lama who gave tours at Ivolginsky explained to me, "great lamas can choose their times; past, present and future are all the same to them."

From the perspective of a bodhisattva like Maitreya or Etigelov, time is malleable, not linear. From the perspective of a human being who exists within linear time, past prophecy becomes meaningful in the present, as the present reveals the meaning of the past. Through physical contact with the bodhisattva, the meaning of past events become clear, one's soul is lightened, and one's body can be healed. While Maitreya has not yet returned, Etigelov has: he is "the scientifically proven miracle" that you can see and worship in the flesh. For most of the attendees at the Maidari festival I attended, those who lined up at midnight the night before and waited in the heat, the current bodhisattva, Etigelov, and the rumors of his healing powers were the main attraction.

After the procession had circumambulated the monastery complex, the temple was closed for lunch, and the crowd was told to wait another hour to see Etigelov. This news was not well received, and people began to push and shove and mutter angrily. Lamas and police talked urgently on walkie-talkies, and eventually the temple was re-opened. The leadership of the monastery was not prepared for the masses of people, but Ianzhima Dabaevna Vasil'eva, the director of the Etigelov Institute, was pleased with the turnout. In her view, Etigelov has a task to fulfill and the more people he touches, the better.

After waiting hours in the sun, the inside of the temple was cool, despite the crowds and sickly sweet smell of *aia ganga*. Immediately inside the first set of doors is a vestibule, and through its glass we could see the inner temple and its altar wall, filled with statues and *thangkas* (paintings on silk), most prominently a portrait of the Dalai Lama.[4] Running down the center of the room, rows of padded benches for the lamas faced each other, two on each side. Along the left and right walls, visitors could sit on benches and purchase prayers at tables. In the right corner by the exit, a kiosk sold prayer beads and souvenirs. Patchwork fabric covered the ceiling and the brightly colored walls were hung with painted silk *thangkas*, depicting mandalas and multi-armed, blue Tibetan protector deities. It smelled of incense, oil candles, and musty coats. The shuffling feet and muted whispers of the visitors were muffled by the lamas' chanting, which swelled together into one stream of sound, occasionally interrupted by drum or gong beats.

Etigelov sat in the middle of the altar wall, in a glass box above eye level, looking down on the proceedings (see Figure 4.5). He was placed in the position of honor at the head of the chanting lamas, seated in the lotus position, the same position in which he was buried in 1927. This fact alone was presented to me as miraculous by several locals, who argued that the weight of his body should have collapsed his skeleton. Only his face and hands are uncovered. The texture of his skin is leathery, but the color of his skin resembles that of a living person, not the waxy grayish color of the dead. His eyes are closed and sunken. He is dressed in monastic robes, with silk scarves (*khadaks*) in different colors, around his shoulders. The *khadaks* hang out of the box, and as pilgrims filed past, they bowed to Etigelov, with their hands pressed palms together, while the attending lamas held the end of the *khadaks*

FIGURE 4.5 Etigelov at the Maidari Festival, Ivolginsky Monastery, July 2005.

to the pilgrims' foreheads. Some pilgrims kissed the *khadaks,* as one would a Russian Orthodox Christian icon, but most pressed their foreheads against the silk.

Two young student lamas at the front kept the line flowing in an orderly manner and made sure that no one lingered or tried to touch the box. After bowing and touching the *khadak,* the pilgrims passed another statue of Green Tara and a portrait of the Dalai Lama. On the right side of the temple, pilgrims could make an offering for the construction of a new temple to house the body; buy oil lamps, pamphlets, or a DVD about Etigelov; or leave slips of prayers, purchased for themselves or on behalf of others.[5]

Over the year and a half that I lived in Ulan-Ude, I visited the Ivolginsky *datsan* each time Etigelov was on view to the public, on a total of eight holidays, and also attended other Etigelov-focused events, including the inauguration discussed in Chapter 1. I spoke to a lot of people at these events and elsewhere about what Etigelov meant to them. For the vast majority, the "scientifically proven" claims about the imperishable nature of his body was what captured their attention and produced the most fascination—more than anything, they talked about this phenomenon. Each time I attended a viewing, I asked people why they had come; while a good number were driven by curiosity, or by the karmic merit they would acquire, most were drawn by rumors of his renowned healing powers.

Imperishable Buddhist Bodies and Healing the Embodied Post-Soviet Soul

As the lamas at Ivolginsky are quick to tell you, Etigelov is not the only miraculously preserved body of a Buddhist monk. Buddhist traditions throughout Asia include the veneration of both relics and living persons, and the Etigelov phenomena shares elements with this broader field. A growing body of literature argues that relic veneration has always been an essential component of Buddhism (see, e.g., Trainor 1997; Germano and Trainor 2004; Strong 2004) and that it testifies to the long tradition, especially within Mahayana Buddhism, of taking imperishability and other "signs of saintly death" (Martin 1994) as markers of the spiritual development of prominent figures (see also Sharf 1992).

Both official statements by the Etigelov Institute and comments by lamas link Buryatia to a broader Buddhist world by emphasizing that his preservation is not unique. At the same time, however, both lamas and laypeople often stressed to me that no other Buddhist saint or mystic had been subjected to scientific testing. In fact, other than noting that this type of miraculous preservation exists elsewhere, the discussions of Etigelov's condition that I heard were only rarely, if ever, framed in terms of Buddhist doctrine. Bernstein, who worked with Tibetan lamas in Buryatia and Buryat lamas studying in India, discusses Etigelov in the context of Tibetan Buddhist religious traditions and inter-organizational rivalries, but notes that lay people in Buryatia have little awareness of this broader context (Bernstein 2013, 28). I never heard anyone mention specific instances of preserved or venerated corpses in other countries. Other than referring to him as a bodhisattva, most commentators were far more interested in his status as a scientifically proven miracle than in how his preservation related to Buddhist doctrine or Tibetan practices.

It should not be surprising that most contemporary Buryats—even those who identify as Buddhist—know very little about Buddhism. Most of my adult interlocutors had been educated during the Soviet era, when giving religious instruction to minors was technically illegal and public discourse about religion was extremely limited. What they do know is often derived from newspaper articles or word of mouth. A majority of Buryats identify themselves as Buddhist, claim that Buddhism is their "national" religion, and are both sympathetic to and interested in Buddhism, but this sense of ethnic affiliation is mitigated by a lifetime of Soviet secular education and habits (Amogolonova 2014, 1167; Holland 2014, 171). For several of the laypeople I spoke with, curiosity first brought them to the temple, after which they began to seek out more information about Buddhism. Although Etigelov can be understood within a broader Buddhist framework, and locals were enthusiastic that Etigelov's recognition as a miracle might help forge links to the broader Buddhist world, their desire to make these links also marked the distance between them and this Tibetan Buddhist world. However, although post-Soviet subjects were drawn to Etigelov for his healing potential, as they engage with Etigelov, they encountered a new historical genre and a Buddhist chronotope within which time flows very differently than in the familiar linear chronotope. This genre of history is a Buddhist genre, grounded in Etigelov's recursive reincarnated presence in Buryatia.

The Etigelov Institute, which under the auspices of the Traditional Buddhist Sangha is responsible for managing the administrative aspects of the Etigelov phenomenon, collects stories of miraculous cures, but they do not release any figures or information about them. Ianzhima Dabaevna insists that the institute cannot publicize information about healings if they have not been scientifically confirmed, but the lack of confirmation only contributes to the power of the rumors. Although the institute started surveying visitors, the completion rate was so low it was impossible to know how many of the visitors were healed or what types of illnesses they had. During my visits I saw people on crutches, with twisted limbs, or carrying sick children, and once I saw a Russian family with a severely disabled boy on a stretcher.

During one visit, I asked an older Buryat woman next to me in line why she had come. She showed me her hand, twisted and partially paralyzed, as if from a stroke. "Is this your first time?" I asked.

"Oh no, I've been twice before."

"And may I ask, did it help?"

"Yes. I mean . . ." she paused, aware that her twisted hand seemed to belie her claim. "The hand is a little better," she explained, "but mostly I'm lighter/better in my soul" (Russ.—*mne legche na dushe*). I heard this explanation of the attraction of religious practices in Buryatia many times. People go, whether to a shaman, to Etigelov, or to a Russian Orthodox church, because their souls feel heavy, and doing whatever they do there, makes it lighter.

The term Russian term for soul (*dusha*) has a long history in Russian literature.[6] While you might expect discussions of the soul to vary significantly among people who identified themselves as Russian Orthodox, Buddhist, or shamanist, I did not find any difference in how they used the term. Buddhist laypeople were just as likely to describe a "heavy soul" as ethnic Russians who identified themselves as Russian Orthodox, and I often heard the term in shamanic circles as well.[7] I almost always encountered the term in reference to the feeling that people got from religious rituals: A heaviness on the soul (or of the soul) is a condition that requires healing or intervention through ritual. Sometimes people would say "*mne tiazhelo,*" which translates as "I feel a heaviness" or, more accurately, "it is hard for me." Usually people would explain that they knew a ritual had worked because their soul felt lighter (*mne legche na dushe*). People told me that visiting Etigelov and praying to him lightened their soul. A young Russian college student told me that she attended Orthodox services whenever she needed to lighten her soul. A Buryat woman whom I met at the Tengeri shaman's offices told me that her soul gets heavier and heavier, and then she knows that she needs to make an offering. She would come to the shamans to make an offering to her ancestors; she knew it worked when her soul felt lighter.

A heavy soul is an embodied sensation.[8] People described it as a palpable weight in their chests, and sometimes more generally throughout their body. Accordingly, a lightened soul is also a sensory experience, one that is described as a form of healing. Some people linked the feeling of a heavy soul to other physical symptoms, whereas others described it as the condition that required healing. For example, on the third anniversary of Etigelov's exhumation, I sat on the bench on the left side of the temple, watching pilgrims file past. An old Russian lady scooted over next to me, eager to talk to a foreigner. She was Russian, but since childhood, she explained, she had been sympathetic to Buddhism. She wanted to visit Etigelov, but her son and daughter-in-law—both good Orthodox Christians—were too busy with work and family to take her. So she ran away from home: She took her pension money, told her daughter-in-law she was going to the store, and instead went to the train station, where she bought a ticket and traveled the twelve hours to Ulan-Ude. She was spending her days at the monastery and her nights on a bench at the train station, and after the festival she would go home again. In her opinion, the trouble was well worth it, as the experience had lightened her soul.[9]

I met people who had traveled nearly a week by car from the Republic of Tuva to see Etigelov, motivated by rumors and the desire to learn more. Pilgrims came by the busload from Aginsky okrug, a smaller Buryat national territory to the east of the Republic, and by the carload from Kalmykia, another Buddhist republic farther west in Siberia. Each pilgrim offered personal reasons for their desire to visit: a sick child, an undiagnosable paralysis, an alcoholic son. Despite their differences, they found that Etigelov either healed their bodies or lightened their souls.

The miraculously imperishable quality of his body was extended to those who came into contact with him. At the inauguration of a monument marking Etigelov's birthplace described in Chapter 1, a lama pointed out an elderly man who had helped find Etigelov's body. This man had witnessed the 1973 exhumation and remembered the burial site. "He is nearly 100 years old. You know the life expectancy of the average Russian man is in his 50s. Elders like that are very rare these days. Etigelov kept him alive so that he could show us where he was buried," said the lama.

Just as pilgrims are concerned with Etigelov's effects on their bodies, they are also concerned about the state of his body. Since his exhumation in 2002 there has been a running debate about his condition. Several people who had never been to see him asked me with ghoulish fascination, "So, does he look alive?" Newspapers report on the results of medical tests that confirm he is not as dead as he might seem. "His blood is still alive, still active, and his cells are those of someone who died twelve hours ago," a doctor told me, wondering if perhaps the lack of decay was due to a genetic anomaly. "Of course he's alive," one person insisted, "he sweats." "Oh, that's just condensation," another countered. (Neither speaker had seen him.) Others shuddered at the idea that he is somehow both alive and dead, insisting they were too afraid to go see him.

Those who had been to see him many times were concerned that he seemed to be "drying out" and shrinking. By 2005, people were debating whether or not he should be reburied to preserve the condition of his body. For the lamas and the members of the institute, the debate centered on whether or not he had fulfilled his mission yet. Was he ready to be reburied? Ianzhima Dabaevna insists that when he is ready, Etigelov will let them know. But what exactly is his mission? What did he come back to heal?

The "Scientifically Proven Miracle"

In January 2005, a press conference was held in the offices of the Etigelov Institute to release the results of scientific analysis performed on nail, hair, and skin samples taken from Etigelov's body. At that time the Etigelov Institute consisted primarily of Ianzhima Dabaevna and her assistant, Darima. A number of other individuals volunteered occasionally, and Ianzhima's husband was often recruited to help with projects, but Ianzhima Dabaevna was the heart of the organization. A former NGO coordinator and a distant relative of Etigelov, she was asked by Khambo Lama Aiusheev to run the practical aspects of the Etigelov phenomenon. The institute's mission, as described during the press conference, is to provide information, conduct research, and publish Etigelov's writings. Research, as Ianzhima defined it, included both historical research on his life and scientific research on the state of his body—and the latter dominated discussions at the press conference.

The samples were collected and analyzed by members of the Russian Academy of Judicial Medicine, under the direction of Victor Zviagin, director of the Department for Identifying Individuals.[10] Zviagin was not present, so Ianzhima Dabaevna reported the official findings in his stead. The report confirmed that there were no embalming chemicals present in the body; it had not been frozen; and it did not qualify as mummified. Quoting Zviagin, she said that "the body of Khambo Lama Etigelov, in my professional opinion, resembles the body of a person who had died twelve hours earlier."

The analysis revealed that his body appears to have 70 percent fewer elements present than the average human body. For example, most human bodies have traces of iron and zinc, but these elements were not present in the tissue samples. A reporter asked what this meant. Although they could not explain it, Ianzhima Dabaevna and several lamas linked this test result to the concept of "emptiness" (Russ.—*pustota*), a Buddhist theological concept that Etigelov wrote about extensively. Ianzhima Dabaevna, quoting one of the scientists, described the results as "the feeling as if it were emptiness." The lamas present began a long discussion of Etigelov's philosophical writings on the concept of "emptiness," in which the everyday reality we perceive is in fact an illusion, thereby implying that the results of the laboratory tests were confirmation of Buddhist philosophy. Perhaps, they suggested, Etigelov was dissolving the illusion of himself, element by element.

The Etigelov Institute and the leadership of the Traditional Buddhist Sangha argue that Etigelov is unique because his miraculous state has been scientifically verified. Local newspaper reports echoed their claim, and people repeated this to me when I asked them what they thought about Etigelov. Buddhist adepts have left behind bodies before, they explained, but none has been scientifically verified. Bodies have been declared miraculously preserved by religious leaders the world over, but none, the institute stresses, have been verified by scientific analysis. Etigelov's lack of decay is not merely a miracle, it is a scientifically proven miracle.

Herein lies Etigelov's power to fascinate and to heal. During the press conference, Aiusheev presented his opinion (from the transcript):

> I think, he [Etigelov] came, to definitely help his own (Russ.—*svoim*) . . . in the 1920s he told his countrymen that difficult times were coming, that their home temple, the Iangazhinskii temple, would be destroyed. He saw that difficult times were coming for religion, and that must be why he left his body, to help with even his body, the rebirth of spirituality. . . . when people meet the body of the Khambo-Lama, in atheists some sort of doubt appears, and for believers, belief is strengthened . . . Before if they were told, then they believed. But now people ask questions: Was there a Christ? Buddha? In our scientific times, without analysis, there is less faith. And then when people meet with Etigelov, we are modern people, [we need to] certify for ourselves that there is spiritual teaching. That's why he [Etigelov] did this, because he saw that people would believe less in these times. He stayed for us, so that we can touch him, bow to him, see him to provide support, to verify and then we can decide, that yes.

In Aiusheev's statement the materiality of the experience, the ability to touch and to see with your own eyes, is essential to belief; "modern" people need scientific proof, or (at the very least) scientific verification of religious claims. By using the language and authority of science, the Traditional Sangha of Buryatia seeks to restore the power of religion. Aiusheev embeds the encounter with Etigelov onto a historical teleology from "before"—when people believed because they were told to—to "modern people" who need to "certify for themselves that there is spiritual teaching." Etigelov, as a reincarnated bodhisattva, could see that these modern times were coming, so he stayed in this reality in the unique form of a miraculously un-decaying body. The progression from "before," when people believed, to the "modernity" when people require proof is recognizable as a Soviet genre of progress. In his explanation, Aiusheev subsumes this Soviet teleology into a longer Buddhist chronotope. Etigelov, from his position outside this linear timeline, can see all of it, and intervene accordingly, leaving his body behind in 1927 in order to meet the needs of post-Soviet Buddhists in 2003.

Scientific imagery is also prominently used in the film about Etigelov produced by the institute. Filmed in his lab coat surrounded by equipment, Zviagin, the forensic specialist who was not able to attend the press conference in Ulan-Ude, states: "We don't know of any case of this type of preservation. He is a scientific riddle." The narrator continues: "This sensational result was produced in 2004 from spectroscopy analysis of skin, hair, and nail samples. Modern science is not in a position to explain his condition" (Blinnikov 2005). Modern science fails to explain Etigelov, but it succeeds in proving his miraculousness.

In conversations with people throughout the city, I found that the scientific proof of his imperishable condition was indeed what aroused their fascination, and, in many cases, fear. Quite a few of the people I spoke to were profoundly disturbed by the idea that he was "undead." Representatives of the Etigelov Institute and the Traditional Sangha emphasize his "undead" quality by using the verb "to leave" (Russ.—*uiti*, as in *on ushël*—past tense, he left) to describe what occurred in 1927, and laypeople often echo this usage.

"I don't know what he is," a man told me after seeing the body, "but you can't argue with science." But of course people did precisely that.

The Traditional Sangha and the institute's interpretation of Etigelov's physical condition is by no means uncontested, and the types of scientific testing that have been performed have been deliberately limited. People speculate on alternate causes, including the soil he was buried in and whether he had a genetic anomaly that could prevent decay. During the press conference a journalist asked whether there were any plans to exhume other bodies from the same cemetery to determine if perhaps the soil conditions were responsible. Aiusheev responded that it was an interesting question, but as far as they could tell, it was a completely average cemetery. There were no plans for either further exhumations or further analyses of Etigelov's body.

Critics of the Traditional Sangha range from those who say the preservation of Etigelov is a freak of nature and the display is a disgusting publicity stunt to devout Buddhist scholars who agree that Etigelov is in a state of deep meditation and object to his display because it will disrupt this state of deep meditation and kill him. Much of the debate and disagreement centers on whether or not he can or should be considered dead. A local scholar of

Buddhism told me that "the whole business merely displays the ignorance of the Traditional Sangha." Worshiping a dead body is antithetical to the spirit of Buddhism that seeks to transcend the material world, she argued.

"The idea that something dead can heal the living is ridiculous. Only living energy can heal," a shaman told me. Neither of these critics questioned that he was dead, and, like them, those who believe Etigelov is dead do not necessarily object to his display. Those who spoke of him as a place spirit (Russ.—*khoziain mesta*) had no qualms about displaying his body, nor did the monks who spoke of him as a bodhisattva on whom they could model their own behavior. His imperishable corpse is merely a sign that he had achieved enlightenment.

For those who considered Etigelov to be dead, the scientific proof was unconvincing. However, for most of the pilgrims at Ivolginsky, it was precisely the scientific "proof" that drew their interest. They worried and imagined that he was something more or other than dead. For them the scientific testing produced uncertainty, and this uncertainty created the space to endow him with the potential to transform bodies, souls, and history.

When pilgrims to Ivolginsky encounter Etigelov and experience the healing effect he has on their bodies, they encounter new historical events from the pre-Soviet and early Soviet years. Like the other rituals discussed in this book, Maidari is not explicitly about Etigelov, and these festivals do not narrate historical events. However, information about Etigelov's life and the world he lived in is distributed in pamphlets, books, and posters, explained by lamas, and repeated in newspaper articles. Pilgrims repeated these explanations to each other and to me. The festivals are sources for new knowledge about historical events that were not included in the Soviet history that they learned in school. Their experiences at the festivals often induced them to learn more about Buryat history once they got home.

Buddhist festivals are not the only places that pilgrims may encounter these historical events. Buryat intellectuals are deeply invested in producing knowledge about pre-Soviet Buryat history, and the pre-Soviet generation of early nationalist Buryat scholars is a favorite topic of books, newspaper articles, and museum exhibits.[11] However, the experience of Etigelov does not merely offer new historical information. Etigelov's unique biography offers a Buddhist genre of history that embeds both new historical events and already known Soviet historical events into a Buddhist chronotope in which the Soviet experience becomes part of Etigelov's larger project of spreading Buryat Buddhism. Grounded in Buddhist theological conceptions of reincarnation and treasure texts, this recursive chronotope is both extremely old and yet new to the pilgrims, who grew up within Soviet linear time.

There is a methodological challenge in writing about a chronotope that is not linear. Do I present the information in chronological order? Chronological order will be most familiar to the reader versed in conventional history, but it distorts the way in which time becomes meaningful within a Buddhist chronotope. Instead, I will present these historical events in the order in which local residents encountered them, and make them meaningful. I will begin in the Soviet period, move to the post-Soviet period for Etigelov's arrival, and then return to his life and departure in the early years of the 20th century.

A History of Bodies

In February 1917, the Russian tsar was overthrown. In October 1917 the Bolsheviks seized power, and from 1917 until 1923 they waged a civil war throughout Russia to consolidate that power. In 1923 the Buryat-Mongolian Autonomous Soviet Socialist Republic was founded to allow the Buryat people to develop as full members of the Soviet brotherhood of nations.

When Lenin died in 1924, the Bolshevik party was faced with a decision: whether or not to bury him or to preserve his body as a relic. By all accounts, the Politburo was aware that preserving Lenin's body was an explicit reference to the preservation of saint's bodies (Tumarkin 1997; Zbarsky and Hutchinson 1998; Buck-Morss 2000, 70–79). Nina Tumarkin argues that the Lenin cult drew on Russian traditions of the saintly prince, protector of his land and people, who accepts death as the inevitable consequence of leadership and for whom "political assassination becomes sacrificial and the victim a holy martyr" (Tumarkin 1997, 6), as well as Russian Orthodox beliefs that the bodies of saints do not decay. Stalin claimed that the workers and peasants wanted Lenin's body embalmed, but Leon Trotsky objected:

> I would very much like to know who these comrades are who, according to the words of Stalin, propose that with the help of modern science the remains of Lenin should be embalmed, transformed into a relic. I would tell them that they have absolutely nothing to do with the science of Marxism (Tumarkin 1997, 175; see also Zbarsky and Hutchinson 1998, 10–16).

Trotsky explicitly accuses Stalin of trying use a religious form (the embalmed body as relic) to bolster the power of the state. For Trotsky, this was a betrayal of Lenin's modernist project, which sought to replace superstition with atheist science. For both Stalin and Trotsky, science and religion are in opposition to each other. Trotsky argued they should be kept apart, while

Stalin argued that religion could be co-opted to serve science. Stalin won the argument, and the scientific "miracle" that preserved Lenin's body became a visible symbol of the power of the Soviet regime. A keystone of the legitimacy of that power was the argument that it was grounded in the absolute truth of science. Alexei Yurchak argues that instead of a relic, which preserves the biological matter of a saint, the Politburo and the scientists who worked on Lenin sought to "maintain the form of this body (its 'physical appearance')," grounding the Soviet state's sovereignty in representations of Lenin's image, including his body, which was a scientifically maintained representation of itself (Yurchak 2015, 128). Marxism was presented by the government as a science, and as such, it offered the possibility that the power of human rationality could conquer even death (Aronowitz 1988; Zbarsky and Hutchinson 1998). Lenin's body was the icon of that future victory, to which generations of Soviet pilgrims, Buryats included, paid homage. This preservation was the opposite of what the Traditional Buddhist Sangha is doing now: by using the age-old religious form of venerating a saint's earthly remains, the Politburo sought to reaffirm the power of science, and by extension, the power of the still-fragile Soviet state.

The transformative power of Soviet science took on added importance in relation to non-Russian native Siberian populations, such as the Buryat, who were the "most backward" of all the Soviet Union's citizens. Both Slezkine (1992, 1994) and Hirsch (2005) argue that the Soviet government legitimized its nationality policies through the rhetoric of liberating Siberian populations from their "backward" religious practices, which in many cases, were considered to contribute to poor health (see, for example, Solomon 1993).

As we have seen in both Chapter 2 and 3, Soviet-produced histories and ethnographies of Buryatia painted a picture of Buryats as illiterate nomadic herders. The chapter on Buryats in Levin and Potapov's encyclopedic collection *The Peoples of Siberia* is typical. Each chapter in the reference book is devoted to a "people" (Russ.—*narod*) and contains entries on occupations, food, and clothing, as well as the final section on "Socialist Reconstruction." The author of the Buryat chapter, Soviet ethnographer Vyatkina, writes: "Before the Revolution the Buryats had no form of writing or literature of their own, but oral folklore was found among them extensively" (Vyatkina 1964, 229). Note the term "their own"; the author does mention that "religious literature was printed from word blocks in the Tibetan and, to some extent, Mongol languages, and the lamas studied theology, religious-mystic philosophy . . . . Dogmatism, scholasticism, and conservatism were characteristic features of this 'teaching' " (Vyatkina 1964, 228). These "teachings" were presented as not authentically Buryat, but rather foreign religious claims inaccessible to the average Buryat herder. Although produced by Buryats, this scholarship was deemed "not their own."

The "Socialist Reconstruction" section of the Buryat chapter lists the achievements of the Soviet regime, beginning with reforms to agriculture, industry, and daily life. Medicine is singled out as a socialist achievement:

> On account of the abysmal poverty, lack of medical aid and low cultural level of the Buryats, there was always a high death rate, especially among children.
>
> Over the period of the Soviet regime there has been developed an extensive network of medical establishments in the republic. Hospitals and maternity homes are being built on collective farms. Over the last few years there has been progress in medical aviation, enabling first aid to be given to the population of the more distant and inaccessible *aymaks*. Every year many millions of rubles are assigned for public health. The numbers of trained medical workers among the Buryats have also increased along with the hospitals. The number of doctors in 1953 was 30 times greater than in 1923 (Vyatkina 1964, 236).

Bringing medicine to Siberia was a point of pride for the Soviet government (see also Anderson 2011). The Soviet government also brought a new, more accessible alphabet, enabling mass literacy: "For the first time in their history these people had a newspaper in their own language," writes Vyatkina (1964, 239), perfectly embodying the Soviet genre of history.[12] This is the story of how the Soviet regime brought modernity and science, embodied in education and medicine, to Buryatia, replacing religious superstition with truth, and illness and ignorance with health and vitality. Science, modernity, and health were the Soviet gift to the Buryat people, and the justification for consolidating Soviet power in the region.

In 2005, however, for many residents of Ulan-Ude the Soviet promise of scientific progress has been betrayed by the post-Soviet neo-liberal state. The salaries for intellectual professions, which are the most likely to be funded by the state, did not keep pace with the changing economic situation. Once highly paid, professors, scientists, doctors, and those in the arts were struggling to survive. Academic institutions and medical clinics often lacked basic resources and struggled to provide the services they still believed were valuable, but for which they were meagerly paid.

The loss of prestige once commanded by scientific and intellectual labor was felt especially keenly in the medical field, where the average person is most likely to come into contact with Soviet-style science. Without state support, medical institutions no longer had adequate supplies and charged for services that were once free. Doctors and nurses, like other intellectuals, were underpaid, and the effects were particularly destructive in the medical professions. The doctors I met told me that they felt overwhelmed and underappreciated; they insisted that they did not accept bribes, but knew of colleagues who did. One doctor told me that while she understood why her colleagues were tempted by bribery, it made her angry; not only was she not making extra money, but her patients suspected her of taking bribes anyway. Patients told me that they were never sure if a particular medicine or treatment was really not available, or whether it was reserved for those who could pay bribes.[13] The result is a general loss of faith in the medical system. Some patients have begun to leave a "donation" on a doctor's desk, just as one leaves a donation for treatment from a shaman or a lama, in the hopes of getting better attention or better medicine.[14] They also increasingly turn to both shamanism and Tibetan Buddhist medicine as an appealing and cost-effective alternative.[15]

The change in state power has also changed Lenin's status. The lines to visit Lenin's mausoleum are shorter now that he is a historical monument and not a symbol of political power, but the experience of visiting the mausoleum follows the same pattern it always did. Visitors wait in line in Red Square to enter the dark, cool interior of the stone building. Soldiers keep you from lingering too long and looking too closely at the waxy face and hands and the draped body that seems surprisingly small for a grown man. The line circumambulates the body, encased in glass, and then you are once again squinting at the sunlight in Red Square, dwarfed by the walls of the Kremlin and the graves of other Soviet greats, like Yuri Gagarin and Joseph Stalin. The Soviet regime's mummification and display of Lenin's body once demonstrated the power of science over death, but now, without the regime that it once legitimated, Lenin's body is a tourist curiosity, a relic of history.

As a foreigner, it is hard to look at a venerated body in Russia and not think of Lenin, but when I asked locals in Buryatia what they thought of this comparison, most were scandalized, insisting that Lenin and Etigelov were not at all the same thing. The connection has been made by the Russian mainstream media (Klin 2006), but when I tried to discuss it, most people in Ulan-Ude vehemently denied any connection.[16] "I suppose, but Etigelov is real. Lenin is artificial," Aldar, a university student, told me.

Only once did someone spontaneously make the comparison to me. I was drinking tea in a friend's office at the university with another American researcher, who said that on her recent trip to Moscow, she had to go through a metal detector to enter Lenin's mausoleum. The Buryat professor asked how Lenin looked. "Isn't he small?" she remarked. The discussion of Lenin prompted her to ask me if I had seen Etigelov.

"Yes, of course, two times now," I said.

"Oh! what a brave girl!" Both she and a Buryat graduate student drinking tea with us shuddered. Neither had been to see Etigelov, and they wanted to know what he looks like; in the photos, they said, it seems like he has no face, no nose. I asked what she found so disturbing.

"In the beginning, we just thought it was another mummy, but now that scientists confirmed it, well, there are just some things in the world that are miracles." She said she had read all about it in the newspapers, but she hadn't gone to see him. Her husband thinks it's wrong, she explained; that it's an unhealthy obsession with the dead, like Lenin. He thinks that when someone dies you should bury them and that's the end of it (Russ.—*otpustit' ego*). All this hubbub, going to see a dead body, is in his view, unhealthy and wrong.

But as Aldar said, Lenin is artificial while Etigelov is the "real thing." Etigelov is the real thing because he is a scientifically proven miracle, while Lenin is merely a miracle of science. We know how Lenin was embalmed; there is no doubt or transcendent meaning in his body, from Aldar's perspective. During the Soviet period, the verifiable, non-mysterious nature of his preservation was the whole point: it verified the power of science, and suggested that everything, including death and decay, was knowable and subject to human intervention. Now in Ulan-Ude, although the statue of Lenin's head still looks out over the city, the promises of Soviet science ring hollow. But that is okay, because as it turns out, the Soviets did not bring science to Buryatia. It was always already there.

Buryat Science

In the 19th century, Buryat intellectual production and literacy was embedded in Buddhist monastic structures. For Vyatkina, and other Soviet scholars, this discredited the scholarship, whereas from the perspective of contemporary Buryat Buddhists, the relationship gave Buryats access to a whole world of Buddhist cultural production (see Bernstein 2013, 34–60). As noted in earlier chapters, most literate Buryats used classical Mongolian, a vertical calligraphy shared with other groups in the broader Mongolian Buddhist cultural area. Buryat lamas traveled to Tibet to study, achieving high monastic ranks and returning to foster Buddhism in Buryatia. By the end of the 19th century there was a small but vibrant and rapidly growing Buryat intelligentsia who wrote in both Russian and Buryat in the classical Mongolian script.[17] Some, like Etigelov, pursued their scholarship within the purview of Buddhist monastic structures. Some, like Tsyben Zhamtsarano (1880–1942) were educated in Russian institutions of higher education, and others, like Genin-Darma Natsov (1901–1942) were originally trained in monasteries and pursued Russian educations. Piotr Badmaev (ca.1850–1920), for example, was educated in Russian institutions and converted to Russian Orthodoxy, but practiced Tibetan medicine at the tsar's court in St. Petersburg. Natsov became a member of the Bolshevik party, but also catalogued and preserved Buddhist artwork and manuscripts confiscated from monasteries during collectivization (Natsov 1998).

In the biographies of Etigelov reproduced at the Ivolginsky monastery, he is presented as a great Buddhist philosopher who produced important philosophical works. Unlike the secular intellectuals documented by Rupen (1956), Etigelov was exclusively a Buddhist scholar. As discussed in Chapter 1, he was identified during his lifetime as the reincarnation of Damba Darzha Zaiaev, the first Russian Pandito Khambo Lama.

According to Tibetan Buddhist conceptions everyone reincarnates, but only individuals of sufficient spiritual development are able to retain control over the process, thereby directing where, when, and if they will be reborn. When the current Pandito Khambo Lama states that "Etigelov chose to leave his body in this condition," he is referring to the spiritual power that enables an enlightened being, referred to as a tulku, to control reincarnation and extend beyond a single human body. Tulkus "may physically incarnate into another body, transmogrify into other forms or permeate the body of another" (Zivkovic 2010, 123). Physical contact with tulkus and their relics can convey spiritual power, enlightenment, and healing (Sharf 1992; Mills 2002; Makley 2007; Zivkovic 2010).

In this situation, Tibetan Buddhist doctrines intersect with the specific local conditions of post-Soviet Buryatia. Etigelov is not merely a Buddhist philosopher, a former Pandito Khambo Lama, state figure, and enlightened being: He was also anti-Soviet. Etigelov's firm anti-Soviet stance is illustrated by a story I was told on several different occasions about his encounter with Agvan Dorzhiev (1854–1938), the most well-known of the turn-of-the-century Buryat intellectuals. Dorzhiev was also a Buddhist monastic, trained in Tibet, a personal friend of the Dalai Lama, and a sophisticated diplomat, who promoted an alliance between Tibet and Russia (Samten and Tsyrempilov 2012; Snelling 1993). After the Bolshevik Revolution, Dorzhiev became a leader of the Buryat Buddhist Renovationist movement, which sought to reform their faith and coexist with the Bolsheviks.

After the revolution, adherents of religious groups across Russia attempted to coexist with the officially atheist government (Freeze 1995; Gerasimova

1967). Buddhists, like Russian Orthodox Christian clergy, were divided into two groups, Renovationists and Traditionalists, who believed compromise was not possible. The Renovationists argued that Marx's idea of false consciousness is compatible with the core tenet of Buddhism: that existence is an illusion. They argued that Soviet criticisms of clerical corruption were often valid, and that since Buddhist salvation does not come from a deity, but through an individual's realization of the illusion of existence, Buddhism is essentially an atheist religion, and therefore compatible with communism (see Gerasimova 1967). They also asserted that Buddhist virtues of asceticism, love for all living beings, and the desire to help others mirrored Bolshevik values. At the All-Buryat Buddhist Congress in 1922, Renovationist clergy suggested that "there must be established a procedure for keeping and maintaining the property of Lamaist communities that is not opposed to the interests of the toiling masses and the policy of the state" (cited in Snelling 1993, 208). In addition to condemning greed and corruption among the clergy, the reformers at the 1922 conference also tackled aspects of Buddhism that linked it to shamanism and thus appeared "primitive," banning oracles and reincarnate lamas (tulkus) (see Snelling 1993, 207, 211).

Traditionalists, including Etigelov, argued that compromise with the Bolsheviks was not possible, and the Bolsheviks eventually agreed. From 1922 to 1928, the Communist Party supported both Orthodox and Buddhist Renovationist movements, but in 1929, the League of Militant Godless Congress changed that policy, and the Renovationists were accused of being "the disguises for a more effective struggle against the Soviet power. By comparing ancient Buddhism and ancient Christianity to communism, the Renovationists are essentially trying to replace the communist theory by a cleansed form of religion, which therefore only becomes more dangerous" (Yaroslavsky, cited in Pospielsovsky 1987, 1, 55).

Etigelov is also credited in contemporary narratives with recognizing the essential incompatibility of Buddhism and communism. An informational pamphlet produced by the Etigelov Institute tells the story of his meeting with Dorzhiev. In 1921 their paths crossed somewhere along the Mongolian border; Dorzhiev was coming from Tibet, via Mongolia, and Etigelov was heading in the opposite direction. The two men shared a fire, drank tea together, and talked of their views of the future. Etigelov told Dorzhiev he would do better to turn around and head back to Tibet, because the government was about to begin arresting lamas, and if they caught him, he would not escape alive. Dorzhiev, expressing his faith in the compatibility of Buddhism and Soviet reform, dismissed Etigelov's concerns. He then asked Etigelov why, if he believed as he did, he did not flee to Mongolia. Etigelov responded, "They won't catch me." As he predicted, Etigelov "left" shortly before the repressions started, while Dorzhiev died in a Soviet prison in 1937.

From a contemporary perspective, Dorzhiev's death in a Soviet prison represents the betrayal of Buryat participation in the Soviet project. During the 1930s thousands of Buddhist monks were killed. Most of the non-religious pre-revolutionary Buryat intellectuals were killed in the 1937 purges. These intellectuals were not only killed, they were also effectively silenced. As discussed in Chapter 2, the alphabet reforms of the 1930s, which the government presented as necessary for widespread literacy, rendered pre-revolutionary Buryat scholarship inaccessible to Soviet-educated Buryats. The combination of the purges and the alphabet reforms made true the Soviet claim that "before the Revolution the Buryats had no form of writing or literature of their own" (Vyatkina 1964, 229). The history of pre-Soviet Buryat Buddhist scholarship was effectively erased from public awareness, accessible only to a handful of scholars who curated historical manuscripts.

Etigelov is both a great Buddhist intellectual and a great Buryat intellectual. As pilgrims come to see Etigelov, to touch his *khadaks* and marvel at the state of his body, they are confronted with the material proof of his existence. His biography, published by the Etigelov Institute and sold at kiosks at the monastery, repeated orally by those visiting him, and reproduced in newspapers, proves that there were great intellectuals in Buryatia before the revolution. His body is proof that he was not merely a scholar and theologian but a bodhisattva, a being so wise and learned that he transcends both time and death. From his position outside time he foresaw the Soviet repressions, as well as their consequences. He knew not only that the Soviet government would seek to destroy Buddhism, but that post-Soviet subjects would need proof in order to believe. Etigelov's prophecies, burial, and return incorporate the Soviet period within a longer historical narrative that is Buddhist and that invokes the pre-revolutionary and ongoing history of Buryat intellectual production. This history refigures science and scholarship, from something that was brought to Buryatia by the Soviets, into something that was already inherently Buryat and Buddhist.

This argument, that science was already always Buryat and Buddhist, is extended to the Tibetan medical treatments offered by lamas at the monastery. Tibetan medicine has always been part of Buddhist practice in Buryatia. As noted above, Piotr Badmaev practiced Tibetan medicine at the imperial court in St. Petersburg, and Etigelov is said to have organized lamas trained in Tibetan medicine to treat wounded soldiers at the front during the Russo-Japanese war. A very rare Tibetan medical atlas, which is part of the collection of the Khangalov History Museum in downtown Ulan-Ude, documents

Buddhist medical theory and treatments. This medical atlas was part of a local controversy in the 1990s, when it was loaned to an international exhibition on Tibetan medicine (Avedon et al. 1998). The current Pandito Khambo Lama Aiusheev protested this loan, arguing that sacred Buddhist objects should not be allowed to leave Buryatia, and that the History Museum should respect the wishes of the Traditional Sangha, even if they had no legal authority over the atlas. However, most Buryat Buddhist intellectuals were in favor of the loan, because they felt that it was a unique opportunity for Buryatia to show the world its contributions to Buddhist culture. In fact, the 14th Dalai Lama, in his foreword to the exhibition catalog, wrote, "It gives me great pleasure that the public will be able to see for the first time the unique set of medical paintings that were taken from Tibet to Buryatia for the purpose of training doctors in the Tibetan tradition" (Avedon et al. 1998, 11). The Khambo Lama was not able to marshal much support against a loan that the Dalai Lama supported.

Viewing a portion of the atlas on display at the history museum, Marianna Dorzhievna,[18] a Buryat friend of mine and a local intellectual, explained:

> The Tibetan Atlas shows illnesses in the form of a tree. One half of the tree is illness, and the other shows health. In the 19th century, Buryatia was forming its own branch on this tree. Every *datsan* had its *emchi* lamas and many, including Etigelov, were writing texts about their own medicines, ones that they had developed using local flora and fauna. They even used parts of animals more than herbs. Siberian nature (Russ.—*priroda*) has a lot of specially suited plants and so they were developing treatments for the local context. In the 1930s, this development was broken, cut off, and now, we are discovering the tradition again. People are re-learning these treatments, and so Tibetan medicine is being re-valued and developed, and starting to be valued by Western medicine.

She knew very little about this herself, she said, although she had visited a specialist in Tibetan medicine and taken some herbs that he had prescribed. As she spoke, she qualified most of her explanations by saying that someone else had explained it to her that way. It was clear that she felt regret for not knowing more about Buddhism, and at the same time, pride in the idea that something once thought worthless was being re-valued by contemporary doctors. Almost every time anyone in Buryatia spoke about Tibetan medicine, they usually mentioned that it prefigured forms of knowledge that Western bio-medicine was only now beginning to understand.[19]

These descriptions of Tibetan medicine parallel the way people spoke about Etigelov's theological scholarship. Both offer material proof that scholarship and science were always already present in Buryatia, prior to the Soviet period. Their return closes the circle, surrounding the Soviet period as a brief interlude within a longer history of Buryat Buddhist history, intellectual scholarship, and medicine.

Proof

In Soviet ideological discourse, the existence of "backward" religious beliefs necessitated and justified the imposition of science. In contemporary post-Soviet Buryatia, the instability of Soviet scientific institutions and the failure of Soviet medicine to provide healing necessitate a turn to religion, and the efficacy of religion is in turn proven by relying on scientific evidentiary regimes.[20] The Buddhist historical genre presents science and scholarship as always already Buryat, but the Sangha's leadership proves their case using scientific methods to verify their miraculous claims.

I do not wish to argue merely that Soviet science replaced religious faith and that subsequently post-Soviet faith is now replacing science. Rather, I am arguing that, in Ulan-Ude and perhaps elsewhere in the former Soviet Union, as a result of the Soviet atheist experience, science and religion exist in a longstanding dialogic relationship to one another. During the Soviet period, the regime was legitimized by the promise that atheist science and Soviet biomedicine were replacing religion with truth. However, as power relations between institutions shifted in the post-Soviet period, so too, did the possibilities enabled by these discourses (see also Petryna 2004). The scientifically proven inexplicable imperishability of Etigelov's body opens up the possibility for the transfiguration of all the bodies and souls that come into contact with him. Yet in neither of these instances is science or bio-medicine invalidated. Instead, in both cases, it is precisely because the limits of science are scientifically verified that transfiguration is possible.

The disarray produced by the post-Soviet rearrangement, and, in many cases, decay of Soviet bio-medical institutions and economic redistributive networks has produced a population with high levels of un- or underemployment, alcoholism, and a host of other social, familial, and physical ills that require forms of healing that bio-medicine cannot provide. Whether Etigelov can heal these ills cannot be proven, but he is able to lighten the souls of the suffering by offering the promise of something that exceeds bio-medicine, that is nonetheless authorized and confirmed by bio-medicine.

As a bodhisattva, Etigelov transcended the human condition and has returned to help others transcend it. However, he has not just transcended the universal Buddhist understanding of the human condition of suffering, but a specifically local, Buryat, and post-Soviet condition of suffering, rooted in the dislocations of post-Soviet transformations. Etigelov's imperishable body presents the possibility of transfiguring death and decay. Lenin's body did the same during the Soviet period, but Lenin merely offered material proof that a body can be preserved eternally. Etigelov is the "real thing" because he offers material scientific proof that the spiritual can heal and preserve the material.

Lenin "lived, lives, and will live," as the saying goes, but both Maitreya and Etigelov lived and return, bringing a historical cycle full circle. Lenin represents stasis, while both Maitreya and Etigelov fulfill prophecies and transcend time. Maitreya walked with the Buddha, and will return to bring enlightenment to all those who live at the same time. Etigelov brings knowledge, faith, and healing back to Buryatia, where they always already were. His biography subsumes the Soviet period into a longer, Buddhist chronotope, within which the Soviet anti-religious repressions were merely a test of faith, a bump along the road by which the dharma is spread. The scientific proof of Etigelov's imperishability proves science to be inferior to faith, thereby enabling people who believe in science to also have faith. However, by using science as means of proving this faith, this proof also reconciles a perceived dichotomy between science and religion, recuperating the temporal divide between religion and modernity that was created in the Soviet genre of history. Just as science is subsumed by (and placed in service to) religious faith, through Etigelov's biography—his departure and return—the Soviet era is subsumed by Buddhist time. The narrative does not erase, deny, or change the content of the Soviet genre of Buryat history, but by making it a part of a larger Buddhist chronotope, it completely reconfigures what the Soviet period means to those who experience Buryat history by visiting Etigelov.

5

Opening the Center, Opening the Roads

I WAS FIRST introduced to Tengeri in 2003 by Professor Dashinima Dugarov of the National Humanities Institute at the Buryat State University, where I had been taking Buryat language classes. A few minutes after meeting me, Professor Dugarov said, "If you are interested in shamanism I have some people you should meet. Meet me in 20 minutes on the corner of Lenin and Revolution Square." I followed him into the oldest section of Ulan-Ude, which still has pre-revolutionary wooden houses with intricately carved woodwork and no plumbing. Around the back of a grocery store, we opened a rickety, unmarked door on one of these wooden houses and entered a two-room office. The waiting room was bare. Inside the second room I met Budazhab Purboevich Shiretorov.

I don't know what exactly I expected, but Budazhab Purboevich was not it. On that day, he was dressed in a suit jacket and dress slacks, with a cell phone on his hip and stylish little sunglasses. He was the only one in the office, and, out of respect for Professor Dugarov, was very generous with his time, explaining the organization's mission to me at length. Contemporary Buryats, he argued, suffer from a wide range of social problems, including rampant alcoholism, broken families, and ill health. People no longer had good relationships with their ancestors and their gods. They had forgotten the ceremonies, no longer honored their ancestors, so their ancestors, angry at this neglect, persecute them. Some people have the calling to be a shaman, but no longer know how to recognize it, and so they suffer. Tengeri's mission is to re-introduce shamanic practices, and to re-teach traditions that have been lost, in order to heal contemporary social problems. To do that, they needed to build an institutional form for shamanism, a center where people can come to be healed and educated.

Tengeri's mission is grounded in a narrative of degeneration, which sees the present as a state of loss, the sum of a long history of religious oppression. Their religious practices presume a past golden age when the living knew how to maintain positive relationships with their ancestors. Through their attempts to restore these shamanic ritual traditions, Buryat shamans produce knowledge about the past, and thus a particular shamanic chronotope.[1]

The shamanic genre of history is widespread in Buryatia and is generated through shamanic ritual practices of various kinds, but I will engage with it primarily through its particular instantiation in Tengeri. As an urban and institutional form of Buryat shamanism, Tengeri is not typical of Buryat shamanism and has critics as well as supporters.

Shamanism is a label given to a wide variety of indigenous ritual practices that predated the arrival of Buddhism and Russian Orthodox Christianity. Shamanism became a "religion" through the contrast with these two traditions and has been called a "religion" locally, for a very long time, at least since Dorzhi Banzarov's (1846) dissertation on "The Black Faith of the Mongols" (reprinted in Banzarov 1997). Banzarov labeled shamanism the "black" faith, in contrast to Gelugpa Buddhism, which was the "yellow" faith. Shamanism in Buryatia, as it is elsewhere, is a creative practice that draws on particular ritual forms to interact with a wide variety of other-than-human persons and animate landscapes. Humphrey and Onon (1996) usefully argue that the focus on individual shamans is misleading, and that scholars should, in contrast, focus on the conceptions of the world that render a shaman's intervention occasionally necessary. A shaman's intervention into this animate world is creatively adapted to solve the problem that provoked the intervention, and as such cannot be effectively evaluated by categories of "tradition" or doctrine. As a result, however, it is difficult to offer a baseline description of Buryat shamanic practices against which to measure Tengeri's innovations.

In general, Buryat shamanic practice relies on three main ritual forms: a *tailgan*, which is an offering ceremony to an other-than-human being on behalf of a group (often, but not necessarily, a clan); shamanic initiations, in which shamans establish relationships to specific other-than-human persons; and healing ceremonies, which can vary widely. Buryat shamanism posits a hierarchy of spirit beings, with Tengeri, the Eternal Blue Sky (Bur.—*khukhe munkhe Tengeri*) at the pinnacle. Although shamans will make offerings to Tengeri, he is too far away to intervene in human affairs.[2] Below Tengeri there are 99 Tengerins, and below them a variety of deities and ancestors. The spirit beings that shamans interact with are usually ancestor spirits and masters of place, which are the spirit protectors of particular territories (see Chapter 1). Shamans communicate with these beings in positive ways: by making offerings; through dreams; and by calling them to a ritual or calling them into their bodies. While both the spirits and the method of communication vary regionally and from shaman to shaman, shamans learn to interact primarily with their own ancestral shamans, those clan members who carried the clan's shamanic gift in previous generations (*ongons*).[3] Shamans can also interact with malicious beings, who are often the spirits of shamans or the unhappy dead, but usually only to remove their influence from the living. There are three main types of shamans: black, white, and blacksmith, although there are a number of other types of healers that are considered to have shaman-like powers, such as bonesetters and massage therapists. Prior to the revolution there were also inspired oral epic singers (Gesar bards), but this tradition is, to my knowledge, not reviving in Buryatia.[4]

The distinction between black, white, and blacksmith shamans is a good example of the trouble with "tradition." While pre-revolutionary ethnographic texts describe black shamans as interacting with evil spirits and white shamans with good spirits, this distinction does not map onto the cosmologies described in the same texts and is likely to have been a missionary perspective. In contrast, Dugarov (1991) argues that Buryatia is the geographic border between Siberian forms of shamanism, represented by black shamans who use drums to go into trance, and Central Asian forms, represented by white shamans who use bell-staffs and chant a Buddhist mantra to induce trance (see also Skrynnikova 2002; Bolkhosoev and Pavlov 2006). The shamans at Tengeri, who knew and valued Professor Dugarov's opinion, adhere to this explanation. In their practice, the type of shaman you become depends on the type of shaman your ancestors were. However, at least half the shamans at Tengeri are initiated as more than one kind. At the same time, there are village shamans who only conduct offering ceremonies, for whom these distinctions are relatively meaningless.

The Tengeri shamans draw on this broader body of shamanic practices and on a broader shamanic genre of history in idiosyncratic ways. However, because the shamans at Tengeri are specifically engaged in rebuilding shamanism among urban Buryats who have lost their connections to village shamanic practices, Tengeri offers a particularly sharp lens through which to refract the shamanic genre of historical knowledge production.

The shamanic genre of history incorporates many of the same historical events as the Buddhist, Soviet, and hospitality genres described in previous chapters. In contrast, however, the shamanic genre timeline begins much earlier, in the age of Chinghis Khan, when Buryats were one of many seminomadic pastoralist tribes united into the Great Khan's empire. The shamanic genre reaches back to the pre-Buddhist and pre-Christian past, which links

Buryats to a broader Central Asian and global indigenous identity. The Buryat nation, as produced through the shamanic genre of history, is a very different Buryat nation than the Buddhist Buryat one.

Like the Buddhist genre, the shamanic genre of history re-frames the meaning of the Soviet years, but it does so by focusing on the effect that Soviet reforms had on families and their knowledge of the past. Within the longer shamanic timeline, the losses of the Soviet period are only the latest in a long history of oppression. Like the hospitality genre, the shamanic genre tells the history of Buryatia as a history of multi-ethnic intermarriage and border-crossing. Unlike the Buddhist genre, which re-inscribes the boundaries of the Buryat nation, the shamanic genre is produced through kinship and genealogy, offering an easy way to incorporate other ethnicities. By reaching toward a broader indigenous identity, Tengeri is able to see their mission as not just about restoring Buryat shamanic knowledge for Buryats, but for everyone.

Although Tengeri's shamanic genre of history is, on one hand, a much longer history, Tengeri produces historical knowledge through the relationships between individual shamans and patients, and in that sense, these histories are on a smaller scale. Although Tengeri makes the claim that shamanism is a Buryat religion, they are not claiming to tell the history of the Buryat nation. Instead, as discussed in Chapter 6, they produce knowledge about individual families, in most cases filling gaps and silences produced by Soviet state violence. Patients come to Tengeri with problems ranging from physical symptoms of illness that do not respond to medical treatment, to stretches of bad fortune that extend across entire families. The shamans presume that the source of a patient's problems is that they neglect their ancestor spirits, because the patients are ignorant about the past. Accurate knowledge of the past can help the living solve their problems. To gain this information, patients and shamans combine archival and oral history with new knowledge obtained from the spirits that enter the shaman's body during shamanic rituals. The accuracy of this new information is measured by its effect on the bodies of the living. If embodied suffering is relieved, then the knowledge is deemed accurate. If the embodied condition of the living is not improved, then the knowledge is wrong, and the search for new information continues.

The chronotope produced by the shamanic genre is different than either the Soviet or Buddhist chronotopes. In Tengeri's rituals, the living converse with their dead ancestors, resolving conflicts that limit the ability of the living to prosper and thrive. Through these ritual interactions, the past (in the form of embodied ancestors) is continually present; the past is not really past at all. Cause and effect are linear, in that past actions produce effects in the present, but these effects can be reversed through ritual action, so that these past actions no longer affect the future. Time is both linear and continually co-present, rendering the effects of linear time malleable. But to intervene in linear time and repair the fortunes of the living, you must have a good relationship with your past. The shamans at Tengeri produce a version of the Buryat past at the institutional level, one which makes an institutional form of shamanism absolutely necessary.

Local Religious Organization of Shamans, Tengeri

The "Local Religious Organization of Shamans, Tengeri" [Mestnaia religioznaia organizatsiia shamanov (MROSH) Tengeri] was officially registered as a religious organization in the Republic of Buryatia in 2003 by Budazhab Purboevich Shiretorov and Victor Dorzhievich Tsydypov.[5] When I worked with Tengeri in 2004–5, Budazhab Purboevich was the vice-chairman, but when I returned in 2012, both Victor Dorzhievich and Budazhab Purboevich had split off to form their own organizations and many of the core members had left. The current director, Bair Zhambalovich Tsyrendorzhiev, who was originally from the Aga area east of Buryatia, had a new group of shamans, along with a few of the original members. In 2005 the membership rolls listed about 50 members, including at least 13 practicing shamans, apprentices who had received a protective initiation (Russ.—*zashchita*) but were not yet practicing, friends and family members of shamans, and several local scholars.[6] By 2012, the list had doubled, and the membership had changed significantly.

In both 2005 and 2012, the youngest practicing shamans were in their twenties, and the oldest in their fifties and sixties. Some grew up in villages speaking Buryat at home; others were raised in urban homes speaking Russian. Several are of mixed Buryat, Russian, and Tartar parentage. All of them experienced debilitating illnesses that did not respond to mainstream medical treatment and came to interpret these illnesses as a shamanic calling (see Quijada 2011). They are neither the first nor the only registered shamans' organization in Buryatia. The first shamans' organization, Bo Murgel, was founded in 1992 by Nadezdha Stepanova (Humphrey 2002a, 211; Zhukovskaia 2004). However, in 2005, they were the most active and ambitious organization in Ulan-Ude.

Registration as an officially recognized religious organization was a hard-won prize and source of great pride for the Tengeri members. They relished the legitimacy it offered and were especially pleased by the right to issue visa invitations, which enabled them to invite shamans from other countries to attend their annual International Shamanic Conference on Olkhon Island. It also offered the possibility of participating in shamanic tourism, something they had heard a great deal about, but had very little idea of how to organize. In the summer of 2005, they were able to move out of the tiny office where I first met them and into a more spacious center on Kuibysheva Street in the heart of downtown Ulan-Ude.

At the same time, they were in the middle of a lawsuit seeking possession of a larger site. As an officially registered religious organization, Tengeri had the right to request land from the city to build a religious center. They had received a piece of property on the outskirts of the city, in a suburb called Novaia Komushka, but the land was occupied by squatters. The lawsuit would determine whether the squatters would have to move. Even as they inaugurated the center downtown, they set up a donation box with a sketch of the planned ceremonial center that would supersede the one they were inaugurating. Tengeri eventually won the lawsuit and took possession of the property, moving out of the downtown offices. By 2012 they had built several buildings and were regularly conducting rituals at the new site.

The Inauguration

The ritual began with speeches. Everyone gathered outside in the back yard. Wood was set up for a bonfire, and the October morning was cold, so everyone was eager for the fire, even in their coats. It was difficult to hear the speeches, because the new office was down the street from Ulan-Ude's main Russian Orthodox cathedral, Odigitrievskii (Hodegetria), and the bells rang all morning for a special service in honor of another imperishable body: a Russian Orthodox saint, St. Innokentiia (1680–1731), former bishop of Irkutsk, had arrived in Ulan-Ude and was being carried from the train station to the cathedral at the same time as the Tengeri inauguration. The multi-religious context of Ulan-Ude was literally drowning out the shamanic ritual.

Victor Dorzhievich began the inauguration by explaining that this ritual celebrated the opening of the new center, the opening (later that same day) of a museum exhibition at the Ulan-Ude City Museum, and the second anniversary of the organization's registration. He introduced the members of Tengeri who would later be going into trance. Then Victor Dorzhievich introduced two men, both professors at a local university, who were also shamans. One of them, Professor Bazarov, was the author of a book called *Secrets and Practices of Shamanism* (Bazarov 2000).[7] Later, the wife of one of the shamans explained to me that these two men had been part of the initial revival of shamanism in

Buryatia, and when Victor and Budazhab had first started out, they had sought their advice and counsel.

Professor Bazarov spoke at length in Buryat, although at least half of the audience could not understand what he said, including myself.[8] I asked several people afterward what he had said in Buryat and was met overwhelmingly with shrugs. Most of the audience had either not understood or not paid attention (and to be fair, the church bells were working hard to drown him out). What mattered in the context was that he spoke Buryat fluently, something that marks a speaker as "more Buryat."[9] By speaking in Buryat he established his own authority as an arbitrator of "tradition" and marked the ritual as a Buryat space, one in which Buryat "tradition" would be practiced. This effect was not lost on the audience, even if the content of his words was.

In the Russian portion of his speech, he situated Buryat shamanism within a broader Central Asian context, noting the similarities between Buryat shamanism and shamanic practices in Kalmykia, Tuva, and Khakassia. In doing so, he further authorized shamanism as not just a local tradition, but as a local variant of a broader Central Asian religion.[10] He also noted that "we are all shamans here," diffusing any assumptions about tension between the two organizations. After the speech, his companion lit the bonfire, and they were joined by six other shamans. Tengeri, the Eternal Blue Sky (Bur—*khukhe munkhe Tengeri*), was invoked in Buryat, and offerings of white foods and vodka were made into the bonfire. Although few people present understood what they said, their presence provided the validating authority of both religious and intellectual predecessors.

Several government officials attended, including representatives from the Ministry of Culture (in association with the museum exhibit) and the Bureau of Religious Affairs. The director of the republic's Bureau of Religious Affairs called shamanism "the oldest of our religions" (Russ.—*samaia drevniaia religiia nasha, shamanizm*) and noted that Tengeri's center was filling a gap in the city's religious landscape: "Ulan-Ude had churches and *datsans*, but nothing for our oldest religion." The "us" in this speech is interestingly vague; by including Christianity (churches—Russ. *tserkvi*) the speaker seemed to be referring to a multi-ethnic civic "us"—the residents of Ulan-Ude or Buryatia—rather than a Buryat "us." Although I met a handful of Buryat Christians of various denominations, and many more Buryats who avail themselves of the resources of the Russian Orthodox Church (such as holy water) when it is useful, I never heard anyone refer to Christianity as a Buryat religion. His speech evoked the multi-ethnic, multi-religious Friendship of the Peoples rhetoric that characterizes the hospitality genre and which was so prevalent at City Day (see Chapter 3). As a government employee, he was well versed in the hospitality genre, which is the default genre for public speeches. By evoking this genre, the official was praising Tengeri for participating in the local neighborly ethic of performing and preserving traditions. By opening the center, Tengeri was making a geographic space for shamanism as a religion, within the ranks of the other officially recognized religions of the republic. He then cut a blue ribbon strung across the yard, further granting official recognition to the organization.

A representative from the Buryat People's Congress[11] also gave a speech congratulating Tengeri, stating "all people have the right to revive (Russ.—*vozrozhdat'*—rebirth) their religion," while another speaker lauded Tengeri for embodying the "traditions of the Buryat people (Russ.—*narod*)." All of these speeches very explicitly referred to shamanism as a religion, and a Buryat religion. However, this emphasis reveals a tension in Tengeri's stated mission. The name of the organization is "Local Organization of Shamans, Tengeri." The members chose the designation "local" rather than "Buryat" to be explicitly inclusive, to make space for local Russian, Tatar, and Evenki shamans to join as well. Tengeri—the Sky God—and the other deities mentioned, propitiated, and called down are Buryat deities. The traditions Tengeri purports to be reviving are Buryat traditions, and yet the boundaries of who may be represented by Tengeri are more fluid. Although in the beginning all the shamans were Buryats, over time their ranks have expanded to include several shamans of mixed ethnic backgrounds, Russians and even a German.

During an interview with a Russian reporter, Budazhab Purboevich explained "now, in new times, with new situations, shamanism has to find new forms. As long as there were only Buryats, clan ceremonies were fine, but now, if we do only clan ceremonies, we would be praying for only Buryats to live well. That isn't right. We have to pray for all the residents here, after all the years of people marrying each other, the ancestors are all mixed. This is a new situation, so we need new rituals." The shamans at Tengeri find themselves walking a fine rhetorical line between emphasizing that they are reviving Buryat shamanism, and the claim that they are reviving a universal shamanic practice that many peoples share, and which is a resource available to all.

After the speeches, the ritual moved inside, where the practicing shamans of Tengeri had set up altar tables. Several of the new initiates, who passed their initiations that summer, joined the more senior shamans. They were now able to perform *kamlanie* (the opening chant) and call down their *ongons* (ancestor spirits). *Kamlanie* informs the spirits and deities that the ritual is beginning, and calls them to the ritual. Each shaman has his or her own *kamlanie*, which includes the details of their genealogy and all the names of the ancestral spirits with whom they have relationships. During a ritual, everyone begins the *kamlanie* at the same time, drumming (in the case of black shamans) or shaking a bell-staff (in the case of white shamans) along with the chant. A few of the newer initiates read their *kamlanie* from notebooks, whereas the more experienced shamans, like Bair Zhambalovich and Seseg Garmaeva, recited theirs by heart, based on years of practice.

The effect of everyone chanting and drumming in the small space was overwhelming, and many of the audience members escaped the noise inside by stepping out into the courtyard to chat. The audience consisted primarily of family members of the shamans; patients and clients; a few government representatives, most of whom did not stay for the whole ceremony; and the employees of the City History Museum who had been working with Tengeri.

After the *kamlanie*, individual shamans began drumming and chanting to call their *ongons* down into their bodies. The *ongon's* descent is marked by an immediate change in behavior. If the shaman is seated, as they were in the indoor ceremony, they usually jump up; several shamans at the opening ran outside into the yard (see Figure 5.1). In outdoor ceremonies, shamans usually run to induce a trance; once the *ongon* arrives, they will stop running and their movements are noticeably different. *Ongons* and other beings, such as place spirits or deities, usually have signature songs or chants that they

FIGURE 5.1 A shaman in trance/an *ongon* in a shaman's body during the Tengeri inauguration ceremony. The audience is covering their faces so as not to look the *ongon* in the eyes. Note the fire for offerings and the stone cairn on the right. Official opening of the Tengeri Shamanic Center, Ulan-Ude, October 6, 2005.

begin to sing when they enter a shaman's body. These songs and the posture and behavior of the shaman's body help the assistants and other shamans know who has entered, how to address them, and what to ask. New initiates such as Yuri usually have only one *ongon*, but senior shamans such as Bair Zhambalovich and Seseg Garmaeva may bring down several beings over the course of a ceremony.

As Victor Dorzhievich and Bair Zhambalovich explained it to me, *ongons* and other place spirits may be disoriented, confused, or angry at being drawn away from whatever they were doing before they were called. The shaman's assistant, usually a spouse or another shaman, approaches the *ongon* and offers a cigarette and a cup of vodka or milk tea to show respect and to induce the *ongon* to settle down. Some settle quickly, while others run and sing for several minutes before accepting the drink and sitting down. After they accept the smoke and the drink, the rest of the cigarette and the drink are passed to someone else attending the ceremony, who must finish them. Everyone present bows and looks down or covers their eyes, so as not to offend the *ongon* by looking directly at them (see Figure 5.1).

After the *ongon* has settled down, the shaman's assistant will bring clients or patients to ask questions. Sponsoring your own ritual is complicated and expensive, so shamans will often tell their clients to come to larger ceremonies. It is a convenient way to get a few questions answered and determine whether an individual ceremony is necessary. The assistants knew who was there for questions and helped them to know when the right *ongon* had entered the shaman, how to approach, and how to ask their question in Buryat.

Other questions were specifically focused on the inauguration. Aldar Andanovich, the commercial director of Tengeri, asked whether the roads were open for him. He was concerned that without divine support, he would not have the moral authority to do his job. "Shamans," he explained to me, "are very powerful people. Without the support of the gods I won't be able to scold them (Russ.—*rugat'sia*) or get them to do anything. I just won't be strong enough." Aldar Andanovich was concerned that unless he could get the shamans to behave more like other professionals, especially in respect to schedules, the organization would falter. For example, Aldar had drawn up a schedule of office hours so that clients would know when any particular shaman would be available in the office, but no one adhered to it. They would often be waylaid by clients at home, rituals would take longer than expected, or sometimes they simply forgot to show up. As the office manager, Aldar would have to explain these absences and track down shamans on their cell phones, and he argued that if the *ongons* supported his efforts he'd have more authority in relation to the shamans. The *ongon* gave a positive response. Aldar's roads were open. Aldar was pleased, and everyone at Tengeri felt reassured that this new enterprise would be successful.[12]

Ongons speak in verse, in formal, often rhyming (and sometimes archaic) Buryat. Their answers often need to be decoded, especially for the many patients who do not speak Buryat or do not speak it well. A shaman's assistant will usually write down the answer, and then the assistant, shaman, and client puzzle over it. Darima, a Buryat woman in her late 30s who was the primary organizer of the museum exhibit, also asked a question of an *ongon*. She had never visited a shaman before, and the Tengeri members encouraged her to participate. I asked her if she had gotten an answer, but like other skeptical clients, she was not satisfied with it. "Yes," she said curtly. She did not choose to share the question or the answer but from the look on her face it was clear that it had made no sense to her.

The phrase "the roads are open" is a characteristic response on the part of *ongons*. It means that there are no spiritual obstacles between the person and what they hope to accomplish. Success in any endeavor, the shamans explain, is a dual affair. Human beings must do their part to bring about the things that they want to achieve. However, despite all efforts, these attempts sometimes fail. In those cases, some spiritual obstacle is presumed to be blocking the road. These obstacles may have been put there by neglected ancestor spirits who need to be propitiated, negative spiritual karma carried over from the actions of previous generations, or curses (Russ.—*prokliatie*) caused by the anger and jealously of the living. If something is blocking the roads, then *ongons* can help to diagnose the problem and suggest an appropriate resolution. For neglected ancestors, a *tailgan* ceremony may be held to offer them a sheep, and the promise of regular ceremonies is exchanged for ongoing protection for their descendants. A cleansing ceremony may be enough to resolve curses.

Negative karma from previous generations is more difficult to resolve, and depends on the situation. As with the Russian term *dusha* (soul), discussed in Chapter 4, the Buddhist term "karma" is used conversationally across religious contexts in Buryatia in ways that do not correspond to strict Buddhist doctrinal conceptions. I heard the term used by shamanic practitioners, Russian Orthodox Christians, and confirmed atheists to refer to the idea that negative energy from the past affects the present. In these contexts, karma is used to refer to negative or positive energy that can be passed forward across generations, an understanding that fits within the shamanic chronotope. Within Buddhist doctrine, karma is earned by an individual, and carried forward by that individual into future rebirths. However, as used conversationally in Buryatia, karma is carried forward within families. I heard stories about people who suffered in the present because of things their grandparents did during collectivization. Turning a neighbor, a family member, or especially a shaman or lama over to the government during the violence of the 1930s left an indelible mark on the karma of a family and brought bad luck to succeeding generations (see also Leykin 2015).

These stories produce a shamanic chronotope in which the past continues to exist in the present. As a young Buryat college student told me, "If you want to have a good future you have to have a good relationship to your past." The past has already happened, but it continues to exercise influence on the present. The living need accurate knowledge of the past to understand and manage its influences and to function successfully in the present. Ancestors (Russ.—*predki*) may be dead, but they are not gone. They have the power to harm or protect the lives of their descendants; the worst thing a family can do is forget or ignore them. And yet, both the state violence of the early Soviet years and the entire Soviet modernizing project required people to forget their ancestors and their obligations to them.

Tengeri does not seek to undo these socio-economic changes. The shamans and their clientele are, as Victor says, "modern people" who want to work with scientists like myself. Instead, they are looking to develop a new form, an institutionalized and more formal form of shamanic practice that resembles a universal religion that is not tied exclusively to ethnicity. They are trying to reconnect people to traditions by restoring their relationships with their ancestors without necessarily being traditional. It is a fine line to walk, but in the inauguration ceremony, the ancestors declared that the roads were open. The new offices had their blessings. The shamans chanted their closing *kamlanie*, and offered the milk, vodka, and cookies from their altars into the fire, closing the ceremony. Then everyone changed out of traditional *degels* and into suits to walk the few blocks to the City Museum for the exhibition opening.

History in the Shamanic Genre

As with other historical genres discussed in previous chapters, I have pieced this history together from various sources, primarily personal discussions with shamans. However, it is different from the other histories in significant ways. While Buddhists look to the period from the turn of the 19th to 20th centuries as a golden age of Buryat nationalist intellectual life, shamans and shamanists consider that period to be part of the age of colonial domination and decline. Their genre of Buryat history focuses on a more distant past, the golden era of shamanism, when the Buryat tribes were part of Chinghis

Khan's empire. In this view, the history of the Buryat people since the golden era is marked by cultural degeneration under the influence of Buddhist missionaries and Russian colonization. "The Buddhists were persecuting us long before the Soviets," Aldar told me.[13] Like the Buddhist genre, the shamanic genre reframes the Soviet genre, but because it embeds Soviet history into a much longer timeline, Soviet repression is not historically unique.

Although the shamanic genre has a longer timeline, it has a narrower focus. Knowledge about the past is produced by recreating family and clan histories. The ancestors that matter are not ancestors of the Buryat people generally, nor the intellectuals and politicians that constitute the Buddhist genre, but the ancestors of particular clients and shamans.[14] The "us" invoked in this genre is a shifting and uncertain "us" that is Buryat, but unlike the Buddhist Buryat identity evoked by the Traditional Buddhist Sangha, it has porous boundaries. This Buryat "us" is a Central Asian "us" that recognizes the generations of intermarriage and border-crossing resulting from Russian expansion and seeks connections to a global indigenous identity.

A focus on kinship, genealogy, and ancestors enables a more porous approach to ethnic identity. Russians may have Buryat ancestors and Buryats may have Russian ancestors. Any individual may have ancestors from any number of ethnicities. These differences are irrelevant to the shamanic genre, in that all these ethnicities are presumed to have ancestor spirits and people like shamans to communicate with them. The ethnic or national identity of an ancestor is only relevant if it helps to determine their name and the language they speak. The shamans at Tengeri have adopted a broader academic and New Age view that sees shamanism as a universal ur-religion. As such, Bair Zhambalovich and his students argue that they are reviving a Buryat method for communicating with ancestors, even if the ancestors are not all Buryat. Buryats who turn to Tengeri and its practices can therefore participate in reviving Buryat traditions and their Buryat identity, even while they acknowledge and form relationships with their non-Buryat ancestors.

My data for this history comes mostly from conversations with members of Tengeri, but the shamanic genre of history is not exclusive to Tengeri. In fact, one of Tengeri's greatest critics told me that if I wanted to understand shamanism I needed to learn about Chinghis Khan. Leontii Abzaevich Borboev, whom several people referred to as the highest-ranking shaman in Buryatia, shares a similar view.

When I met him, Leontii Abzaevich was in his sixties. Unlike most of the shamans at Tengeri, he had received his calling and initiations during the Soviet period, and was therefore one of the few authorities on shamanism when interest revived after 1991. I had hoped to speak to him for a long time.

When I finally got the chance, I was full of questions about what it was like to practice shamanism during the late Soviet years. But he had no patience for my questions, and insisted on talking about Chinghis Khan instead. During our brief interview he told me "anyone who wants to know about Buryat shamanism should study the era of Chinghis Khan."[15] In 2001 he published a collection of clan histories called *Tales of an Old Shaman* that go back to that era (Borboev 2001). Although he is skeptical of much of Tengeri's mission, they both tell history in the same genre.

Heirs of Chinghis: The Buryat Past in the Shamanic Genre

The area around Baikal was inhabited by the Huns in ancient times, but the Eternal Blue Sky (Bur.—*khukhe munkhe Tengeri*), Leontii Abzaevich told me, sent them west to sack Rome.[16] After that, the tribal peoples in the areas around Lake Baikal continued to live their lives and practice their practices, honoring place spirits and their ancestors. Each clan lived on its own, each with its own shaman. At this time, and stretching back into pre-history, as Borboev and the members of Tengeri explain it, everyone everywhere practiced shamanism. Thus, shamanism should be considered the only true and universal human religion. It is not a religion in the sense of having a doctrine or a book or an institution; it is simply the knowledge of how to recognize spirits and deities and maintain the right relationship with them. Some people (shamans) are genetically predisposed to be able to sense energy fields and interact with these beings. The idea that shamanism was a genetic capability was firmly held at Tengeri, and I also heard it from other people in Buryatia, including academic scholars and people who did not practice shamanism, although Borboev did not mention it (see also Bazarov 2000; Zhukovskaia 2004).

At the time of Chinghis Khan, all the peoples of Eurasia, from Siberia through Central Asia, Russia and into the Germanic peoples of Europe, practiced their own forms of shamanism. As universal religions, notably Christianity and Buddhism, began to spread, they suppressed shamanism. However, among the Mongolian peoples, shamanic practices remained strong, and their greatness was proven by the rise of Chinghis Khan. Whether Chinghis Khan was himself a shaman, or merely relied upon the services of shamans at his court, depends on who is telling the history. Everyone agrees however, that at Chinghis Khan's court, shamanism was the official religion.

A tour guide in a museum in Aga once explained to me that "just as Christianity is about Jesus, and Buddhism is about Buddha, so shamanism is about Chinghis Khan." The parallel is instructive. Initially I took it to mean that this young man knew little about Buddhism and Christianity. However, I came to realize that all three are authorizing figures: Jesus authorizes Christian doctrine and scripture through his divinity and sacrifice; and the Gautama Buddha authorizes Buddhist scripture and practice by having achieved enlightenment. If the Buddha, an ordinary human, can achieve enlightenment through the middle path, then in theory, anyone can. Chinghis Khan authorizes shamanic practice by proving that the world's greatest empire can be founded by shamanic practitioners, demonstrating that shamanism can be a great and universal religion of state.

The tribes that eventually came to be called Buryat, or Buryat-Mongolian, were part of Chinghis Khan's great alliance. The Great Khan's mother and his wife are said to have been Buryat, which puts Buryats in the position of maternal uncles to Khalkha Mongols, the dominant ethnic group of Mongolia (Bulag 1998, 89). But all empires eventually fall apart, and the Great Khan's descendants converted to Buddhism. Buddhism spread into the Mongolian area from Tibet, while Orthodox Christianity began to spread as Russians conquered Siberia. These religions of the book suppressed shamanism, with the support of various governments. By the time of the Bolshevik Revolution, shamanism had been severely weakened. The political repressions of the Soviet period, during which shamans were killed or forced to renounce and hide their practices, almost destroyed Buryat shamanism entirely.

As Buyandelger (2013) movingly demonstrates, state violence made forgetting essential to survival for rural Buryats in Mongolia. Entire families could be ruined by relatives deemed to be enemies of the people, due to their religious practices or their class identity, or simply because they ran afoul of the wrong bureaucrat. Family members of the repressed learned to deny any knowledge of or ties to those who had disappeared out of fear that they too would be targeted. Several of the currently practicing shamans told me that they knew a grandparent had been a shaman, but they had explicitly refused to pass on any information or allow their children to attend ceremonies, out of fear that the child might say something to the wrong person (such as an unsympathetic schoolteacher) or because they believed training their children to be shamans would doom them to a life of persecution.

A graduate student, curious about my research, explained to me that her great-grandfather had been a *skazitel'*, an inspired bard who would recite epic poetry (Bur.—*ul'gers*), like the Gesar epic. People would come to him to read their palms, and her great-grandmother would get very upset because "back in those times, it was dangerous, because these things were forbidden." Like shamans, bards who recite epic poetry enter an altered state of consciousness and are often said to have healing powers.[17] Common before 1917, the practice still exists in parts of northern China and Mongolia, but it has not revived in Buryatia. This graduate student's story is a typical one for contemporary Buryats. Her great-grandfather practiced inspired oral poetry, a local form of shamanism. Due to anti-religious persecution, her great-grandfather did not pass down his skills and knowledge. Now a well-educated and relatively prosperous urban resident, she takes an academic and ethnographic interest in the everyday practices of her great-grandparents.

Buryat society underwent tremendous social and economic changes over the course of the 20th century, most of which were enthusiastically welcomed. Rural Buryats encouraged their children to study in the city, to pursue educations and professions that took them far away from their rural and shamanic backgrounds. Pre-revolutionary shamanic practices were embedded in the everyday life of rural herding and fishing communities. As people left that social environment, and as that social environment came under the regimented control of state and collective farms, these practices were attenuated.

Here, however, Tengeri's version of history diverges from both historical evidence and a more widespread shamanic genre in Buryatia. As the members of Tengeri tell it, during the Soviet period shamanic practices all but stopped, and most knowledge was lost; this is true for many urban Buryats, and certainly those I met at Tengeri (see also Quijada, Graber, and Stephen 2015). Due to this loss, many aspiring shamans (including Bair Zhambalovich) travel to northern Mongolia to study with Buryat shamans. At least three of the leading shamans from Aga have studied in Mongolia, and they insist that Buryats who live on the Mongolian side of the border have preserved knowledge that is desperately needed to rebuild shamanism in Buryatia.

This claim is contested by the shamans like Borboev who continued to practice throughout the Soviet period. They argue that the reason their practices differ from those in Mongolia is that the geographic areas had different forms of shamanic practice. The forms of trance that shamans like Bair Zhambalovich learn in Mongolia are not, in fact, traditional for the areas closer to Lake Baikal. Rather than lost authentic practices, Borboev judges them to be foreign and inauthentic.

In fact, I found good evidence that in some rural areas shamanic practices continued throughout the Soviet period, with various degrees of secrecy depending on local politics. Humphrey, for example, documented *tailgan* ceremonies held to make offerings and request blessings on behalf of collective farm brigades or to bless soldiers leaving for the front during World War II and the Soviet intervention in Afghanistan. Humphrey argues that "these, as it were, 'modern' *tailgans* have as their focus crucial points of compulsion, desire and uncertainty in rural Soviet life which are concealed and therefore unsatisfied by official ideology" (Humphrey 1998, 409). In Humphrey's view, shamanism persisted in large part because, as a creative and proactive form, people could use it to cope with the gaps and challenges in Soviet life that Soviet ideology ignored. Ksenia Gerasimova, a noted local religious scholar, told me that she had participated in surveys in the 1960s that proved that shamanic practices were still widespread even after decades of Soviet rule. The results were so scandalous the researchers never published them.

Despite the widespread continuation of shamanic practices in rural areas, urban Buryats lost everyday familiarity with shamanism, and in both rural and urban areas shamanism disappeared from public discourse. Even those who continued to practice did not speak about it. The histories and genealogies in which it was embedded were silenced. Tengeri and the other proponents of shamanism are seeking to rebuild this public awareness of shamanism and shamanic traditions not only for the benefit of contemporary Buryat society, but also, they argue, because shamanism is universally valuable to humanity.

On the way to the organization's Annual Tailgan on Olkhon Island, while we waited to take the ferry across to the island in the middle of the night, Victor Dorzhievich talked about the terrible social problems afflicting contemporary Buryat society. Most of the time, the members of Tengeri seemed more concerned with pre-Soviet *ongons* and Chinghis Khan than with recent history, but that night, Victor Dorzhievich told me that the current social problems in Russia were a direct result of bad karma earned through the Stalinist repressions. "When someone does wrong, offends people, Russia has so many problems because when you harm someone, it makes a very bad energy," he explained.

"Bad karma," Oleg, who is half Buryat and half Tatar, chipped in.

"Yes, karma. This bad karma is visited on your descendants. In the Soviet period so many people were killed. They killed shamans and lamas and priests, so all this bad karma developed from all the brutality in the 1930s. All the brutality from the Soviet period is being visited on the current generation." Victor Dorzhievich made no distinction between Russians and Buryats; the current suffering is not the result of Russian or Soviet oppression, but is something that all former Soviet citizens, including Buryats, have done to themselves.

At other times Victor Dorzhievich attributed social problems to the anger of ancestors who had been neglected and ignored during the Soviet times. Now that some people were making offerings to their ancestors, those ancestors whose descendants were not making offerings get jealous and afflict the living. Family problems, illnesses, alcoholism, and bouts of bad luck are explained through individual family histories, repairing the "bad karma" of the Soviet period one physical symptom and angry ancestor at a time.

Shamanism is valuable beyond Buryatia as well. Bair Zhambalovich and his students argue that shamanism is a universal religion: ancestor and nature spirits exist, and all human beings, at one point in their history, were able to communicate with them. These practices are lumped together under the term "pagan faith" (Russ.—*iazycheskaia vera*). The role of the shaman is to negotiate the relationship of the living to the spirit world, averting the anger of the spirits and gaining their protection on behalf of their community. Some people are born with this genetic capacity. Through the course of history, modernization, and the spread of "religions of the book" such as Christianity, Islam, and Buddhism, people in Europe and America have lost this traditional knowledge, which was preserved among indigenous populations. The time is now ripe for this shamanic knowledge to be re-valued and re-established as a universal religion. As Victor Dorzhievich explained it to me:

> Each place, each person based on his ancestry has his own gods, and these gods are the ones that have the most effect on people's lives, on nature. Shamanism is a universal religion, the earliest religion, the root of all other religions. There are shamans, there are local spirits everywhere, so shamanism has the potential to be a universal religion. There are these cataclysms. You know Nostradamus? I've read Nostradamus's prophecies, and in these prophecies it is written that there will be one world religion, and of course it doesn't say it there, but we know this is shamanism; only shamanism is so fundamental. Shamanism is better than Buddhism or Orthodoxy. Of course, people go there; they can go wherever they want, we are free, after all, but when you go to church you pray, and you can't see the god. Is he gone? Is he listening? Priests and lamas are intermediaries between man and gods, but with shamanism you have direct contact between people and the gods. The gods enter our bodies, they talk to the client, sometimes we tape it so the patient can know exactly what the god said. This is better than going to church because you talk to the god yourself. You can ask the god questions and get answers.

Unlike religions of the book, shamanism's truth can be proven through experience, through the material and visceral experience of talking to a god through the body of the shaman. Unmediated and direct, shamanic experience does not produce belief, but rather knowledge.

The truth of shamanism is also proven by its resilience. "If shamanism weren't real," one of Victor Dorzhievich's friends, an ethnic Russian who supported the organization but was not a shaman, explained to me, "it would have died out by now":

> All these other religions tried to suppress it, and during the Soviet period it was forbidden. There were seeds, but they were not allowed to grow, and now they had to be re-sown from Mongolia, but it must be based on reality or it would have died. Shamanism comes to people despite all these attempts to wipe it out. The Soviets killed so many shamans and lamas but it always comes back. It is a necessity (Russ.—*neobkhodimost'*). We didn't seek it out. The old shamans, dead and gone, they kept watching their descendants. They give little signs, like someone throwing a pebble at your head and you feel it but you don't know what it is, and brush it away, and then they throw another pebble, and if you don't find the source of these problems they can kill you, but it originates from them, not with us.

All the shamans at Tengeri describe a shamanic calling as a physical mandate, manifested in physical symptoms of illness. They argue that they and their clients were skeptics until their practices relieved physical symptoms (see also Quijada 2011). This is the "necessity" that Victor Dorzhievich's friend spoke about, the need to find healing that brings people to shamanism. Since they lack the proper information about the past, the past (in the form of ancestors) makes them sick. Illness drives them to treatment, which requires producing knowledge about their past, their ancestors, and their genealogies. Most of the shamans at Tengeri insisted they knew very little about shamanism before they became ill and came to shamanism as a result of their otherwise incurable symptoms. The course of their treatment requires them to produce new information and new knowledge about the past.

This explanation also allows the shamans at Tengeri to incorporate the existence of New Age shamans from other parts of Russia, Europe, and America, a few of whom have come to Ulan-Ude to be initiated. Tengeri members argue that some of these New Age shamans have inherited shamanic genes, but, like contemporary urban Buryats, they don't know how to use their abilities. Untutored and undiagnosed, these shamanic abilities are interpreted as mental illnesses. Bair Zhambalovich and Victor Dorzhievich interpret the idea that these abilities occasionally appear among Europeans as proof of their claims that shamanism is indeed the true and universal religion of humanity.

The universality of shamanism is also manifested in the similarities between shamanic practices around the world. A Russian translation of Mircea Eliade's book (2000), which makes the same argument, sits on Bair Zhambalovich's shelf. After all, Bair Zhambalovich and Victor Dorzhievich argued, these similarities wouldn't exist if they weren't based on reality. There are similarities in how spirits are described in different cultures because that is how spirits act. Since these phenomena are real, they can and should be verified through scientific inquiry, a project that has a certain urgency. The members of Tengeri interpret the recent rise in natural disasters, such as the 2004 tsunami in Southeast Asia and Hurricane Katrina in 2005, both of which occurred while I was in Ulan-Ude, as an indication that the relationship between humans and the natural world is severely misaligned, something that can be rectified through shamanic intervention. Both this and the increasing presence of neo-shamans is a sign that the spirits are increasingly demanding to be heard. Shamanism is reviving, because as the only true religion, it is the only one that can help humanity in its current crisis.

However, despite the urgency of their project, according to "traditional" Buryat ethical precepts recited to me by both shamans and their critics, shamans are not supposed to advertise their services. "What do you think of Tengeri?" I would ask people, and often was met with the oblique response along the lines of "Well, 'traditionally' shamans aren't supposed to advertise, are they?" Few people were willing to openly criticize a shaman, but phrasing a question about advertising achieved the same effect. Although their stated mission is to raise awareness about Buryat shamanic traditions, Tengeri cannot raise public awareness, and thereby legitimize their organization, without spreading information. Advertising, however, is morally questionable. They will announce spring and fall city *tailgans* in the newspapers and on local television, but anything further threatened to delegitimize their organization. So Aldar Andanovich was thrilled when the perfect opportunity for "PR" arose: a museum exhibit about their organization at the City Museum.

The Museum Exhibit and the Skepticism of the "Modern" Buryat

After the inauguration, Bair Zhambalovich and his students changed out of their *degels* into suits, and we all walked over to the City Museum for the opening of the exhibit on Tengeri (see Figure 5.2).

The City Museum of Ulan-Ude is located in a pre-revolutionary wooden historic house on Lenin Street. Its modest displays include photographs and

FIGURE 5.2 From left to right, the shamans Solbon Bal'chindorzhiev, Seseg Garmaeva, and Budazhab Purboevich Shiretorov with his wife Larissa, along with Aldar Andanovich Rampilov, Tengeri's commercial director, in front of the City Museum for the opening of the "Modern Shamans of Buryatia" exhibit, in 2005. By 2012, most of these individuals had left the organization. Ulan-Ude, October 6, 2005.

objects documenting the history of the city, from its founding as a Cossack outpost through recent renovations, telling the history of the city in the hospitality genre described in Chapter 3. There is a room devoted to the history of the tea trade, photographs of Tsar Nicholas II's visit to the town in 1894, and a set of Buryat and Old Believer costumes that visitors can try on. The museum's special exhibits, which vary widely and often have very little to do with the history of the city, are an important source of income. Members of the museum staff approached the Tengeri organization about organizing an exhibit on Buryat shamanism, and when Tengeri asked my husband and me if we would supply photographs, we enthusiastically agreed.

From the start it was clear that the museum staff and the Tengeri members had very different attitudes toward shamanism. Darima, the same Buryat woman who had asked the spirits a question earlier, who worked for a government ministry in charge of preserving and documenting Buryat culture, considered me, the foreign ethnographer, to be a colleague, while the shamans were the object of our mutual study. While the government officials at the Center and exhibition openings stressed shamanism's claim to the Buryat nation, this was not a claim that Darima was willing to accept. Shamanism, for her, was an exotic tradition, worth studying and preserving, but not one she identified with.

During one of the planning meetings for the exhibit, Victor Dorzhievich told a story that I had heard several times since the conference on Olkhon, which he routinely used as an example of verifiable proof of the existence of place spirits. Shaman's Rock is the residence of Khotun/Hotun Khan (also called Khan Khoto Baabai), the place master of Olkhon.[18] The rock is considered to be a very sacred shrine by all the local residents, one which women should not enter.[19] However, Russian tourists, unaware of local practices, routinely sunbathe and swim near it.[20] A grotto on Shaman's Rock had at one time been blocked by fallen rocks. While possessing Bair Zhambalovich's body, Khotun Khan explained that he had blocked the grotto because he had been offended by a female tourist in a bikini. This year, when they arrived to make offerings, the grotto was open, and the Tengeri shamans took this to mean that Khotun Khan was pleased with their offerings and that their ceremonies were restoring the site to its proper condition. This was, to Victor Dorzhievich, verifiable proof of cause and effect: that the rocks had been there and were now gone, and the possessing spirit told them why the rocks were there, were material proof that Khotun Khan not only exists but acts on the world and that Tengeri's ceremonies were effectively communicating with him. Darima reacted completely differently. At first, she brushed the story aside as uninteresting. Victor Dorzhievich was deeply dismayed and stressed that this was important. When he wouldn't let it go, she said, "Well, we could present it like a miracle (Russ.—*chudo*)." He was not satisfied with this reaction, but was somewhat mollified that at least the public would get to hear the story, and perhaps they would react differently than Darima. What Victor Dorzhievich viewed as incontrovertible proof of spirit intervention struck Darima as an unremarkable and uninteresting coincidence.

The exhibit was called "Modern Shamans of Buryatia," but as we scrolled through photos for the exhibition, Darima's choices illustrated how for her, shamanism was not modern. Shots of the shamans making offerings on Olkhon Island were dismissed because they were "wearing European clothes" (see Figure 5.3). Group shots from ceremonies were selected on the basis of whether or not they showed "European faces" in the crowd, because "we want to show that another people (Russ.—*narod*) are interested." While the shamans hoped for a chance to bring in new clients and spread what they saw as vital information, for Darima this was a display about people who were anachronistically preserving the past. While identifying people in the photographs, Aldar mentioned the allied organization in Aga. Darima explained, for my benefit,

FIGURE 5.3 Members of Tengeri presenting *khadaks* to Hotun Khan at Shaman's Rock, Olkhon Island, July 2005. This photo was not chosen for the exhibit because they are wearing "European clothes."

that "in Aga they have preserved more. We here in Ulan-Ude are Russians really, but in Aga they are still Buryat." Her words betrayed a paradox: on one level, she accepted and through her work promoted Tengeri's claim that shamanism is a Buryat national religion, but the claim represents a Buryat nation that she does not identify with. In contrast to Tengeri, although she is ethnically Buryat, she calls herself Russian.

The challenge that Tengeri faces is how to revive practices that, for many urban Buryats, are merely an ethnographic curiosity from the past. As they do so, they enter a local debate about authenticity and tradition. As Lindquist (2005) has argued in regard to Tuva, the terms "tradition" and "authenticity" in Siberian shamanic revival are fraught with contention. In Western academic and popular New Age discourse, as well as in local debates within Ulan-Ude, shamanism is endowed with the aura of the past, so the question of whether or not a particular practice is considered "traditional" (i.e., similar to the past) becomes a judgment of legitimacy. Within a linear chronotope, "authenticity" is about how similar a present-day practice is to past practices, as defined by archives, historians, and ethnographers. When contemporary Buryats revive 19th century practices based on ethnographic documents or borrowings from Mongolia, and adapt these to the contemporary needs of their patients, they are—from the point of view of linear, progressive history—"inventing traditions" (Hobsbawm and Ranger 1983). Being able to claim similarity and continuity to past practices is part of asserting an identity within a colonial framework, such as the Soviet regime, that associates indigeneity with the past. "In diverse post-colonial contexts, tradition becomes a metonym for 'identity', and, as the latter, it is best seen as an ongoing process of negotiation and struggle" explains Lindquist (2005, 264). People in Ulan-Ude are embedded in precisely such a context and often get caught up in a discourse of authenticity.

It is important to remember that the question of authenticity, and the concomitant devaluing of invented tradition, is a discourse that requires a particular chronotope, and through that chronotope produces particular kinds of subjects. Although the exhibit was titled "Modern Shamans of Buryatia" all the displays and photograph choices erased any signs of "modernity," giving the title an anachronistic feel to it. "Look" it seems to demand of the viewer, "at the evidence of tradition that still exists today." Through the museum exhibit Darima both produced Tengeri and their practices as "traditional" and "Buryat," but also produced herself as a modern, scholarly subject, excluded from the "Buryatness" that she ascribed to those who have "preserved their traditions." Darima approaches Tengeri's project through a linear, modernist chronotope, through which Tengeri's authenticity is measured by the similarity of their practices to past practice; Darima's modernity is measured by her distance from the same. In order to be modern, Darima is willing to take the risk of being inauthentically or inadequately Buryat.

However, this is not the only chronotope available to shamanic practitioners. For the members of Tengeri there was no anachronism in the exhibit's title. From the perspective of a shamanic chronotope, where the past is still present, there are many other possible relationships to the past. The members of Tengeri—several of whom hold advanced degrees—were all raised and educated as Soviet atheists, so they are familiar with and comfortable in a linear, modernist chronotope. But by engaging with ritual practices that produce a fundamentally different relationship to time, they constantly code-switch between chronotopes. Sometimes the shamans at Tengeri emphasize the continuity of their practices, and at other times they emphasize the discontinuity. Sometimes they assert "this is how it's always been done," asserting their similarity to tradition; at other times, they insist "you know, ten years ago, when we started, none of us knew anything about this," thereby asserting the experimental and creative nature of their practices.

The members of Tengeri have various arguments to establish the authenticity of their practices depending on the chronotope in which they are speaking. Sometimes they rely on the authority of ethnographic texts and arguments about preserving and rebuilding traditions that are firmly embedded in a linear, progressive chronotope. Sometimes they vest their claims to authenticity in a history that traces shamanic practices to the court of Chinghis Khan. By referencing shamans at Chinghis Khan's court they establish not only the authority of age, but also directly counter the criticism that institutional forms of shamanism are new, and hence illegitimate. If shamanism was the court religion of the Great Khan, then shamanism has always been an institutional religion. If so, Tengeri and other shamans' organizations are not innovating, but rather re-establishing the order of things as they were before the foreign influences of Buddhism, Russian Orthodoxy, and Soviet atheism persecuted the practitioners of the true religion, not only of Buryatia, but of all humanity. Accepting a linear chronotope, in which authenticity is measured by how similar something is to the past, they seek to change the available knowledge about the past, so that the present institutional practices that most people see as different from the past are actually a lot more similar (and hence authentic) than one might otherwise think.

However, they also push back against the way in which the linear chronotope presents the past as the standard against which the authenticity of their practices should be measured. Because the past, in the form of ancestors, is always present, it is not a static standard against which present-day practice should be measured. The past is not static, but continually interacting with the present, and authenticity is measured by the effectiveness of this interaction. In the shamanic chronotope, evidence of authenticity is located in the condition of present-day bodies. Within a shamanic chronotope, if shamanic practices can heal Buryat bodies, then they are authentically Buryat practices, and these practices have produced the right kind of knowledge about the past. Rather than judging contemporary practice as authentic in relationship to a static past, the shamanic chronotope judges whether knowledge about the past is authentic based on its relationship to contemporary Buryat bodies. Authenticity comes from having a positive and powerful interactive relationship with the past.

The shamanic chronotope offers a way out of the identity double-bind that a linear chronotope forces on Darima. For Darima to be modern, she must be less than fully Buryat. "We here in Ulan-Ude are Russians, really," she says. The shamanic chronotope refuses this identity double-bind by undermining the linear timeline and the evidentiary standards in which it is grounded. Authenticity is still produced in relationship to a past, but that past is not static, and therefore members of Tengeri can be authentically Buryat through their ongoing ritual relationship to ancestors, without giving up a modern identity or denying their intermarried, multi-ethnic, and assimilated Soviet pasts. For people engaging in shamanic practices, the shamanic chronotope produces an entirely different perspective from which to understand both the Soviet past and their own position in the contemporary world.

The members of Tengeri, its offshoot organizations, and other shamanic organizations in Buryatia are engaged in a project to establish shamanism as an institutional religion on par with Buddhism and Orthodox Christianity. They are motivated to do so because for them, engaging in shamanic practices has produced material, physical, and spiritual well-being. However, to do so, they have to convince Buryats like Darima not only of their authenticity, but also that their authenticity does not exclude "being modern." Bair Zhambalovich, Victor Dorzhievich, Budazhab Purboevich, and their colleagues insist on the power of speaking directly to gods and ancestors, because the ritual experience of direct contact with the past is what produces the shamanic chronotope, and the shamanic chronotope is what enables the transformation of the self and community that they seek.

6

Porous Selves

YURI'S INITIATION

YURI NIKOLAIVICH BALDANOV'S 13-year-old son was not at his father's initiation. "He's at home with a fever," his mother explained, blaming the fever on a draft from a recent car ride. Yuri disagreed. "It's always that way in our family," Yuri explained. "Before a ceremony all the men in the family get sick, because the ancestors don't believe we'll go through with it. Once the trees go up he'll feel better." Sure enough, Yuri's wife confirmed by phone later, after the trees "went up" at the ceremony, his son's fever had passed.

The story of Yuri's *shandru,* the ceremony through which he is initiated as a white shaman in the Tengeri shamans' association, is not a story of just one person's transformation. A shamanic calling is experienced as physical illness inflicted on living members of a family by their ancestors. Relief only comes when the initiate promises to serve as mediator between the living and the dead. To become a shaman, the initiate must learn to draw *ongons,* their ancestral spirits, into their own body, thus enabling the living to contact them. The members of Tengeri call this being "under harness" (Russ.—*za lozheno*) to their ancestors, emphasizing the initiate's submission to the will of those family members who carried the family's shamanic gift in the past.[1] All of the shamans at Tengeri insist that their gift was not a choice; shamanhood was forced on them through illness. The inability to recognize kinship obligations is experienced as a physical illness, while embracing these obligations produces freedom from pain. Initiation draws on and creates webs of mutual obligation between family members, who share both the affliction of the calling and the history that relieves it.[2]

Unlike the histories described in previous chapters, histories in the shamanic genre are small, family histories. Buyandelger (2013), who worked with Buryat shamans in Mongolia, finds that these histories are often fragmentary because they focus on identifying specific afflicting ancestors. In most cases, to do this, shamans do not need to recreate their entire genealogy as long as they have identified the *ongons* who are causing their symptoms. The genealogies often skip over a number of generations without relevant ancestors. By focusing on the individual family or clan, they ignore larger social identifications, like the ethnic group or nation. Major historical events are only part of the story if they affected a particular ancestor's life, or affected whether that ancestor is remembered by the living. A genealogy is just a list of names, rather than a history. Yet the fragmentary nature of these histories stands in stark contrast to the impact they have on the people who uncover and embrace them. These lists of names enable families to tell a story about who they are and why they are suffering in the present, and offer a way of resolving this suffering in the future (Lévi-Strauss 1963; Kendall 1985, 2010).

A patient/initiate who is experiencing a shamanic calling has physical symptoms because they have been chosen to be a shaman by their ancestors. The patient either does not recognize or has ignored this calling, and the ancestors are sending the illness to force the patient to accept the obligation. Often the patient does not know that they have shamanic ancestry and does not know the names of their ancestral shamans. This lack of knowledge is experienced as a physical harm suffered by both the initiate and their family. A combination of genealogical research and inquiry by the diagnosing shaman in trance identifies the ancestors and creates a genealogy. The patient enters into negotiations via the diagnosing shaman; when he agrees to become an initiate, the ancestors relieve the symptoms. Filling the gap in historical knowledge by producing a genealogy enables the patient to establish a relationship with their ancestors, which in turn heals the patient/initiate, and reconnects their family to this past, through the family's acceptance of this history.

As Webb Keane (1997) has argued, the ritual act of conversing with the unseen brings about their presence (see also Apffel-Marglin 2011). The power of this effect is not lost on the shamans themselves, who, as mentioned before, often told me that "our religion is the only one where you can speak directly to the gods." Family members of initiates speak to and are spoken to by their ancestors through the body of the initiate. In this interaction, both the living and the dead acknowledge and promise to fulfill the obligations of mutual aid and care expected of family members. The acceptance of this relationship is then verified through the physical condition of the initiate's body: a healthy body indexes a healthy relationship with the ancestors. Participants interpret these experiences, both the visceral experience of speaking to an "other" within the body of your kin and the medical symptoms that are relieved after the ritual, as verifiable proof that the experience was real and effective. Embodied though trance, speech, and illness, the narratives acquire, to paraphrase Clifford Geertz, an "aura of factuality" that renders them "uniquely realistic" (1973, 90). This enables the shamans, the initiates, and their families to insist that they know the ancestors are real. If they were not real, how could negotiating with them relieve medical symptoms? "You don't need to believe," one of the shamans explained to a patient; "try it, and you'll see that it works."

Geertz's formulation of the "aura of factuality" has, however, famously been critiqued for ignoring the effects of power in bringing about this aura of factuality (Asad 1993). Institutional power here is, as we have seen, notably absent. Tengeri is trying to establish an institution. Buddhist and Russian Orthodox religious institutions are weak after a century of Soviet anti-religious policies, and following the collapse of socialism state institutions are also fragile. The power of the shaman, as Humphrey and Onon have argued (1996), lies in the effect produced by their charismatic ability to fill gaps resulting from the collapse of institutions, and produces conviction through performance (Lévi-Strauss 1963; Kendall 2010, 66–129). A key element producing this "aura of factuality" for shamanic audiences in Ulan-Ude is the embodied, experiential perception of inexplicable otherness. The shamanic chronotope becomes compelling through the viscerally uncanny experience of speaking to ancestors through the body of the shaman.

The histories produced through shamanic callings and initiations are, more than any other historical genre I encountered in Buryatia, embodied histories. They are embodied through the physical symptoms experienced by the shaman and their family, as well as through the physical encounter with the ancestors. As in Buddhist claims about Etigelov's "miraculous" physical condition (see Chapter4), the seemingly irrefutable nature of physical experience rhetorically constructs the evidentiary grounds of historical knowledge.

Like the Buddhist genre of history, the shamanic genre contains a deeply rooted critique of the Soviet experience, but it is in a different register. Shamanic callings produce family histories, which weave across and in between narratives of nations, states, and religions. States, nations, and religious institutions appear only in their effects on individual family members. There is very little explicit critique of the Soviet past in the genealogies because most ancestors that possess shamans are at least eight generations removed from the initiate: *ongons* lived well before the Soviet period, and sometimes even before Russian colonization.

Quite a few shamans with whom I have spoken, both at Tengeri and elsewhere, tell stories of how the violence of collectivization and cultural revolution produced "bad karma" for the descendants of those who committed the violence, and often this bad karma is shared by Buryat or Soviet society as a whole. For individuals, relationships with the ancestors were broken and kinship obligations forgotten during the Soviet period. By locating this rupture in the Soviet era, these histories reject the kind of person produced by the Soviet experience, the "new Soviet person" whose social bonds were forged through professional labor and whose loyalties were to society at large. In contrast, the shamanic subject is defined primarily and fundamentally through kinship, and literally cannot live without acknowledging the ties of kinship and building a relationship to their past.

Yuri's Shandru

Yuri's *shandru*—the second initiation for a white shaman—was held in September.[3] At the first initiation, which is also known as the protection ceremony (Russ.—*zashchita*), the aspiring shaman agrees to begin training, and the ancestors promise to help and protect them. At this point, the physical symptoms—the shamanic calling—should abate. A *shandru* is not a healing ceremony; rather, it is a rite of passage that marks the end of a healing process. In the second initiation, the aspiring shaman goes into a trance and embodies their *ongon* for the first time, after which they can begin to take on clients. These initiations can last anywhere from two days to a week, depending on how long it takes the initiate to go into trance. Yuri's *ongons* entered him easily and quickly, and the ritual lasted approximately 24 hours, after several days of preparations.

Yuri is a large man, several inches over six feet, with a booming voice and a charming smile. He was always ready to joke and tease, and his mother, Nellie Innokentievna, chided him for "not taking this all seriously enough." Nellie Innokentievna is Russian, and Yuri's father, now deceased, was Buryat, a member of an ethnically Mongolian (Khalkh) clan that lived on the Russian side of the border between Chita oblast and Mongolia. The cultural boundary between Buryat and Mongolian is a fluid one, and descendants of Mongolian clans who resided in Russian territory assimilated into a Buryat identity. Yuri inherited three white shaman *ongons* from his father's side.[4] Before his shamanic calling, Yuri had lived and worked in Chita oblast and had identified primarily as Russian. At that time, he did not speak Buryat. His wife, a petite blonde named Larissa, is Russian. By the time of his *shandru*, however, he identified primarily as Buryat, but often noted that his clan was originally from

Mongolia. For example, when other shamans teased him about his lack of fluency in the Buryat language, he joked that he is "really" Mongolian and thus cannot be expected to know Buryat, rather than admit that he did not speak a word of Buryat until he became a shaman.

Yuri had turned 40 that year. Several years earlier he had become seriously ill from what he described as "shamanic diabetes," which incapacitated him for two years. At the time, he said, "I didn't even want to think about it [becoming a shaman] then, but now my whole attitude has changed." I asked Larissa, who had been married to Yuri for 15 years, if it was hard for her to accept his calling, especially since they, like most of the people I met at Tengeri, insisted that they knew nothing about shamanism before Yuri's illness. She agreed that it had been very hard to accept, but "Yuri was frighteningly sick (Russ.—*strashno zabolel*). . . . I love him. I was afraid he would die. If this is what it takes for him to be well, then I'll learn what needs to be learned." It was clear that his mother felt the same way. For them, as for most of the people I met at Tengeri, the relief of physical symptoms was the crucial proof they needed to overcome their doubts.

It also became very clear, as the ceremony continued, that the ritual would not have taken place without the efforts of his ethnically Russian female relatives. When shamans at Tengeri speak about shamanic callings they stress the role and will of the ancestors. They explain that the ancestors choose the initiate and that the initiate must accept that obligation. The initiation is presented as a moral transformation, from a sick person who did not know their ancestors, and did not understand or meet their family obligations, to a healthy person who embraces these ties. However, participating in the initiation reveals that the living members of the family are just as crucial to this transformation. Although Yuri was the one to be called as a shaman, the initiation cannot happen without his entire family's participation and support. Members of his father's family had roles in the ritual, and the labor and resources that made the initiation possible were supplied by both sides of his family. By participating in the ritual, these family members came to accept the genealogical history produced through the shamanic calling; conversely, they would not participate if they did not feel compelled either by the narrative or kinship obligation to the initiate. The shamans at Tengeri told several stories of people who were meant to become shamans but whose families or spouses could not or would not support them in the process, and who ultimately died as a result. For the initiate to become a shaman, both living and dead members of a family must come to terms and agree to accept the family history. The initiate is the focal point between these two factions, and the negotiations are carried out through his or her body.

Preparations

Tengeri conducts initiations all summer in a big open space outside of Ulan-Ude. In 2005, during Yuri's initiation, there was not enough space to hold initiations near their office in Ulan-Ude, but when I returned in 2012 they were still using the open field, even though they had since acquired more space. They rented the field for the summer because the location, about a 15-minute drive outside the city, enabled them to spread out undisturbed. The endless stream of clients and visitors that dropped by the Tengeri offices on a regular basis would not disrupt the initiations, each of which can last from two to five days.

I arrived at the site by taxi before noon on the first day, and found that none of the main participants had arrived yet. A few young women were there; most were Yuri's female cousins from his father's side, who had traveled from Chita oblast to participate. Two young women from Ulan-Ude—friends of one of the relatives—had come out of curiosity. None of them had ever attended a shamanic ceremony before, so no one really knew what they were supposed to do.

Yuri's cousins were helping to set up a large army-style tent, where part of the ritual would take place and where we would all sleep. The day before, a group had gone to cut birch trees in the forest. Solbon, who had undergone his own *shanar* a few weeks earlier, selected nine unbroken ones to be decorated with ribbons and embedded into the ground near the tent to make a grove (see Figure 6.1). Yuri would run around this grove to go into trance, and he was expected to climb it while in trance. His ability to "fly" up the tree while in trance would determine if the trance state was legitimate. Solbon instructed us in how to tie the ribbons, which had been prepared in advance, on the trees.

The work, which took most of the day, was clearly divided by gender. Together with Yuri's female cousins, I tied ribbons on the trees. I was the only person other than Solbon who had attended a shamanic ceremony before, but I had only attended *tailgan* (offering) ceremonies; this was my first initiation too.

At most initiations I attended during my fieldwork, the initiate's family members are new to the process. Most of the shamans at Tengeri learned the procedure from the organization's director during their own rituals. After being initiated themselves, they help instruct new initiates and their families, but the result, like the children's game of telephone, is far from smooth. Instructions are often misinterpreted, work has to be repeated, and in some cases, everyone must wait while a crucial missing ingredient is located. When initiates came from further away—occasionally as far as St. Petersburg or even Europe—the process is even more complicated, since the initiate lacks a local network of family members and friends. Over the years since the organization

FIGURE 6.1 Male shamans and Yuri's paternal relatives setting up the birch grove around which he would run during the *shandru*, Ulan-Ude, 2005.

was founded, the process has become somewhat streamlined, with an established network of suppliers. For example, in 2012, a helpful sign at the ritual site listed the name of a farmer from whom one could purchase a sheep for the sacrifice.

In 2005, at Yuri's initiation, supplies were handled by his wife and mother, both of whom arrived later that afternoon. Larissa spent a good part of the day on the phone, organizing who would deliver what, when, and where. In addition to the ribbons on the trees, the trees were decorated with nine bird's nests made out of sheep wool, one for each tree. The women sewed tiny cups of birch bark, which were filled with butter and then strung on a string, seven cups per string, on three strings, and hung from the trees as offerings to the spirits (see Figure 6.2). Several men from Tengeri and Yuri's male cousins set up the trees, built a makeshift yurt out of birch trees, and built a still out of a barrel. Later, parts of the sheep's body were added to the still, in which *tarasun*, a vodka-like alcohol made from mare's milk, would be distilled and siphoned into two bottles, one for Yuri's mother's side of the family, one for his father's.

After we had tied ribbons for several hours, Larissa arrived with a huge pile of *degels*. Everyone participating in the ritual had to wear Buryat traditional clothing, but *degels*, which must be handmade from Chinese silk, are extremely expensive. Since Ulan-Ude was originally a stop along the trade routes that connected China to Russia, Buryat traditional clothing is made from trade fabric that is not produced locally and is difficult to obtain, despite

FIGURE 6.2 Yuri's female relatives and I prepare gifts for the *ongons* to decorate the birch trees, Ulan-Ude, 2005.

the prevalence of Chinese traders in the city. People who want or need a Buryat national costume generally travel to Ulan-Bator in Mongolia to purchase the fabric and then have the *degel* and its accessories sewn by a tailor in Ulan-Ude. Until the 1960s, it was customary for a bride to sew a *degel* as part of her wedding trousseau. These days, however, since *degels* are only worn on special occasions, very few people own them, aside from performers and shamans. None of Yuri's relatives owned one and they needed at least ten for all the ritual participants. Larissa scrounged and borrowed from friends of friends, gathering enough for the participants.

A lot of people take part in an initiation. In addition to the initiate, two more senior shamans will go into trance and coach them through the experience. All three shamans have assistants, usually either another shaman or a relative, who help the shaman get dressed, keep track of paraphernalia, speak to the possessing spirits, and otherwise help out. All of these participants are members of Tengeri and familiar with the ritual procedure. Several other shamans from the organization took part, such as Solbon, who directed the preparations. Bair Zhambalovich and another white shaman, Donduk, went into trance with Yuri. However, an initiation requires the participation of the initiate's relatives, which is where things get complicated.

Since the ritual was for *ongons* on Yuri's paternal side, Yuri's parents had to present him to the *ongon*. Sadly, Yuri's father had died the year before, so an uncle and his wife were filling in. At Yuri's first initiation, Nellie Innokentievna and her husband had participated, but this time she could not. One participant erroneously told me it was because she could not speak Buryat; during the first initiation, parents did not have to speak, but in the second, they do. However, Yuri's uncle correctly explained that the man in the couple must be the father or a paternal relative, and the woman had to be his spouse. Since the relative must represent the patriline, the woman in the couple is not important, so Nellie would be unable to stand up for her son alone. But the alternative explanations highlight his family's lack of experience and the resulting confusion. The potential for giving and taking offense at being or not being included was high.

In addition to his "parents" (who were actually his uncle and his uncle's wife), nine unmarried paternal cousins (five men and four women) had to run with Yuri, helping him go into trance. For the duration of the initiation, they were tied together in a row at the waist, first the men and then the women, in order of age. They had to remain attached to each other the entire time—even while they slept, ate, and went to the bathroom—which caused a lot of awkward hilarity. The officiating shaman places their souls in the keeping of the *ongons* at the beginning of the ceremony and returns their souls to them at the end. Running with a shaman during an initiation is both a great responsibility and an honor. It is also exhausting, but all of Yuri's runners were eager to participate. The willingness of relatives to support the initiate, by running or by contributing to expenses, is crucial. In return, they know that Yuri will be there for them as a shaman, should they ever need him in the future. He owes them a debt that can only be repaid by serving as his family's intercessor with their ancestors. This bond of mutual obligation will last a lifetime.

All of Yuri's relatives had traveled here from Chita oblast, a journey that took between 12 and 18 hours by car or train. They had to be housed and fed, loaned *degels* to wear, and taught their roles. None of this would have happened without the efforts of Yuri's wife and his mother. Despite their hard work and unflinching support for Yuri, neither his wife nor his mother played a formal role in the ritual itself, because neither is a member of Yuri's patriline. When we showed them the photos we had taken, Larissa lamented that she was not in any of them, and confessed that the *ongons* made her nervous. Another time she told me that she was worried that the *ongons* would object to her, because she is Russian. A friend of hers, a Buryat woman whose sister is a shaman, reassured her that the *ongons* would not care. Her friend insisted that her support for her husband mattered more than her nationality. Since shamanic rituals are based on genealogies and membership in particular patri- or matrilines, the presence of non-Buryat family members does not disrupt the logic of inclusion. Whether or not Yuri's wife or his mother are ethnically Buryat has no bearing on their ability to participate. Likewise, non- or partially Buryat members of his patriline, such as Yuri's brother and Yuri himself, are included based on their membership in the patriline. Their respective "Buryatness" is irrelevant either way. As I have noted elsewhere (Quijada 2008), families of mixed ethnic background were far more common at shamanic ceremonies than at Buddhist ones, possibly because grounding participation in kinship (which often crosses ethnic lines) offers more room for participation than claims to ethno-national identity.

While Larissa was in charge of logistics, Nellie and her friend Elvira took charge of food. With 30 to 40 people spending 12 hours of preparation at the site and 24 hours of ceremony, she had a formidable task, but we ate well. Yuri's family had supplied two sheep: one for the sacrifice, and one just for food.

As they prepared for the ritual, the cousins who ran for Yuri wrote out in Buryat what they had to tell the *ongon*, including information on their clan. But none of them knew their clan affiliation. "Auntie Nellie," they asked Yuri's mother, "What's our clan (*rod*)?"

"Write *Khamnigan*," she said, adding, "the *ongon* will tell you what it is."

"Khamnigan" is an ethnic term for a mixed-heritage Buryat/Mongolian/Russian population (Zhukovskaia 1994). One of Yuri's cousins told me that the area they were from, in Chita oblast, had very few Buryats, "so no one speaks Buryat, and my family never participated much in rituals before Yuri became a shaman. All the Buryats get together for Tsagaalgan, or maybe a blessing at an *oboo*, but not really."[5] Although sometimes treated like an ethnicity, the term "Khamnigan" indexes a history of border crossing and intermarriage. An English-speaking Buryat friend once translated it as "mestizo."

When Yuri became extremely ill, visiting a shaman was his last resort. A treating shaman will ask a patient what their clan is, and whether they have shamanic ancestors.[6] Patients who do not know, which is often the case, are tasked with recreating their family's genealogy. These missing genealogies are produced by asking family members, by researching census records in the national archives (if available), and by asking questions of the ancestor spirits that are channeled by the diagnosing and officiating shaman. Several people have told me that Bair Zhambalovich is particularly skilled at identifying ancestors while in trance. The information gleaned from relatives is used to ask questions of the spirits, and the answers are then reported back to the rest of the family.

Over the course of several diagnosing sessions, the shaman identifies and negotiates with the ancestral shamans. In Yuri's case, his *ongons* were identified as one grandmother and two grandfathers from his father's patriline. These ancestors, who had carried the family's shamanic calling during their lifetimes, had chosen him to be the next bearer of the gift. Although these ancestral shamans are no longer living, they become social actors. Their desires and demands are manifested in the initiate's physical condition and that of their family members, such as Yuri's son's fever. The ancestors afflicted his son to remind him what was at stake: not merely his own health and well-being, but that of his entire family. If Yuri himself had gotten ill, he would not be able to meet his ritual obligations.

During his first initiation, Yuri offered these ancestors a sacrifice and promised to begin training as a shaman. He received his *toli*, the brass mirror that all shamans wear to protect them from the malicious energy of others. After the first ritual, his illness began to respond to the medical treatments his doctors had previously prescribed. His symptoms abated. This physical evidence confirmed that he had been chosen to be a shaman, and his family embraced the process and the genealogical claims it was grounded on. It was not enough for Yuri to accept this history; his family had to accept it too, and support him in the arduous process of learning a language and a new profession.

Other would-be shamans at Tengeri could not muster the resources and support of their extended family, and as a result, their transformations stalled. One man told me that his parents, who were devout Buddhists, absolutely refused to consider the possibility that he should become a shaman; they would neither help him raise the funds for an initiation, nor participate in it.[7] In contrast, Nellie Innokentievna asked us to take photographs of the ritual to share with relatives in Chita; it had been a long road to get this far, and the whole family was eager to see Yuri succeed. By participating in Yuri's initiation, his whole family took possession of this family history, embracing this particular version of Buryat-Mongolian identity and community.

Through this process, Yuri produced a family history, albeit fragmented. His father's clan is a Mongolian clan with the same name as Chinghis Khan's. At some point in the past centuries, these distant relatives of Chinghis Khan moved to the Russian side of the boundary between China and Russia, and intermarried with Russian settlers. This history of border crossings and intermarriage connects his family to a Buryat identity; to his mixed Buryat-Russian relatives; and even to the empire of Chinghis Khan and greater Inner Asian nomadic identity. Although this mixed identity enabled Yuri to be Russian during the late Soviet and early post-Soviet period, the *ongons* could not be ignored, and claimed Yuri as their mouthpiece. By claiming this genealogy, Yuri's family become the (distant) descendants of a great empire, instead of just members of a mestizo ethnic minority population living on the fringes of Russian territory.

Thus, history in the shamanic genre is both smaller (in the scope of its historical events) from other genres, and also bigger, in terms of the impact on the people who are producing this new historical knowledge. The family's genealogy has a new relevance and meaning, because knowing their ancestors and clan's heritage is what saved Yuri's life. Following his initiation, Yuri's family now have a new relationship with their past and their *ongons*, mediated by Yuri's body.

The Shandru

The ritual itself did not begin until midnight on the first night. Yuri, Bair Zhambalovich, and Donduk, who would go into trance with Yuri, set up their altars and chairs inside the tent, facing the back wall. Outside, a fire was lit. Water, milk, and herbs were boiled in a big pot and the mixture was sprinkled around the area and on the participants with a birch branch (*venik*) to purify the site.[8] Bair Zhambalovich marked the ritual site with a string, which participants were not supposed to pass; when we needed to leave to use the makeshift outhouse, we had to douse our hands with the liquid from the pot before re-entering the site.

After the ritual site was marked, all three shamans who were to go into trance put on their robes, which indicated their level of experience. Bair's, made over a decade earlier, was worn and faded. Yuri's robe, which he wore for the first time that night, was shiny and stiff, glittering in the light of the candles and the fire. Bair Zhambalovich and Donduk began their *kamlanie*, and Yuri soon joined them, calling the *ongons* to the site and informing them that the ceremony was beginning. After the *kamlanie*, Bair Zhambalovich sprinkled the herb-scented water into the fire, and Donduk swept each of the participants with the birch branch dipped in the herb-scented water. Coals from the fire were put in a metal pot, and Yuri's brother stepped over it, symbolically taking on the sins (Russ.—*grekhi*) of the relatives who were going to run with Yuri. They gave him coins in exchange, "paying" him for this service. At that point, it was nearing 2 AM, and everyone went to bed, either in the tent or in their cars, while Yuri, nervous about the coming day, paced the perimeter of the site.

FIGURE 6.3 Asking the *ongons* if Yuri's runners are acceptable. Ulan-Ude, 2005.

The next day dawned bright and clear, and by 9 AM the chill of sleeping on the ground had burned off. Bair Zhambalovich went into trance, calling down one of his own *ongons* to enter his body. This *ongon* would serve as an intermediary between Yuri's living family and Yuri's *ongons* in the spirit world until they were able to enter Yuri's body, later in the ritual. The *ongon* asked Yuri's uncle and aunt, each of Yuri's runners, and Yuri's brother for their name and their clan. For each, the *ongon* took a cup of milk and flipped it over his shoulder. If it landed right side up, this was a sign that the person was acceptable to Yuri's ancestral *ongons* (see Figure 6.3). As explained to me during the ceremony, if the *ongon* found them acceptable (which he did), then their soul would be taken out of their body and sent up to heaven for the duration of the ceremony, to counter-balance the powers of the gods, which would come down to earth. None of the runners seemed affected by the temporary loss of their soul, and none went into trance. Bair's *ongon* left him, and the ceremony started in earnest.

Yuri and his cousins started to run (see Figure 6.4). Black shamans drum to induce trance, while white shamans shake dragon-headed staffs with bells and

FIGURE 6.4 Yuri and his runners, circling the birch grove. Ulan-Ude, 2005.

chant "*Om mani padme hum.*"[9] Both white and black shamans can also induce trance by running around the grove of birch trees at a ritual site, drumming or chanting while they run.

Yuri and his runners began to circle the stand of birch trees, jogging and chanting together. Whenever they began to slack off, Bair Zhambalovich or Donduk would encourage them to continue, to chant louder, to run faster. Ideally, Yuri would run until he went into trance and his *ongon* entered his body, but since this was his first time, he was having trouble, so periodically, Bair Zhambalovich would call for a break and let Yuri and the runners rest while he gave Yuri advice and encouragement (see Figure 6.5).

During one of these breaks, the sheep was sacrificed as an offering to Yuri's *ongons*. This took longer than expected, because no one knew how to sacrifice the sheep properly, by reaching into the chest cavity to snap an artery, tear the aorta, or squeeze the heart, so that the blood pools inside the animal and does not touch the ground. Although these techniques are common knowledge in Mongolia, very few urban Buryats have the requisite skills. When he realized that no one at the ceremony knew how to do it, Bair Zhambalovich called Aldar Andanovich on his cell phone, and the sacrifice had to wait until Aldar arrived. Once he slaughtered the sheep in the "Mongolian style," the blood was collected, the meat boiled, and the skin, bones, and meat were placed in

FIGURE 6.5 Yuri (left) pauses to catch his breath, as Bair Zhambalovich (right) offers support and urges him to keep running. Ulan-Ude, 2005.

the trees to present them to the spirits. As in *tailgan* (offering) ceremonies, the rest of the sacrificed sheep was eaten by the ritual participants, who share the meal with the ancestors.

Over the course of the day, the energy of the ritual ebbed and flowed. There were intense periods where Yuri and his runners ran and chanted, while all the participants watched, some holding their breath, to see if an *ongon* would descend. Then Yuri and the runners would rest, and everyone else would have lunch or tea. Several times during the day Bair Zhambalovich called down his own *ongons*, and participants were able to ask them questions. Several clients of Tengeri, unaffiliated with Yuri or his family, showed up to take advantage of the ceremony and ask questions. After these lulls, Bair Zhambalovich would decide Yuri had rested enough, and start the running again.

By the end of the ceremony, Yuri had gone into trance three times, once for each *ongon*. While attempting to call the *ongons*, Yuri was running or singing and rhythmically shaking the bell on his staff. When an *ongon* enters a shaman, there is an abrupt shift in stance and posture, in voice, and in

FIGURE 6.6 Yuri "flying" up the tallest birch tree while in trance. Ulan-Ude, 2005.

rhythm, marking the shift in person. The assisting shamans offer vodka in a cup and a puff of a cigarette as a gesture of hospitality, and try their best to get the *ongon* to sit down so they can ask questions. Some spirits sit, others resist. Yuri's *ongons* were reluctant to sit. The assisting shamans attempted to identify the individual *ongon*, and asked whether they accepted Yuri's sacrifice, whether they will help him in his practice. *Ongons* may bless their descendants, stroking them with a staff. One of Yuri's grandfather *ongons* did an eagle dance, the traditional victory dance of a Mongolian wrestler, to celebrate his success (see Figure 6.7). As Yuri continues to channel these *ongons*, their personalities become clearer, so that over time his family and colleagues will come to recognize who has entered his body. In the first initiation, however, these personae are not yet fully developed, so the most powerful effect is the embodied experience of alterity; the *ongon* is primarily recognizable as "not Yuri."

The materiality and embodied nature of this experience is central to the way in which participants talk about the ritual. Yuri, like the other shamans at Tengeri, insists that he does not remember his trance experiences. From his

FIGURE 6.7 One of Yuri's *ongons* performs an eagle dance while inhabiting his body. Ulan-Ude, 2005.

perspective, he is not present in his body. His family shares this perception, as the unfamiliar speech and strikingly different movements of Yuri's body during trance produce the uncanny effect of a person that is both recognizably Yuri and yet also recognizably not Yuri. The ancestral *ongons* who were, up until this point, presumed to be the authors of Yuri's physical symptoms, are now directly experienced in the ritual. Several people told me the effect was frightening (Russ.—*strashno*); the officiating shamans may play up this effect on purpose, scolding participants who don't behave properly, such as those who look directly at the shaman in trance or turn their backs to the *ongon*. For some participants, this heightens the sense of risk and fear that is engendered by encountering a "not Yuri" inside the body of a familiar relative. Sometimes, however, this technique backfires, as happened with one of Yuri's cousins, who was scolded by the shamans and angrily complained, "they know we don't know anything. If it was important they should have told us!" This lack of preexisting knowledge was an essential part of what made the experience convincing for the participants, several of whom told me "we didn't know what to expect." Despite not knowing anything about the ritual beforehand, they were able to speak to their ancestors through Yuri's body. Their lack of experience with shamanism was proof of their objectivity: their ignorance rhetorically transformed them into unbiased observers who were convinced by the effects of the experience.

The final test was climbing the birch tree at the center of the ritual grove. "Flying" to the top, as the shamans say, of the tallest tree is taken as the sign that the initiate has achieved a full embodied trance, because this is a feat that the initiate should not be able to do without supernatural assistance. The moment happened so quickly that it really did appear to me as if Yuri had "flown" up the side of the tree (see Figure 6.6). Given that Yuri is a very large man, and the tree is a cut birch set only about a foot into the ground, it was surprising that he did not pull it over. However, he ascended only about halfway up. "Is it enough?" the woman next to me asked. The rest of the family did not know, and whispered with great concern. "Was that it?" someone asked, mildly disappointed. Bair Zhambalovich, the initiating shaman, determined that it was enough, and that the ceremony was complete. Yuri had successfully embodied his ancestors.

After Yuri climbed the birch, all the participants entered the tent and sat around the edges. We tasted the alcohol (*tarasun*) that had been distilled during the ceremony. The *tarasun* was poured into two small cups, one from each still, and passed around the circle. Each person took a tiny sip of the vile and powerful liquids, and we voted on which we thought was stronger. The more powerful *tarasun* indicated the relative strength of the spirits on each side of Yuri's family: yet another piece of sensory evidence. Everyone concurred that Nellie's side was by far the stronger brew, which was odd, since Nellie Innokentievna is Russian, and Yuri's *ongons* are from his Buryat father's side. "Who knows," one of the shamans suggested, "there may be *ongons* on Nellie's side too."

In fact, it is not uncommon for shamans, even once initiated, to discover more *ongons* from the same or other sides of the family. Several of the shamans at Tengeri are initiated as both black and white shamans, or blacksmith shamans, with one line coming from one family, and the other from the other side. If a ritual does not fully ameliorate the physical symptoms of the shamanic calling and the symptoms return, there are other shamanic ancestors to be discovered.

This initiation was for the ancestors of Yuri's father's family, which represents only half of Yuri's genealogy. Yuri's Russian mother may have Buryat ancestors, like many of the ethnic Russians in Buryatia, or she may have a Russian folk healer in her family, which the Tengeri shamans consider to be a kind of shaman as well. Whether a family's genealogical knowledge is complete is determined by whether the living members of the family are healthy and prosperous. If they are not, the research and rituals will continue. If the physical symptoms are not healed, then the diagnosis was not complete.

Bair Zhambalovich, Donduk, and Yuri—now a fully initiated shaman—put on their robes and performed their *kamlanie* to thank the *ongons* and let them know that the initiation was over. Finally, the birch trees were taken down and burned. When it was over, everyone was exhausted, but also exhilarated that it had gone so well. Yuri's *ongons* had not only entered him, one of them had performed an eagle dance while in his body (see Figure 6.7), and an eagle had circled overhead, which everyone took to be a good omen for Yuri's future as a shaman. Yuri was jubilant, and joked that after a few initiations, maybe he would be able to call down Chinghis Khan. Even though it was a joke, evoking the great Khan reminded everyone that Yuri's lineage ties him and his family back to the great Mongolian empire. The initiation had transformed a half-Russian former businessman into the heir of a great Mongolian shamanic tradition. Yuri was also desperate for a cigarette, since Bair Zhambalovich would not let him smoke during the ceremony. Nellie Innokentievna, who only smiled when he joked about Chinghis Khan, was relieved that her son had done what was necessary to avoid a relapse of his symptoms.

The tent was left standing, because another initiation was scheduled to start in a day or two, but everyone packed up their stuff and went home. A few days later, we met Yuri and his wife to give them copies of the photographs my husband had taken during the ritual. Yuri looked at the shots of himself in trance with great interest and said quietly "I don't remember that part. Of course, I wasn't there." He paused awkwardly, as if trying to remember. "No, I don't remember."

"Look how different he looks," Larissa remarked. "A completely different face."

Possession requires the initiate to open their body to the presence and will of ancestors, and it requires families to open themselves to new historical knowledge. Once an initiate has gotten this far, they have embraced the process, but they and those around them are always aware that it began in physical pain and illness.

Conclusion

Through trial and error, experimenting with what relieves their symptoms, and experiencing trance states, the shamans at Tengeri learn to read the will of their ancestors in the physical conditions of their bodies. By describing a shamanic calling as genetic and ancestral compulsion, the Tengeri shamans insist on the absolute demands that the (at least partially) Buryat body places on an individual. The Tengeri organization seeks recognition as an institution that represents a national religion of the Buryat people, but in practice it works through individual shamans, who in piecemeal fashion assert and accept the demands that Buryat ancestors make on the living, whether or not the living identify as Buryat. Through diagnosing the spiritual causes of physical illnesses they produce family histories, and these histories often cross ethno-national boundaries, reflecting a Siberian history of colonization and intermarriage, rendering the Buryat nation as permeable as the body of a shaman. At the same time, through the experience of embodying and speaking to ancestor spirits, the rituals produce a different sense of time, a shamanic chronotope, in which the past is continuously present.

The Soviet past is only obliquely present in these family histories. Sometimes people invoke the dislocations of the Soviet period to explain why genealogical knowledge of their families has been lost. The purges and state violence during collectivization, when large numbers of Buryats fled to Mongolia and China, left gaps in family histories. Ancestors who were causing symptoms had been forgotten either because they were purged or because the elders who knew the genealogies died or fled. But more often, people simply said, "it wasn't something we thought mattered." This sounds like a simple statement, but it is usually spoken with great intensity. It would be a mistake to dismiss the critique of the Soviet past that lies behind this deceptively simple statement.

The New Soviet Person was one of the key elements of the Soviet modernizing project. Early Soviet social reforms sought to fulfill Marxist ideology by dismantling the nuclear family and fostering emotional ties to society and the Communist Party. Jochen Hellbeck (2006), for example, writes of the way in which diary writers under Stalin identified with and strove to refashion themselves into heroic Soviet individuals. The ideal of the New Soviet Person was a heroic individual, differentiated from the bourgeois individual, in that they worked towards realizing "the enlarged life of the collective" (Hellbeck 2006, 10). The heroic, world-building attributes of the Soviet person were often contrasted with the passive peasant, who vests their agency in a fake God, rather than taking it into their own hands. "Soviet citizens, under the guidance of the Communist Party, had the capacity to will the communist world into existence. This expectation resonated with the belief that man could bend the whole universe to the rhythm of his desires by an act of will" (Hellbeck 2006, 32–33). Although Hellbeck is writing about the Stalinist period, the ideal of the New Soviet Person remained a cornerstone of Soviet ideology, embodied at the height of the Cold War by the cosmonaut (Smolkin-Rothrock 2011), the fearless space traveler who could leave the entire earth behind without a backward glance in the pursuit of Soviet glory.

Although Hellbeck does not use Bakhtin's idea of the chronotope, as a relationship between a hero and the contours of time and space within which the hero exists, it is useful in understanding this ideal. The New Soviet Person was always located within a historical teleology of progress and modernization, the linear, progressive time of the Soviet genre of history. As explained in Chapter 2, within the context of Soviet nationality rhetoric, this teleology took on added importance. If the New Soviet Person was a hero combatting backwardness and striving for progress, the "backward" Siberian native had further to go. Although the idea of the New Soviet Person is usually presented as a uniquely Soviet phenomenon, it should be understood as a uniquely Soviet interpretation of the Western Enlightenment secular project, a variant of what Elizabeth Povinelli calls the autological subject: the "discourses, practices, and fantasies about self-making, self-sovereignty, and the value of individual freedom associated with the Enlightenment project of contractual constitutional democracy" (Povinelli 2006, 4). The imagined autological subject is the ideal of the free individual, subject only to their own rational thought, seeking to discover and fully embody their own true and authentic self. For the Soviet autological subject, the New Soviet Person, the authentic self is cultivated and fulfilled through heroic labor for the collective good. The New Soviet Person leaves behind the specific ties of family, clan, and religion in favor of the universal ties of citizenship and a commitment to universal human progress.

The genealogical society, in contrast, stands for the social and familial ties that render certain types of individuals—usually indigenous, but also peasant and female individuals who are obligated through kinship, custom, and tradition—less than fully free. In this aspect, Soviet nationality rhetoric was comparable (if slightly different from) other forms of colonial logics, in that the ties of "tradition," "kinship," and "clan," often (but not exclusively) expressed in religious practice, were stumbling blocks on the road to turning indigenous subjects into modern citizens. Within the linear, progressive chronotope of the Soviet genre of history, religious practices and kinship obligations were the markers of "backwardness" that rendered some Soviet subjects unable to fully participate in the construction of the radiant communist future, and which the New Soviet Person should leave behind. Although the rhetoric of the Friendship of the Peoples offered the possibility of full inclusion into Soviet modernity, participation in that modernity required a transformation of self. Buryats were not excluded by virtue of being Buryat in a purely ethnic or biological sense, but as Darima's dilemma in Chapter 5 shows, Buryats who embraced Soviet forms of self-hood distanced themselves from the kinship and religious practices that they most associate with Buryat identity.

I cannot say to what degree Soviet-era Buryats actually aspired to these rhetorical ideals. Family and kinship ties remain enormously important to the contemporary Buryats I have worked with. However, regardless of whether they embraced Soviet ideals, over the 20th century the Buryat population overwhelmingly participated in the Soviet "modernizing" initiatives that were designed to overcome "tradition" and "backwardness." As I have noted in the introduction, in the 1930s, "almost 85 percent of the Buryat population still practiced some form of nomadism" (Chakars 2014, 8), whereas by 1989, 44.5 percent of all Buryats in Russia were urban residents and were over-represented in cultural, education, medical, media, government, and other white-collar professions in their republic.[10] Individuals could not participate in these professions and openly engage in either Buddhist or shamanic religious practices. Although they would not have needed to repudiate kinship ties to pursue these professions, the ways in which kinship obligations are expressed and managed was by necessity profoundly altered by the shifts in everyday life that resulted from these socio-economic transformations.

Yet it is precisely these highly educated urban Buryats who are remaking themselves into subjects of their ancestors' will and establishing a relationship with the past. Among the ranks of shamans at Tengeri at the time of Yuri's initiation were an engineer, a veterinarian, an agronomist, and, like Yuri, several entrepreneurs. Other shamanic organizations are filled with former scholars. All of them re-imagine their lives, which were professional successes in Soviet terms, as a failure to heed kinship obligations, which in turn made them sick. The process of becoming a shaman is a process of self-making, through which a previously autological Soviet subject becomes a Buryat shamanic subject, defined and subjugated to kinship obligation.

An initiation ceremony is the culmination of this process of self-making, in which the initiate produces their true and authentic self as a self that is subjected to the will of the ancestors. Rather than a backward past to be left behind on the linear path to modernity, the past (as ancestor) is embodied in the present, physically present as social beings with whom one has negotiated a relationship. The initiation is the final rite of passage marking the endpoint of this transformation of self.

The way in which Yuri remakes himself and his family as shamanic subjects has a complicated relationship to the idea of the New Soviet Person. Both are projects of heroic self-making, one in which literally life-threatening obstacles are overcome. These heroic projects, however, are undertaken within different chronotopes, thereby changing the kind of personal agency that is possible. The New Soviet Person's agency rests in destroying the bonds of the past. In contrast, the new shaman is forging new bonds to the past, completely subjugated (Russ.—*za lozheno*/"harnessed") to the will of the ancestors. Shamans constantly stress their lack of choice and agency in the process. It is the ancestral *ongons* who choose the candidate, who direct the process, who interact with family members. This effacement culminates in the initiation ceremony, when the *ongons* completely take over the initiate's body. Rather than a person who "could bend the whole universe to the rhythm of his desires by an act of will" (Hellbeck 2006, 33), the shaman must bend him or herself to the will and desires of the *ongons*, an empty vessel to be filled by their powers. "I don't remember that part," Yuri said. "Of course, I wasn't there." Yuri's individual survival depends on a radical decentering of his will and his personhood.

Yet the shaman is hardly passive. The effort required to subject oneself to the ancestors and build this relationship is enormous. Yuri, who from his sickbed sought out a cure, learned a new language, discovered new genealogical information, convinced his family of this genealogy, produced a new family history, and called the ancestors into his body, is not passive. Yuri actively produced his relationship to his ancestors, and he will continue to maintain this relationship for his family's greater good. Like the New Soviet Person, and unlike the bourgeois individual or neoliberal entrepreneur that the New Soviet Person stands in contrast to, the shaman works towards the positive good of the collective, which, in this case, is their family and community. A shaman must use their relationship to the *ongons* to heal others, and the shaman who turns away a patient will lose the protection of their *ongons*. The initiation ties the shaman to the living, through bonds of moral obligation, as much as to the dead. During the Soviet period, as most of the shamans say, "we didn't think these things mattered." Within the Soviet chronotope, which was ascendant during the Soviet period, the past was past. In the post-Soviet period, for urban shamans like Yuri who have come to accept a shamanic chronotope, the past has become vitally and sometimes dangerously present, and "these things" have become matters of life and death. The family histories produced through shamanic practices do not contest or re-evaluate the events of the Soviet genre of history. Instead, the shamanic genre of history rejects the kind of person that the Soviet project sought to produce: a person who doesn't recognize the signs of obligation to their ancestors. Instead, by producing genealogical information and by interacting with their ancestors, who are present in the shaman's body during the ritual, the shaman and their family produce themselves as the kind of people who have a relationship with their past. Ritual practices, in which the past is embodied in the present, produce a shamanic chronotope, which provides the practitioners a different subject position from which to engage with the world.

For Yuri, who has invested tremendous effort into becoming a shaman, the shamanic chronotope will most likely be the primary way Yuri orients himself in time and space, but the Soviet and hospitality genres of history will still be familiar and available ways of interacting with the past. However, many of his family and friends will continue to participate in Buddhist rituals and sometimes relate to the past through a Buddhist, recursive chronotope. While some people, especially shamans and lamas, will favor one chronotope over another, for laypeople these historical genres are all resources, not commitments. None of these chronotopes will completely supplant the others in people's lives. Contemporary Buryats code-switch between them, producing a relationship to the past that is appropriate to the context in which they are interacting at the moment. These chronotopes remain in dialog with each other. For Yuri, as for the other shamans who trained at or remain affiliated with Tengeri, learning to live embodied within a shamanic chronotope has the capacity to heal the ills caused by a linear, modernist, Soviet one.

Epilogue

IN 1991, AS the Buryat Autonomous Soviet Socialist Republic was becoming the Republic of Buryatia, Shirab Chimitdorzhiev, a Buryat historian, wrote the following in an academic book whose title translates as "Who are we Buryat-Mongols?":

> Radical changes have occurred in our country in all spheres of life. New thinking is happening about the historical past and a reevaluation of cultural heritage. National consciousness is awakening, striving to revive the language and traditional culture, and the desire to determine the status of the nation in the contemporary world has strengthened interest in historical knowledge, in our sacred ancestors. In the Republic of Buryatia the process of establishing historical truth,[1] the rebirth of many-centuries traditional culture and national language, national folk customs and rituals has not been simple, although our people have achieved notable successes on the path of rebirth (Chimitdorzhiev 2004a, 12–13).

In his book, Chimitdorzhiev argues against Soviet narratives of history, stating that:

> The contemporary generation of Buryats with a European education, studying the history and culture of their people from works composed during the period of totalitarian ideology, have a distorted idea of the Mongolian state system, about Mongolian tribes, about Mongolian civilization and about the Buryat participation in them. If these people commanded the old Mongolian script, which was the foundation of the Buryat literary language over the course of several centuries before 1931,

> and were familiar with the sources in this writing system, they might begin to speak differently, to say with great respect and pride "we are Buryat-Mongols" (Chimitdorzhiev 2004a, 5).

For Chimitdorzhiev, history is not merely a question of re-reading existing history books or opening previously closed archives. For him, history is about reconnecting to cultural heritage and "sacred ancestors." To know one's history is a political act, in opposition to the "distorted" history of the "totalitarian period" (i.e., the Soviet years). This history, moreover, is located in material practices: in "national folk customs and rituals" and in the old Mongolian script, which was replaced by the Latin and then the Cyrillic alphabet by state decree under Stalin. For Chimitdorzhiev the consequences and the stakes of these practices are clear. Rediscovering a forgotten past will change how Buryats think about themselves in the present. For him, the past will produce a Mongolian identity in the present, but as the preceding chapters have shown, this is only one of the pasts available to contemporary Buryats.

I have a copy of Chimitdorzhiev's book because the popular text was reissued with a new introduction in 2004, the year I began my dissertation fieldwork, its publication financed by a local businessman. The questions raised by the book still mattered, even though over the past 15 years many Buryats have profoundly shifted their relationship to their past. For some, involvement in shamanic practices have filled in family genealogies, connecting contemporary Buryats to their ancestors, their clan identities, and a broader Mongolian identity, through which they become the heirs of Chinghis Khan. For many, Buddhist practices have introduced them to a pre-revolutionary Buryat intelligentsia, a world of religious and secular scholars whose knowledge were silenced by the Soviet regime. Both of these historical genres coexist with, enrich, and complicate the linear, modernist, Soviet genre of history that most Buryats learned in school.

Chronotopes describe not only time, but also how time and space interact. A shamanic chronotope not only brings past ancestors into the present, but also situates them in space, reconnecting people to ancestral clan territories and to the spirits that are immanent in the landscape. Buddhist histories and reconstruction projects uncover an already Buddhist landscape that ties Buryatia both to the imperial Russian past and to a global Tibetan Buddhist community. The hospitality genre, in contrast, ties Buryats to their neighbors, retelling Siberian colonization as a story about different national groups becoming locals, redefining a multi-ethnic Buryatia in contrast to an ethnically Russian center. In all of these chronotopes, time, space, and community stand in a particular relationship to each other. Each of these chronotopes is indexed by, and becomes real, through ritual practices.

I see these chronotopic projects as comparable to similar efforts by indigenous people around the world who are recuperating their own histories from a linear, modernist, state-driven colonial historical genre. The stakes of these projects are not merely revealing new historical facts, but rather a way of orienting communities in time and space. In order to improve their situations in the present, they must change their relationship to the way their history has been told and challenge the evidentiary standards that favor state genres and render oral, religious, and other forms of history-making less than authoritative.

To repeat Trouillot's insight from the introduction, "the collective subjects who supposedly remember did not exist as such at the time of the events they claim to remember. Rather, their constitution as subjects goes hand in hand with the continuous creation of the past. As such, they do not succeed such a past: they are its contemporaries" (1995, 16). Merely writing more accurate histories is not enough to grasp this kind of historical poesis. In order to understand the continuous creation of the past, of alternative chronotopes that constitute communities in the present, we need an anthropology of history.

I have borrowed a terminology from Austin and Bakhtin to help us to analyze this continuous creation of the past. The idea of the chronotope allows us to examine the relationship between time, space, and the subject, reuniting the past with those who are its contemporaries (in Trouillot's sense of the term). I use the term historical genre to identify the relationship between a chronotope and the evidentiary standards and contexts within which it is produced. By separating historical events from the performative effect of producing knowledge about them, I hope to give us a terminology that will help us to think analytically about how people produce historical knowledge.

What we can see by taking a comparative approach to indigenous revitalization projects in post-Soviet secular Buryatia is the contingent nature of human conceptions of time and space and the vast creative ability of human beings to code-switch between chronotopes. By drawing on linguistic analogies, the chronotope, genre, and code-switching, I hope to index my own adherence to Silverstein's caution that, while ritual indexes shared cultural concepts, these concepts live in the daily interactions of people, including rituals (2004, 626). Chronotopes do not exist as overarching sacred canopies, but as constantly negotiated, contingent, performative evocations of pasts that continuously produce us as subjects in the present. We all exist as the products of various pasts, and I see that as a strength, because it enables us to imagine ourselves as part of multiple identities and provides the grounds from which we can reimagine ourselves more meaningfully in the present.

Although the social sciences have long embraced the realization that "a culture," as a bounded entity, is impossible to find, we often act as if a culture (whatever that may be) has one conception of time and space, or that human beings need a singular conception of time and space. Ritual is one of many frames where we play with alternative chronotopes. If religion is, as J. Z. Smith defines it, "the quest, within the bounds of the human, historical condition, for the power to manipulate and negotiate one's 'situation' so as to have 'space' in which to meaningfully dwell" (1978, 291) then the chronotopes in rituals are a resource within this negotiation. Ritual, which indexes chronotopes rather than narrating them, facilitates this play, negotiation, and code-switching, allowing us to explore historical genres without committing to one. For people in Buryatia, who move between and across different ritual spaces, the different chronotopes offered become imaginative resources as they seek to meaningfully dwell in a post-Soviet space where the Soviet modernist chronotope no longer dominates public discourse.

That modernist chronotope is, however, not gone. To return to Chimitdorzhiev's words, he notes that "our people have achieved notable successes on the path to rebirth," a phrase that sounds a great deal like "notable successes on the path toward Communism." Is this merely a habitual turn of phrase, or the substitution of one utopian future for another? From an analytic point of view, it urges us, as I hope I have done, to take seriously the question of how Soviet habits shaped post-Soviet subjectivities, and ask to how post-Soviet religious revival projects are shaped by a secular context.

I argue that the emphasis I encountered on materiality as proof for belief is a secular conception that undergirds religious practice in both Buddhist and shamanic genres. Etigelov and his recursive Buddhist chronotope becomes real through the results of scientific tests and the material condition of his body and that of his visitors. People who "didn't know anything about this before" come to know shamanic ancestor spirits through miraculously cured symptoms, medicine that didn't work until ceremonies were held, and the visible encounter with uncanny and unfamiliar ancestor spirits through the bodies of familiar relatives. In both Buddhist and shamanic contexts, people insisted to me that they overcame their skepticism and came to believe because they were confronted by material, physical proof. All of these chronotopes, Buddhist, shamanic and Soviet are grounded in embodied evidence, in the sensory experience of ritual, the ubiquity of lived environment and the physical symptoms of healed bodies. The embodied experience of ritual renders religious imaginaries, religious conceptions of time, space, and personhood, compelling, and that is precisely why ritual becomes an important locus for re-imagining the self in a highly secular, post-atheist population with multiple religious and nonreligious commitments. The materiality of ritual appears to participants to exceed its explanations, enabling people to re-imagine themselves in relation to a past, even if they are not sure what to believe. In code-switching between chronotopes, Buryats inhabit indigenous, shamanic, Buddhist, atheist, Asian, Mongolian, Russian, Soviet, neo-liberal, and multi-cultural subject positions from which they can build a relationship with the past, and from which they can stake claims on the future.

Notes

INTRODUCTION

1. The official name is the "Local Religious Organization of Shamans, Tengeri" [Mestnaia religioznaia organizatsiia shamanov Tengeri].
2. As should be evident from the dates of my fieldwork I am using the term "moment" loosely, to mark the period between the end of the Soviet Union (1991) and the amorphous shift into whatever comes next, which ethnographers are beginning to call "neo-liberal Russia" (see, e.g., Collier 2011; Zigon 2011). Although 2005 was 14 years after the end of the USSR, Soviet institutional structures still shaped social life, and as such, parts of Russia remain post-Soviet even a quarter of a century later. The transformation of Soviet institutional structures happened at a different pace throughout the former Soviet Union. In 2005, when I asked locals if they thought the term "post-Soviet" made sense, they agreed it did because "Moscow may not be post-Soviet anymore, but we still are," which is, in and of itself, an interesting chronotopic perspective.
3. I use the term "nationality" to translate the Russian term *natsional'nost'*, but readers unfamiliar with Soviet nationality studies should be aware that the term is used much as "ethnicity" is used in other polities. One's nationality (which was, for a long time, an official category in the passport) is different from one's citizenship (*grazhdanstvo*). However, unlike "ethnicity," "nationality" was linked to the existence of territories, such as the republic.
4. A *bodhisattva* is a being who has achieved enlightenment (nirvana) but has chosen to continue to exist on this plane of being so as to help others achieve enlightenment as well. Whether or not Etigelov is a bodhisattva is a matter of local debate.
5. Amogolonova (2014, 1167) cites data that 70 percent of Buryats identified as Buddhist in 2011, and Holland's (2014, 171) survey data found that 83 percent of Buryats identified as Buddhist. However, it is important to remember that

survey data measures how people identify when asked for the purposes of a survey. These numbers should not be read as indicating that 70–80 percent of Buryats actively participate in Buddhist practices or do not participate in the religious practices of other religions.

6. In addition to the two dominant ethnic groups, Russians and Buryats, Buryatia is home to people who identify as Evenki, who usually practice shamanism; the descendants of a Jewish trading community, who largely identify as atheist; the descendants of Polish exiles, who may identify as Catholic, but until 2005 had no access to Catholic services; and traders from the Caucasus, who are predominantly Muslim. These are the generally recognized "national" religions of these groups, but as post-Soviet citizens, members of all of these ethnic groups may or may not actually engage in any practices relating to that religion, and may or may not call themselves atheists.
7. "Alphabet reform" refers to Soviet state reforms to "modernize" the Buryat language. Prior to 1917 most literate Buryats used Classical Mongolian (also called Written or Literary Mongolian) orthography, especially east of Lake Baikal, where most education was offered in Buddhist settings. Written Mongolian was slightly different from spoken forms of the Buryat language, but was close enough to allow a shared literary culture across a wider range of Mongolian speakers. West of Lake Baikal there were attempts to write Buryat in Cyrillic (see Montgomery 2005 for a detailed history of Buryat literacy and alphabet reforms). From 1929 to 1937, the Soviet state worked to shift the Buryat language to an adapted version of the Latin alphabet. In 1939 all Soviet minority languages using the Latin alphabet were switched to the Cyrillic alphabet. While these reforms may have contributed significantly to the Soviet Union's high literacy rates, the result is that the vast majority of Buryats educated after 1939 cannot read documents written prior to that date.
8. Etigelov's name comes from the Buryat world for faith and trust: Etigel. His name is spelled "Etigelov" when transliterated from Buryat, and "Itigelov" or "Itigilov" when transliterated from Russian. I have opted for the Buryat spelling, even though the Russian spelling is more commonly used, including by the Traditional Sangha of Buryatia.
9. *Okrugs* are both smaller than republics and administratively less autonomous. Both okrugs and republics have titular nationalities (i.e., are the homeland of a particular ethnic group). Okrugs have independent administrations, while republics have a president, an independent legislature, and, in theory, more autonomy in regard to internal legislation. Since all participants in the political process during the Soviet period were members of the Communist Party, during the Soviet period this distinction was theoretical. After 1991, however, the Union republics (like Ukraine) declared independence, while autonomous republics were able to make use of the existing political structures and negotiate membership in the Russian Federation on different terms than okrugs. *Oblasts* are larger

than both republics and okrugs, and are not "national" and therefore not autonomous. I have chosen to retain the Russian terms because English translations do not add any explanatory value. Six of ten autonomous okrugs were dissolved between 2005 and 2008.

10. The 2010 Census results show a lower overall population for the Republic of Buryatia, down from 981,238 residents in 2002 and from 1,038,252 in 1989. Although the overall population of the republic has dropped, the population of Ulan-Ude has grown slightly, due to migration from rural areas. Ulan-Ude had 404,426 residents in 2010. Within the Republic of Buryatia, the percentage of Buryats has grown since 2002, when there were 272,910 (27.8 percent) Buryats. The number of ethnic Russians in the republic has decreased from 665,512 (67.8 percent) in 2002 to 630,783 (64.89 percent) in 2010, and the remaining 5 percent are a mix of different nationalities. There are 461,389 Buryats in the Russian Federation overall, an increase from 2002, when there were 445,175 Buryats. In 2002 Buryats constituted 0.31 percent of the Russian Federation's 141 million residents. There are just under 1 million Buryats worldwide, predominantly in Russia, Mongolia, and Inner Mongolia in China. Statistics from 1979 indicated that 58.6 percent of all Buryats lived within the republic (Humphrey 1989). However, Buryats who lived outside the republic are increasingly moving within its borders, predominantly to Ulan-Ude. The 2002 census indicates that 61.3 percent of all Buryats in the Russian Federation live in Buryatia, and in 2010, 62.16 percent of all Buryats lived in the republic. Census results at: *Vcerossiiskaia perepis naceleniia 2002 goda* [All-Russian population census 2002] http://www.perepis2002.ru/index.html?id=87 (accessed June 29, 2009), and www.gks.ru/free_doc/new_site/perepis2010/croc/perepis_itogi1612.htm (accessed January 14, 2016).
11. It should also be noted that the following applies only to Buryats within the Russian Federation; those living within China and Mongolia have very different histories, and different forms of political identifications. Shimamura (2011, 88–91), for example, treats Buryats in Mongolia as a diaspora population, since they emigrated from Russia to Mongolia around the time of the 1917 Bolshevik Revolution. Buyandelger (2013) does not explicitly identify Mongolian Buryats as a diaspora but does discuss the trauma of being dislocated from the territory they consider to be their homeland (Lake Baikal). It is ironic that Russian Buryats, who continue to live on their "traditional" territory, consider Mongolian and Chinese (Shenekhen) Buryats to be less assimilated to Western/Russian culture and therefore the bearers of "traditional" Buryat culture.
12. During my fieldwork there was a conference and protest focused on the 1937 partition, in relation to the proposed dissolution of the okrugs. Chimitdorzhiev's edited volume (2004b) is a collection of original documents and essays pertaining to the partition originally published by the Congress of the Buryat People (a civil organization) in 1997 and republished in 2004. It is notable that the partition

and loss of territory receives far more public attention than the concomitant purges, in which tens of thousands of Buryats were killed, but I do not wish to suggest that this is due to the value of land to Buryat self-identification. The 1937 purges are a very sensitive topic throughout Russia, and I suspect that the loss of territory figures so prominently in part because it is a placeholder for the loss of life.

13. See Murray (2012) for a fascinating discussion, drawn from missionary archives, of how individual Buryats (especially women) used the legal possibilities of conversion to negotiate their domestic situations.
14. See Graber (2012a, 38–40) for further discussion of this question.
15. See Oushakine (2009, 82–109) for an excellent discussion of ethnos theory and its impact on ethnic Russian identity in the Siberian city of Barnaul.
16. Examples of English-language work that situated Buryats within a larger Mongolian cultural sphere include Krader (1963) and Rupen (1964).

CHAPTER 1

1. The two terms are used interchangeably in Buryatia. In Tibet these structures are also called *chorten* (Fisher 1993, 84).
2. Tibetan Buddhism uses a lunar calendar to calculate holidays, so the dates shift each year. Services held at a temple are referred to as *khural*, which is the same term used to refer to parliamentary assemblies in Buryatia and Mongolia. In 2005, there were seven *khural* where Etigelov could be seen by the public, whereas by 2012 there were eight. They are: Sagaalkha / Lunar New Year (early February); Ganzhur Khural (March); Duinkhor Khural (late April); Donchod Khural (late May); Maidari Khural (the festival of the future Buddha Maitreya) in early July; Etigele Khambyn Khural, the anniversary of Etigelov's exhumation in early September; Lkhabab Duisen Khural (late October); and Zula Khural (late November or early December). Each year the Traditional Sangha publishes calendars that list the dates on which Etigelov will be available for viewing, along with the dates of holidays, *khurals*, and days that are lucky or unlucky for undertaking new events, starting trips, or cutting hair. One of the criticisms leveled at the Traditional Sangha is that "ordinary people" and women can only see Etigelov on holidays, while notable or powerful men are able to schedule private viewings.
3. Richard Gere, as a famous Hollywood Buddhist, occupied a powerful place in local imaginaries about Etigelov's relevance to the world. Local Buryats told me that Richard Gere was coming to visit Etigelov in 2003, 2005, and 2012, and these rumors continue to circulate, in part due to the existence of a photograph of Ianzhima Vasil'eva taken together with the actor. Amogolonova states that Richard Gere's name can be seen in the visitor's book at the Ivolginsky *datsan* (2014, 107), but I have not been able to corroborate this visit, and in September

2017 Infopol.ru reported on a video Gere had recorded expressing his desire to visit Buryatia. See: https://www.infpol.ru/news/society/132460-v-buryatiyu-vozmozhno-priedet-richard-gir/ (accessed March 11, 2018).

4. The Institute has hosted five conferences bringing together local scholarship on Etigelov in 2007, 2009, 2011, 2013, and 2015. The conference proceedings are all available at http://etegelov.ru/conf.
5. There are numerous accounts of Tibetan Buddhist adepts who are able to control the process of death by engaging in meditation, a condition referred to as *thukdam* or *thugs dam*. Those who argue that Etigelov is meditating rather than dead are probably referring to this condition. However, I never heard this term used to refer to Etigelov by laypeople in Buryatia.
6. This argument is further explored in Chapter 4.
7. Within a Buddhist context, as Bernstein (2013) argues, Etigelov's return parallels the Tibetan tradition of *gterma*. *Gterma* are sacred texts that were "ahead of their time" and were hidden by the founding figures of Tibetan Buddhism. When the time is right for the knowledge they contain they are "discovered," sometimes in written form, sometimes through inspiration. The chosen "discoverer" often receives instructions on where to find the text in dreams. Although outsiders are often skeptical about the validity of these revealed texts, classifying them as a form of "retroactive prophecy," within Tibetan Buddhism *gterma* are an accepted practice, and there is an internal system of judging whether or not a particular text qualifies as an authentic *gterma*. However, Etigelov is not a text, and *gterma* were a practice specific to the Nyingma school, which did not spread into Buryatia. Nevertheless, Bernstein (2013) argues that Etigelov is posited as possessing wisdom appropriate for the current moment, and he sent instructions, through a dream, to a young lama, asking to be recovered because his "time had come." There were also several other "treasures" including a collection of statues and rock art discovered around the same time. Although the monastic community and some Buddhist Buryat intellectuals would be aware of the tradition of *gterma*, I never heard Etigelov compared to one. See Gyatso (1996) and Davidson (2002) on *gterma*.
8. Many springs throughout Buryatia are considered by local residents to have healing properties. See Metzo (2008) on the commodification and ritual economy of the healing springs in Arshan, Buryatia.
9. Verkhniaia Beriozovkha, meaning Upper Birches, is an area just outside the city of Ulan-Ude where the City Hippodrome, the open-air Ethnographic Museum, and this Buddhist temple are located.
10. "White" foods are contrasted to "red" or "black" offerings, which are sacrificed animals that are offered in some shamanic ceremonies. Sacrificed animals are also eaten by the participants, which in this case includes the spirits present at the ritual. Buddhist deities are vegetarian and hence only accept "white" offerings.

11. I translated the Russian text into English and transliterated the Sanskrit mantra into the Latin alphabet from the Cyrillic alphabet. The mantra may be a phonetic transliteration of the following: *oṃ namo daśadiśe trikāle sarvaratnatrayāya mama pradakṣa supradakṣa sarvapāpaṃ viśodhani sukha*, which may translate very roughly as: OṂ, homage (*namo*) to all the Three Jewels (*sarvaratnatrayāya*) in the Ten Directions (*daśadiśe*) in the Three Times (*trikāle*); my (*mama*) circumambulation (*pradakṣa*), excellent circumambulation (*supradakṣa*) for the sake of purifying (*viśodhani*) all sin (*sarvapāpaṃ*); happiness (*sukha*) [this may be a misspelling of *svaha*, which is a standard closing for prayers]. My thanks to Ryan Overbey for his help in deciphering this text.
12. A Tibetan monk who teaches at Ivolginsky told me that this ceremony is a local addition to Buddhism, and not performed in Tibet. He added, however, that Buddhism always adapts to local conditions, and he saw nothing inappropriate or un-Buddhist about the practice.
13. A *surkharban* is a festival featuring the three "traditional" national sports. The first "r" is silent, so it is sometimes spelled *sukharban* in English. During the Soviet period *surkharban* was coopted as a national festival and a government-sponsored *surkharban* was (and continues to be) held at the City Hippodrome in mid-summer. However, since 1991, it has become common to hold smaller *surkharbans* after religious festivals. Many people attribute the interest of Damba Aiusheev, the current Pandito Khambo Lama, in *surkharbans* to the fact that he is a former physical fitness teacher. He has constructed a stadium outside the Ivolginsky *datsan* where *surkharbans* are held Buddhist festivals in the summer. However, I have also seen wrestling matches with prizes held after shamanic rituals. For more on *surkharban* see Krist (2005, 2009). Both the dance performance and the *surkharban* indexed the "Buryatness" of this and other events.
14. Naj Wikoff's account of the ceremony is available at: http://www.northcountrypublicradio.org/news/naj/naj10.html.
15. Although I never heard anyone mention it, I think it is relevant that the Buddhist calendar organizes years into cycles of 12. Local residents explicitly identify three as an auspicious number, and the auspiciousness of the numbers were probably so obvious they did not need to be explained. Ritual activities such as circumambulations or prostrations are more effective if they are done in multiples of three, and both 12 and 24 are multiples of three.
16. Although the Traditional Buddhist Sangha of Russia presents itself as a continuous institution since the time of Zaiaev, from the perspective of state recognition it is not. There was a gap in state recognition during the Soviet years, until the Central Spiritual Buddhist Authority was formed in 1946, which has since been renamed the Traditional Buddhist Sangha of Russia (Bernstein 2013, 99; Belka 2014, 88–89).
17. See also Etigelov's biography on the webpage of the Ivolginsky datsan, Traditional Buddhist Sangha of Russia. https://web.archive.org/web/20131212040107/

http://www.datsan.buryatia.ru/itigelov/life accessed 9/22/2015). The website has since been re-designed.

18. Bernstein instead notes, "Although it claims to be heir to the Buryat Buddhist golden age, technically the Sangha is a successor to the Central Spiritual Board of Buddhists (Rus. Tsentral'noe dukhovnoe upravlenie buddhistov), a Soviet-era organization formed in 1922 and reorganized in 1946." (Bernstein 2013, 99).
19. Tulku is the common English usage for the Tibetan term *sprul sku* (*khutukhtu* or *khubilgan* in Mongolian and Buryat). Buryat Buddhists recognize reincarnations, and several famous Buryat figures have been recognized as specific incarnations of previous teachers, but unlike in Tibetan and Mongolian monasticism, Buryat monastic institutions do not pass titles or property through reincarnation. The Etigelov Institute does not generally use the term tulku; instead it refers to Etigelov as a reincarnation (Russ.—*pererozhdenie*) and calls the list of his 11 previous incarnations a line of succession (Russ.—*liniia preemstvennosti*). I am using the term tulku because this is the most familiar term for English-speaking readers.
20. Although I heard many people say that the Traditional Sangha received state financial support, all representatives of the organization insisted that this was not the case, often arguing that as the "national religion" they ought to receive such support and: do not.
21. Belka (2014, 89–90) likewise argues that the Traditional Sangha's 2004 declaration that Etigelov, the *Atlas of Tibetan Medicine*, and the Zandan Zhuu sandalwood statue of the Buddha are a "Triad of National Buddhist Symbols" is an attempt to bolster the authority of the organization. In 2004–5 I heard very little discussion among laypeople of the "Triad of National Buddhist Symbols."
22. The dividing line between those who make offerings and those who do not appears to be how long they have been residents. I have met both Russian Orthodox Christians and Muslims who refuse to make offerings on the grounds of their religion, but in all cases the individuals had moved to Buryatia as adults. Other Orthodox Christians and Muslims observed the practice, explaining to me "we live here, so we have to respect the local practices." These individuals had all been born in Buryatia and considered it their *rodina* (homeland), which implies a sense of origin or heritage, rather than merely being their place of residence. This is discussed further in Chapter 3.
23. I was surprised when she used the term "Christian" (Russ.—*khristian*) instead of "Orthodox" (Russ.—*pravoslavnyi*), which is the more common statement in Buryatia. When I pressed her, she specified that she was Catholic. I was told by several people that there were nearly 40,000 ethnic Poles in Buryatia, all descendants of exiles. Until 2005, however, there was no Catholic church in Ulan-Ude. See Quijada (2009, 98).
24. See Paxson (2005) for an extensive discussion of the term *khoziain* and its flexibility, as well as the role of place spirits among Russian peasants in Leningrad

oblast. For Paxson, the category *svoi* versus *chuzoi*—own versus other—is an important analytic distinction. While I found the same thing in Buryatia, in contexts where Paxson's villagers used "*svoi*," both Buryats and Russians use "*nash*"—ours, versus "*ne nash.*" "*Chuzoi*" is reserved for extreme marks of difference, and I almost never heard it used. "*Svoi*" is a reflexive pronoun, while "*nash*" is a standard personal pronoun.

25. See also Buyandelger (2013) and Humphrey (1998) for descriptions of Buryat place spirits.
26. See Chapter 2 for a discussion of the 2005 Victory Day celebrations.
27. The original Russian is *Voiny—Orongoitsy Kavalery Ordenov "Slavy,"* which might also be translated as Military Orongoi, or Veterans of Orongoi.

CHAPTER 2

1. Average life expectancy for men has since increased to approximately 65 years.
2. Almost everyone who mentioned the opera house told me that it was built by prisoners, but several historians told me that this popular misconception is not in fact true. I do not think it is a coincidence that popular rumor credits World War II with producing the biggest and most notable cultural building in the city.
3. See, for example, "In the Center of Lamaism," which states: "In 1922 during the retreat of the Red partisans from the White bandit Ungern, the retreating groups came under fire from the monastery. Yes, and it's not surprising. This *datsan*, then as now, was the main center of Lamaism. Lamas, just like priests, were faithful servants of tsarism in the enserfment of the working masses" (Mashchekke 1930, 10–11; see also Klimovich 1931, 12).
4. A Cyrillic-based alphabet was also introduced in Mongolia. Modern literary Buryat and Mongolian are written in this Cyrillic-based alphabet, but Buryats living in China's Inner Mongolia still use the classical Mongolian script. Classes in old or Classical Mongolian script were introduced at the Buryat State University in 2004, and it is taught at the Buddhist University Dashi Choinkhorlin at the Ivolginsky *datsan*, but very few people can read it. A small percentage of Buryats are literate in Buryat, and an even smaller percentage are literate in the classic Mongolian script. This places sharp constraints on historical research because all documents produced in the Buryat language prior to 1930 were written in the old script. Although the old script is not widely read, young Buryat intellectuals are increasingly learning the script in order to have access to these texts, and there is now a computer program to allow those who can read it to type in old Mongolian script using a standard computer keyboard.
5. A year later, Erbanov was executed in the 1937 purges along with most of the Buryat members of the Communist Party elite (see Chakars 2014, 75, for both estimates of population losses under Stalin and the difficulty in deriving these estimates).

6. "Elena Mikhailovna" is a pseudonym. The following is taken from my notes from the conversation, slightly edited and sometimes paraphrased for length and clarity. The conversation took place while walking through the woods and was not tape-recorded.
7. I presume that she was referring to purchasing gold jewelry and handing it down through families. I did not interrupt her narrative and was not able to clarify it with her later, but it would not be unusual for semi-nomadic herders to keep wealth in the form of jewelry.

CHAPTER 3

1. These numbers seem to be fairly consistent, although the cause of the deaths remain highly contested. I have taken the numbers from a website that displays the photos and names of the victims: http://www.pravmir.ru/angelyi-beslana-imena-i-litsa-vseh-pogibshih/ ("Angely Beslana. Imena i Litsa Vsekh Pogibshikh [Angels of Beslan. Names and Faces of All Those Who Died]" 9/1/2015), compiled by the editorial staff of Pravoslavie I Mir (Orthodoxy and the World), a Russian Orthodox internet newsletter, accessed March 25, 2018.
2. See for example (Vlasova 2004; *Nomer Odin Ulan-Ude* 2004; BMK Informatsionnoe Agentstvo 2014). Murray also notes that during her research people often contrasted Buryatia to the Caucasus (Murray 2012, xi).
3. It must be noted that while residents of Buryatia speak of themselves and this ethic as unusual, Luehrmann documents similar rhetoric and behavioral standards in Mari-El, another multi-ethnic republic in the Volga region. She states: "By the term neighborliness, I am referring to the ambivalent set of relations between households and villages that evolved in this region, whose inhabitants had lived with religious and linguistic diversity for centuries and where religious affiliation had served as a marker for legal and political distinctions up until the Bolshevik Revolution" (Luehrmann 2011, 27–28). It is likely that similar ethical orientations towards multi-ethnic and multi-religious tolerance are more common than usually thought.
4. United Russia (Edinaia Rossiia) is the political party of Putin and has been the majority party since 2003, although technically once elected the president is no longer affiliated with a party. United Russia posters and images were not on display during Victory Day. United Russia posters and flyers were very visible, however, at the city-sponsored *surkharban*, a Buryat sporting festival held in mid-summer that has been sponsored by the government since the Soviet era.
5. It is also profoundly gendered. Although a few of the dance troupes had male performers, the vast majority of the dancers and all of the singers were women. But beyond noting that women are often the bearers of culture and tradition, I will not address gender here.

6. Tsam performances have been performed at the Ivolginsky *datsan* since 2011. For descriptions of Tsam in Mongolia see Fedotev and Fedotor (1986); Galli (2009).
7. At both shamanic and Buddhist ceremonies, food is blessed with the Buryat exclamation "*Akhai!*" When blessings are specifically identified they are usually for "*blagopoluchie*," which means well-being or prosperity.
8. For general English-language histories of Russian and Cossack expansion into Siberia see Forsyth (1992); Bobrick (1992); Lincoln (1993); Naumov (2006); Hartley (2014). For an English-language text that focuses on indigenous Siberia generally, see Slezkine (1994).
9. For example, Cossack was not a recognized official nationality on the 1920, 1926, or 1937 Soviet census, but Hirsch notes that this point was debated, and they were included on some lists for the 1927 census because people had self-identified as Cossack (Hirsch 2005, 123, 133, 327–35). On the post-Soviet revival of Cossack identity, see Skinner (1994).
10. I later observed a similar ritual offering of bread and salt to visitors to an Old Believer (Semeiskie) village during a conference. For a similar ritual elision in a colonial context, see Grimes's description of the Entrada from the Santa Fe Fiesta, in which the narrator describes the ritual as a "request for forgiveness" on the part of the Spanish, for conquering the Pueblos, but in fact during the ritual the Pueblos are "offered pardon" for having rebelled against Spanish colonizers and all New Mexicans are presented as "the children of 'that historic reconciliation' " (2013, 110–13). In both cases, the ritual produces an ambiguous "we" that encompasses both colonizer and colonized, and as Grimes argues "fiesta performances also encode conflict while simultaneously masking it. Masking conflict is not the same as living in peace" (Grimes 2013, 120).
11. This is a bilingual book; this quotation is taken from the book's English text and is not my translation.
12. See Humphrey (1998, 23–32) and Chakars (2014, Chapter 1) for good, concise English-language summaries of what we may know about these historical events. During the early Soviet period this history was usually presented as colonization, so that the Soviet government could argue that it was superior to its tsarist predecessor, whereas in the post-War period (like the 1959 anniversary) the "unification" narrative was favored. Since this is a highly contested historical argument with political stakes for contemporary Buryat scholars, I am choosing not to cite any contemporary Buryat sources.
13. Personal communication with several local historians in Ulan-Ude.
14. See Lenin (1975a, b, c, d) for his views on national self-determination, and Pipes (1997) and Carr (1985) on early Bolshevik policy debates about nationality policy, especially in the western borderlands. Both Pipes and Carr argue that Lenin's views on nationality were a *realpolitik* measure to gain support from minority groups during the Civil War. Slezkine (1994) includes a detailed review of shifts in policies regarding Siberian nationalities. The current prevailing view

of Soviet nationality policies, as defined by Suny (1993) and Slezkine (1996), argues that Soviet nationality policies "naturalized" national identities, and that when the Soviet Union fell apart, the national minority territories established by Stalin, regardless of how arbitrary their boundaries, appeared as natural political entities. Following Suny's and Slezkine's argument, both Martin (2001) and Hirsch (2005) have examined nationality policies in detail. Hirsch and Martin agree that nationality categories were "naturalized" by Soviet policy, but they have opposing arguments about how Soviet bureaucrats interpreted Lenin's and Stalin's proclamations that nationalities should be "national in form, socialist in content." Martin argues that Soviet nationality policy is contradictory, drawing a distinction between "affirmative action" policies that fostered equality (which he terms "soft-line") and repressive (hardline) policies that led to purges of national elites in the 1930s and assimilationist policies in the post-war period. Hirsch rightly argues that Martin's use of the term "affirmative action" is an anachronism. She convincingly argues that Soviet nationality policy is not self-contradictory, but rather that both violent and non-violent policies were an expression of "state-sponsored evolutionism" designed to drag backward minorities into modernity. However, Martin's use of "affirmative action" usefully points to parallels between social engineering efforts in the USSR and in Western democratic settler societies, which, when combined with Hirsch's argument that "state sponsored evolutionism" can have both violent and nonviolent aspects, meshes well with current critiques of Western multiculturalism.

15. See Hirsch (2005) for a detailed history of the impact of Soviet ethnography on the formation of Soviet census categories and Grant (1995) for a detailed case study of how a "century of perestroikas" has impacted an ethnic group.
16. See Oushakine (2009, Chapter 2, pp.79–130) for an excellent discussion of Bromley, Gumilev, and the impact of these theories on post-Soviet conceptions of Russian identity.
17. See Oushakine (2009) for a discussion of how this unmarked quality produced a sense of ethnic crisis in Russia.

CHAPTER 4

1. Gautama Buddha (Sakyamuni) is commonly thought to have lived in the fifth century B.C.E. There are several prophecies about Maitreya and his return, some of which identify him as a friend, disciple, or successor of the Gautama Buddha, but he is not clearly identified as a historical personage the way the Gautama Buddha is. Maitreya's depictions in different Buddhist contexts varies. For general accounts of Maitreya, see Kitagawa (1981); Sponberg and Hardacre (1988); Tsultemin (2015). Tsultemin argues that in Mongolian Maitreya processions Maitreya is depicted as a cakravartin, a universal ruler, who will reincarnate in the north (i.e., Mongolian lands) (Tsultemin 2015, 149).

2. Finished in 2008, Etigelov now resides there permanently, and the building is only opened to the public during festivals.
3. Since the Russian Orthodox church calculates holy days using the Julian calendar, Kreshchenie (literally Baptism, also translated as Epiphany or Theophany) is celebrated on January 19. Although technically the same holy day as Epiphany in western Christianity (the difference in dates is due to the difference between the Julian and Gregorian calendars) Russian Orthodoxy emphasizes Jesus's baptism by John the Baptist. The holiday is celebrated by cutting a cross-shaped hole through the ice into a river and dunking oneself into the freezing water. Holy water collected from churches is considered to be particularly powerful on this date and in Buryatia both Orthodox and non-Orthodox will bring large bottles to church to collect holy water, which they will take home for consumption by their families. This is a good example of how religious practices often cross denominational lines.
4. *Thangkas* are paintings of Tibetan Buddhist deities made on silk that follow very specific iconographic conventions. See Fisher (1993, 80). For a discussion of the role of *thangkas* within the Western study of Tibetan Buddhism, see Lopez (1998, 135–55). For examples of Buryat *thangkas*, see Bolsokhoeva and Soktoeva (1998).
5. To purchase prayers, visitors write the appropriate names on slips of paper, and then pay the cashier at the kiosk, who stamps the prayer slip. The purchaser then deposits the prayer with a monk at the end of the prayer line. The names are read at intervals during the services and are repeated according to how much was paid. Prayers can be purchased at any service, but they acquire more merit on special holidays. When patients visit the medical specialists at the monastery (*emchi lamas*) they will often prescribe attending or purchasing prayers at a particular service.
6. Dale Pesmen (2000) has devoted an entire ethnography to the idea of Russian "soul" or *dusha* in all its complexity. Pesmen argues that *dusha*, while associated with and used in reference to many things, is fundamentally about the ability for human beings to connect to each other in a meaningful way. Having *dusha* means having meaning, in contrast with "this post-Soviet life," a life of scrambling for money and things in an uncertain economy, an everyday life that conspires to destroy *dusha*. In Omsk in western Siberia, Pesmen's friends "attributed certain ways of feeling ill to a 'pressure' that was not simply blood, barometric, or any other clearly defined pressure" (Pesmen 2000, 38).
7. After the centuries of coexistence, it is difficult, if not impossible, to parse distinctions between Russian, Buddhist, and Buryat pre-Buddhist conceptions of the soul in practical usage. There are definitely theological differences between Russian Orthodox conceptions of the soul, Buddhist conceptions of the soul (which is ultimately the reincarnating self that seeks to dissolve itself), and pre-Buddhist (shamanic) Buryat conceptions of souls (as documented in early ethnographies), which become ancestor spirits after death. However, I never

heard anyone in Buryatia express any concern that the Russian term *dusha* was being used to refer to potentially different kinds of souls in different religious contexts. People appeared to code-switch between conceptions of souls just as they switched between historical genres.

8. A "heavy soul" sounds like what an American might call depression or anxiety, but it is important not to equate them. For people in Buryatia, depression and a heavy soul are different conditions—related, perhaps, but not identical. Depression and anxiety are meaningful diagnoses within the field of discourse that constitutes psychiatry and psychology. A heavy or light soul is a meaningful diagnosis within a completely different field of discourse, one concerned with religious practice, traditional systems of knowledge, and social relations. Both religion and psychiatry as discursive fields are present in Buryatia, and are seen as related and potentially interchangeable, but not commensurate. A Buryat psychology student once told me this field wasn't very popular in Buryatia, "because people visit shamans instead." Psychiatry and the diagnosis of depression are an available diagnostic option for the people I spoke with. By choosing to treat their condition within a religious framework, not as a psychiatric one, they assert that a heavy soul is not a psychiatric condition.
9. Paxson also describes a similar impulse on the part of rural Russian women who feel driven to return to their birth villages (2005).
10. This is a literal translation of the title; in English, this would be known as "Institute of Forensic Science."
11. Many Buryat intellectuals now see the period around the turn of the century, prior to the 1917 revolution, as a golden age (see, e.g., Chimitdorzhiev 2004a). Many Buryat scholars have spoken to me in reverential terms about Robert Rupen's article on the pre-revolutionary intelligentsia (1956), and the article, translated into Russian, was available for sale in pamphlet form at the kiosk at the Academy of Sciences. In his article, Rupen, a Cold War American scholar of Mongolia, documented the lives and subsequent deaths of Buryat intellectuals from 1900–1930, who were influential in politics during the early Soviet period and subsequently killed by the regime during the 1937 purges. Their lives and scholarship are a direct refutation of the Soviet portrait of Buryatia as a wasteland of illiterate herders, and contemporary Buryat scholars find the fact that their lives were documented by an American scholar in the 1950s, when speaking their names at home was dangerous, to be particularly validating.
12. See Chapter 2 for a more extensive discussion of the Soviet genre of history.
13. Interestingly, Twigg (1998, 585) notes that bribing doctors was a late Soviet-era practice that post-Soviet medical reform was intended to remedy. In my experience, however, people in the former Soviet Union think of medical bribery as being a result of post-Soviet decay.
14. Rivkin-Fish (2004), working with Russian reproductive health advocates, stresses the way in which they understand their activities to be in pursuit of

social, emotional, and physical healing that the bio-medical complex cannot offer. Rivkin-Fish (see also Keshavjee 2006), found that, like in Buryatia, locals do not merely seek healing outside the bio-medical sphere, but rather, perceive the Soviet and post-Soviet bio-medical complex as producing the conditions that require healing: "Pervasive illness and compromised health were linked to the nation's social and spiritual suffering, a diseased social order that affected interpersonal communication and relationships at all levels of society. . . . interpreted the problems surrounding women's reproductive health as symptoms of the social diseases wrought on the nation by the Soviet system" (Rivkin-Fish 2004, 290).

15. See Chudakova (2013, 2015) on the uniquely Buryat project of merging Tibetan Buddhist and Russian bio-medical practices.
16. See Bernstein (2013, 13–17) for a comparison between Lenin and Etigelov, as well as pp 15–20, especially footnote 20 (pp.19–20) for links to online discussions of Etigelov (including http://www.koicombat.org/forum/viewtopic.php?f=7&t=8709 accessed February 1, 2011). Issues discussed in these forums parallel those I observed in 2005, predominantly discussions of the scientific status of his body and whether his condition can be explained through natural causes or not.
17. The classic source on this intellectual movement is Rupen (1956). See Montgomery (2005) for a history of education and literacy in Buryatia. See Samten and Tsyrempilov (2012), Tsyrempilov (2010, 2012, 2014a, 2014b, 2015), and Sablin (2016) for the history of Buryat Buddhism in the 19th and early 20th centuries.
18. This is a pseudonym.
19. See Chudakova (2013, 2015) for ethnographic accounts of the practice of Tibetan medicine in Buryatia, and collaboration between Russian bio-medical and Tibetan doctors.
20. Nor is this unique to Buryatia. Lindquist (2006) offers an extensive discussion of the way in which New Age healers in European Russia integrate and legitimate their practices through medical degrees, diagnostic technology, state licenses, and other trappings of bio-medicine. See also Menzel (2013).

CHAPTER 5

1. Buyandelger (2013) and Shimamura (2011) make a similar argument about Buryat shamans in rural Mongolia. Although the social context of these practices is radically different, shamans from Tengeri have worked with shamans from the areas where Buyandelger and Shimamura worked, so significant parallels are to be expected.
2. Although Tengeri is usually referred to as male in contrast to the female earth deity Etugen (mentioned for example in Galdanova 1987), neither Tengeri nor Etugen are anthropomorphized. I never encountered anyone referring to

Etugen in practice and cannot speculate on the reason for this gap between pre-revolutionary ethnographic literature and contemporary practice. Tengeri is not a deity associated with the sky, he *is* the sky. Although in general Tengeri does not intervene in human affairs, there is one notable exception: Chinghis Khan is said to have been chosen and blessed by Tengeri. This may be a fusion between Mongolian cosmology and Han Chinese ideas about the mandate of heaven.

3. *Ongon* (pl. *ongonuud* in Buryat) is the term that Tengeri uses to refer to ancestor shamans who enter the bodies of living shamans during trances. They are not exactly deities, but they are more than just ancestors. Only shamans become *ongons*. Although the Tengeri shamans spoke about their *ongons* as individual persons, the way in which they discussed their calling implied that the (singular) shamanic force of a clan had been embodied in each of these individual ancestral shamans, and the living shaman was the current holder of this power, which is referred to as *onggor* by the Daur Mongols. Humphrey and Onon (1996, 183–93) describe the *onggor* among Daur Mongols as "the soul-spoor of previous and now dead shamans."
4. See Coleman (2013) on a contemporary Gesar bard in China.
5. For more descriptions of Tengeri rituals see Quijada (2008, 2011); Quijada, Graber, and Stephen (2015); Quijada and Stephen (2015); Jokic (2008).
6. Jokic (2008) notes a significantly larger number of practicing shamans, based on the official list of members kept in the office, which included people who were only loosely affiliated. There were 13 "core practicing members" identified in the pamphlet produced for the museum exhibition (Tengeri 2005) and who were regularly at the offices.
7. At the time (2005) I was told that Bazarov was part of a shamans' organization named Bo Darkhan ("Bo" is the Buryat term for a male shaman, "Darkhan" is a blacksmith). On the jacket of his book published in 2000, he is identified as the vice president of Bo Murgel, the organization founded by Nadezhda Stepanova (Bazarov 2000).
8. Although I have studied some Buryat, to the despair of my long-suffering and excellent teacher, my oral comprehension of formal and elaborate speech remains very low. Everyday life in Ulan-Ude in 2005 was conducted in Russian, and while many Buryats do not speak Buryat, every Buryat I met also spoke Russian, rendering knowledge of Buryat, while desirable, not strictly necessary.
9. On the symbolic and performative aspects of Buryat language use, see Graber (2012a, 2012b).
10. There were allusions in his speech to "Tengerianism," the idea that the worship of the Sky God Tengeri, which exists in many Central Asian shamanic traditions, is (or should be) a religion. The name of the organization evokes this deity, who is the primary (but distant) shamanic deity in both Mongolia and Buryatia, and the members occasionally refer to Tengerianism as a related phenomenon.

However, the members of Tengeri call what they do shamanism and distinguish it from Tengerianism. The Sky God is a very distant and abstract deity who is occasionally invoked in blessings but is not called down into the bodies of shamans and is not petitioned for help. For more on Tengerianism see Urbanaeva (1996) and Laruelle (2007).

11. The Buryat People's Congress is a civil organization and has no political authority.
12. However, it appears that Aldar Andanovich's roads led elsewhere. By the time I returned in 2012, he had left the organization, and the position of commercial director no longer existed. Administrative work was conducted by shamans as needed or by the woman who ran the sales kiosk in the office.
13. See also Buyandelgeryin (2002) for similar arguments made by Buryat shamans in Mongolia.
14. However, by 2012 Tengeri members were regularly calling down Bukhe Noion, the bull ancestor of the Buryat people as a whole. I did not witness this deity in 2005, but the shamans may not have yet been proficient enough to summon him.
15. Personal communication, June 26, 2005.
16. There is an archeological site attributed to the Huns outside the city of Ulan-Ude.
17. Geser or Gesar is a mythic king sent to earth to battle demons. The epic was performed throughout a broader Tibetan Buddhist culture area, including Tibet, Mongolia, Buryatia, and northern areas of China. See, for example, Coleman (2013), a documentary film about a Gesar bard in China.
18. This being is referred to by various versions of similar names and is also identified as Khan Khoto Baabai (Manzhigeev 1978, 61; Bernstein 2008, 27). According to the Babushkin dictionary, *baabai* means grandfather in Buryat, and *khaan baabai* is translated as *tsar'-batiushka*, which is an affectionate diminuitive calling the tsar father often encountered in fairytales (Babushkin 2000, 31). All these are variant titles for the being named Khoto/Khotun/Hotun. Buryat has an "h" sound (and letter when spelled in Cyrillic) while Russian does not. Hotun Khan would be Lord Hoton, while Khan Khoto Baabai would be Grandfather Lord Khoto. Furthermore, Bernstein worked with Valentin Khagdaev, who is from Olkhon Island, which may explain why Khagdaev refers to Khotun Khan as "grandfather" when the Tengeri shamans, who are from Ulan-Ude and Aga, do not. When I was on Olkhon in 2012 one of the Tengeri shamans insisted the original Buryat name was Hotun, with the Buryat "h," although I have only ever seen it written with "Kh." I do not wish to endorse one or the other spelling of this name as more accurate, but rather point to it as an example of what happens when oral traditions are reduced to written forms.
19. See Dugarova (2005) on how female Buryat shamans relate to this restriction.
20. See Bernstein (2006) for interactions between Russian tourists and Valentin Khagdaev, a local shaman on Olkhon Island.

CHAPTER 6

1. The phrase *za lozheno* is apparently an archaic Russian phrase, but it is the one the shamans use. Images of horses or the idea that spirits "ride" mediums are not uncommon (Bourguignon 1964). For example, horse imagery is widespread in Siberian and Central Asian shamanism (Eliade 1964, 466–70) as well as trance possession practices such as Haitian vodou and Bahian Candomble, where those in trance are described as "ridden" by a spirit, or as the "horse of the spirit" (for examples see Brown 1991, 56, 61 for Vodou; van der Port 2005, 168 for Candomble).
2. See Leykin (2015) on Rodologia, an ethnic Russian movement that, in a slightly different form, also seeks to produce healing in the present through gathering and understanding genealogical knowledge.
3. The second initiation for a black shaman is called a *shanar*; see Dugarov (1991, 41–61) for a detailed account of a *shanar*. See Tkacz et al. (2002) for a photographic description of a *shanar* initiation in the Aga Buryat Okrug. Yuri's ceremony followed a very similar procedure to the one documented in that text. Both Bair Zhambalovich and Bair Rinchinov, the officiating shaman in that *shanar*, studied with the same teacher in Mongolia, and therefore follow the same procedure. See Jokic (2008) for another description of Yuri's *shandru* specifically, and Shimamura (2011) for a description of *shanars* among Buryats in Mongolia.
4. On other occasions I was told that white shaman *ongons* pass only through maternal relatives, but as far as I know this was not the case with Yuri.
5. Tsagaalgan, or white month, is the Buddhist New Year celebration, and an *oboo* is the shrine of a clan's ancestors or a spirit place-master (see Chapter 1 for a discussion of spirit masters of places).
6. It must be noted that not all patients are diagnosed with shamanic callings; there is a whole array of illnesses that can be treated by shamanic intervention. See Quijada (2009, 2011).
7. This individual later determined that he did not, in fact, have a calling. Another person who could not complete her initiations died of her illness. Despite the opposed outcomes, both situations are used as proof of the overall logic of the system. See Evans-Pritchard (1976, 154–163) for a classic example of how individual instances of divinatory failure are explained without undermining the overall system of divination.
8. These birch branches, called *veniki*, are similar to the kind used in Russian saunas.
9. This is a Buddhist mantra, and is generally acknowledged as such by white shamans, in my experience, with a shrug of indifference. Skrynnikova (2002), following Dashinima Dugarov (2002) argues that Buryat shamanism is a meeting point between a Central Asian form of shamanism that has incorporated Tibetan Buddhist/Lamaist elements (represented by white shamans) and

a northern Siberian one, represented by black shamans, who use drums to induce trance. Dugarov and his argument are well known and respected by the members of Tengeri.

10. See Chapter 3 in Chakars (2014) for precise breakdowns of the demographic shifts in occupations for Buryats in the post-WWII years. One striking example is that although Buryats constituted only 25–28 percent of the total population of the republic, by 1979 Buryats constituted 60 percent of all writers, journalists, editors, and instructors in higher educational institutes (Chakars 2014, 97).

EPILOGUE

1. The original Russian term is "*istiny*" (pl. of *istina*) which translates as "truth" but is more often used in religious contexts to refer to foundational or existential truths, as opposed to "*pravda*" which was the more commonly used Soviet term for truth (such as for example, *Pravda*—the party newspaper).

Bibliography

ARCHIVES

NARB—National Archive of the Republic of Buryatia.

PUBLISHED WORKS

Adams, Laura. 2010. *The Spectacular State: Culture and National Identity in Uzbekistan*. Durham, NC: Duke University Press Books.

Agadjanian, Alexander. 2001. "Revising Pandora's Gifts: Religious and National Identity in the Post-Soviet Societal Fabric." *Europe-Asia Studies* 53 (3): 473–88.

Aiusheeva, S. G, M. G. Bukhaeva, N. K. Safonova, and L. P. Shchapova, eds. 2001. *Iz istorii religioznykh konfessiĭ Buriiatii, XX vek: sbornik dokumentov* [From the history of religious confessions in Buriatia, 20th century. Collection of documents]. Ulan-Ude: Komitet po delam arkhivov.

Amogolonova, Darima. 2014. "Buddhist Revival in the Context of Desecularization Processes in Russia (on Materials of Buryatia)." *Journal of Siberian Federal University Humanities and Social Sciences* 7:1165–76.

Amogolonova, Darima, I. E. Elaeva, and Tatyana D. Skrynnikova. 2005. *Buriatskaia Etnichnost' v Kontekste Sotsiokul'turnoi Modernizatsiii (Postsovetskii Period)* [Buryat ethnicity in the context of sociocultural modernization—post-Soviet period]. Vol. 3. 3 vols. Irkutsk: RPTs Radian.

Anderson, David. 2011. "Local Healing Landscapes." In *The Healing Landscapes of Central and Southeastern Siberia*, edited by David G. Anderson, 1–13. Patterns of Northern Traditional Healing 1. Edmonton: Canadian Circumpolar Institute (CCI Press) in cooperation with the Centre for the Cross-Cultural Study of Health and Healing, University of Alberta.

Apffel-Marglin, Frédérique. 2011. *Subversive Spiritualities: How Rituals Enact the World*. Oxford: Oxford University Press.

Appiah, K. Anthony. 1994. "Identity, Authenticity, Survival: Multicultural Societies and Social Reproduction." In *Multiculturalism: Examining the Politics of Difference*, edited by Amy Gutmann, 149–64. Princeton, NJ: Princeton University Press.

Armstrong, J. A. 1990. "The Ethnic Scene in the Soviet Union: The View of the Dictatorship." *Journal of Soviet Nationalities* 1 (1): 14–65.

Aronowitz, S. 1988. *Science as Power: Discourse and Ideology in Modern Society*. Minneapolis: University of Minnesota Press.

Asad, Talal. 1993. *Genealogies of Religion: Discipline and Reasons of Power in Christianity and Islam*, Baltimore: Johns Hopkins University Press.

Aurell, Jaume. 2015. "Rethinking Historical Genres in the Twenty-first Century." *Rethinking History* 19: 145–57.

Austin, J. L. 1962. *How To Do Things with Words*. Oxford: Clarendon Press.

Avedon, J. F., F. Meyer, N. D. Bolsokhoeva, K. M. Gerasimova, and T. Bradley. 1998. *The Buddha's Art of Healing: Tibetan Paintings Rediscovered*. New York: Rizzoli.

Babushkin, S. M. 2000. *Buriatsko-Russkii i Russko-Buriatskii Slovar'*. Ulan-Ude: Izdatel'stvo Buriatskogo Gosuniversiteta.

Bacigalupo, Ana Mariella. 2016. *Thunder Shaman: Making History with Mapuche Spirits in Chile and Patagonia*. Austin: University of Texas Press.

Badueva, Nana. 2004. "Katoliki pervymi vstretili Rozhdestvo" [Catholics celebrate Christmas first]. Inform Polis. December 29, 2004. http://www.infpol.ru/newspaper/number.php?ELEMENT_ID=3424.

Bakhtin, Mikhail Mikhailovich. 1981. "Forms of Time and of the Chronotope in the Novel." In *The Dialogic Imagination*, translated by Caryl Emerson and Michael Holquist, 84–258. Austin: University of Texas Press.

Balzer, Marjorie Mandelstam. 1999. *The Tenacity of Ethnicity: A Siberian Saga in Global Perspective*. Princeton, NJ: Princeton University Press.

———. 2005. "Whose Steeple Is Higher? Religious Competition in Siberia." *Religion, State and Society* 33 (1): 57–69.

———. 2011. *Shamans, Spirituality, and Cultural Revitalization: Explorations in Siberia and Beyond*. New York: Palgrave Macmillan.

Banzarov, D. 1997. *Sobranie Sochinenii*. Ulan-Ude: BNTs CO RAN.

Bazarov, B. D. 2000. *Tainstva i Praktika Shamanisma* [Secrets and practices of shamanism]. Ulan-Ude: Buriaad Unen.

Belka, Lubos. 2014. "Buryat Buddhism and Russia: Religion and Politics." In *Religion and Ethnicity in Mongolian Societies: Historical and Contemporary Perspectives*, edited by Karenina Kollmar-Paulenz, Seline Reinhardt, and Tatiana Skyrinnikova, 81–96. Wiesbaden: Harrassowitz Verlag.

Bender, John, and David Wellbery, eds. 1991. *Chronotypes: The Construction of Time*. Stanford, CA: Stanford University Press.

Berliner, David. 2005. "Social Thought & Commentary: The Abuses of Memory: Reflections on the Memory Boom in Anthropology." *Anthropological Quarterly* 78 (1): 197–211.

Bernstein, Anya. 2006. *In Pursuit of the Siberian Shaman*. Documentary Education Resources.

———. 2008. "Remapping Sacred Landscapes: Shamanic Tourism and Cultural Production on the Olkhon Island." *Sibirica: Interdisciplinary Journal of Siberian Studies* 7 (2): 23–46.

———. 2010. "Religious Bodies Politic: Rituals of Sovereignty in Buryat Buddhism." Ph.D. dissertation, Department of Anthropology, New York University.

———. 2013. *Religious Bodies Politic: Rituals of Sovereignty in Buryat Buddhism*. Chicago: University of Chicago Press.

Blinnikov, Aleksei. 2005. *Poslanie Khambo Lami* [Message of the Khombo Lama]. Arig Us po zakazy Instituta Khambo Lami Itigelova.

Bloch, M. 1986. *From Blessing to Violence: History and Ideology in the Circumcision Ritual of the Merina of Madagascar*. Cambridge: Cambridge University Press.

BMK Informatsionnoe Agentstvo. 2014. "Beslan. 12 Let. Pamiati Darimy Alikovoi" [Beslan 12 Years. Memories of Darima Alikova], September 3, 2014. http://www.baikal-media.ru/news/society/277012/.

Bobrick, Benson. 1992. *East of the Sun: The Epic Conquest and Tragic History of Siberia*. New York: Henry Holt and Co.

Boliachevets, Lilia, and Ivan Sablin. 2016. "The Second or the Fourth World: Critique of Communism and Colonialism in Contemporary North Asian Literature." *Ab Imperio* 2016 (2): 385–425.

Bolkhosoev, S. B., and E. V. Pavlov. 2006. "K problem definitsii i genezisa chernogo shamanstva u predbaĭkal'skikh Buriat (po materialam analiza 'korneĭ' "chernykh shamanov zapadnoburiatskogo plemeni Bulagat)" [To the problem of definition and genesis of black shamanism among pribaikal Buriats]. *E'tnograficheskoe Obozrenie* 6: 86–95.

Bolsokhoeva, N. D., and Inessa Soktoeva. 1998. *Buddhist Paintings from Buryatia*. Ulan-Ude: Institute for Mongolian, Buddhist and Tibetan Studies, Buryat Research Center, Siberia Division, Russian Academy of Sciences.

Borboev, L. A. 2001. *Skazanie Starovo Shamana* [Tales of an old shaman]. Ulan-Ude, privately published.

Borowik, I., G. Babinski, and G. Babinski. 1997. *New Religious Phenomena in Central and Eastern Europe*. Krakow: Nomos.

Bourguignon, Erika. 1964. "More on the Equine Subconcious: Comments on Utley's Comment on Gladwin." *American Anthropologist* 66 (6): 1391–93.

Boym, Svetlana. 2001. *The Future of Nostalgia*. New York: Basic Books.

Braeker, Hans. 1989. "Buddhism." In *Candle in the Wind: Religion in the Soviet Union*, edited by E. B. Shirley and M. Rowe. 173-184 Washington, DC: Ethics and Public Policy Center.

Bromley, Yuri. 1975. "Response to Gellner: The Soviet and the Savage." *Current Anthropology* 16 (4): 602–4.

———. 1980. “The Object and the Subject-Matter of Ethnography.” In *Soviet and Western Anthropology*, edited by E. Gellner, 151–60. New York: Columbia University Press.

Brower, D., and E. Lazzerini, eds. 1997. *Russia's Orient: Imperial Borderlands and Peoples, 1700–1917*. Bloomington: Indiana University Press.

Brown, Karen McCarthy. 1991. *Mama Lola: A Vodou Priestess in Brooklyn*. Berkeley: University of California Press.

Brunstedt, Jonathan. 2011. “Building a Pan-Soviet Past: The Soviet War Cult and the Turn Away from Ethnic Particularism.” *The Soviet and Post-Soviet Review* 38 (2): 149–71.

Buck-Morss, Susan. 2000. *Dreamworld and Catastrophe: The Passing of Mass Utopia in East and West*. Cambridge MA: The MIT Press.

Bulag, U. E. 1998. *Nationalism and Hybridity in Mongolia*. Oxford: Clarendon Press.

Burawoy, Michael, and Janos Lukacs. 1994. *The Radiant Past: Ideology and Reality in Hungary's Road to Capitalism*. Chicago: University of Chicago Press.

Buyandelgeriyn, Manduhai. 2002. “Between Hearth and Celestial Court: Gender, Marginality and the Politics of Shamanic Practices among the Buriats of Mongolia.” Ph.D dissertation, Department of Anthropology, Harvard University.

———. 2007. “Dealing with Uncertainty: Shamans, Marginal Capitalism, and the Remaking of History in Post-Socialist Mongolia.” *American Ethnologist* 34 (1): 127–47.

Buyandelger, Manduhai. 2013. *Tragic Spirits: Shamanism, Memory, and Gender in Contemporary Mongolia*. Chicago: University of Chicago Press.

Carr, E. H. 1985. *The Bolshevik Revolution, 1917–1923*. Vol. 1. New York: W. W. Norton & Co.

Chakars, Melissa. 2014. *The Socialist Way of Life in Siberia: Transformation in Buryatia*. Budapest: Central European University Press.

Chimitdorzhiev, Sh. B. 2004a. *Kto Mi Buriat-Mongoli?* [Who are we Buryat-Mongols?]. Ulan-Ude: Buriatskoe knizhnoe izdatel'stvo.

———, ed. 2004b. *Kak Ischezla Edinnaia Buriat-Mongoliia (1937 i 1958 Gody)* [How a unified Buryat-Mongolia disappeared (1937 and 1958)]. Ulan-Ude: Buriatskoe knizhnoe izdatel'stvo.

Chimitdorzhin, G. G. 2004. *Institut Pandito Khambo Lam, 1764–2004 Gg.* [The institute of the Pandido Hombo Lama, 1764–2004]. Ulan-Ude: Izdatel'stvo Buddiiskovo Instituta.

Chudakova, Tatiana. 2013. “Recovering Health: Tibetan Medicine and Biocosmopolitics in Russia.” Ph.D dissertation, Department of Anthropology, University of Chicago.

———. 2015. “The Pulse in the Machine: Automating Tibetan Diagnostic Palpation in Postsocialist Russia.” *Comparative Studies in Society and History* 57 (2): 407–34.

Cole, Jennifer. 2001. *Forget Colonialism? Sacrifice and the Art of Memory in Madagascar*. 1st edition. Berkeley: University of California Press.

Coleman, Donagh, and Lharigtso. 2013. *A Gesar Bard's Tale*. Documentary. Illume Ltd.

Collier, Stephen J. 2011. *Post-Soviet Social: Neoliberalism, Social Modernity, Biopolitics.* Princeton, NJ: Princeton University Press.

Comaroff, J., and J. Comaroff. 1992. *Ethnography and the Historical Imagination.* Boulder: Westview Press.

Connerton, Paul. 1989. *How Societies Remember.* Cambridge: Cambridge University Press.

Daniel, E. V. 2002. "The Arrogation of Being by the Blind-Spot of Religion." In *Discrimination and Toleration: New Perspectives,* edited by Kirsten Hastrup and George Ulrich, 31–53. International Studies in Human Rights. The Hague: Martinus Nijhoff.

Davidson, Ronald. 2002. "GSar Ma Apocrypha: The Creation of Orthodoxy, Gray Texts, and the New Revelation." In *The Many Canons of Tibetan Buddhism (PIATS 2000),* edited by Helmut Eimer and David Germano, 203–24. Leiden: Brill.

Dragadze, Tamara. 1975. "Response to Gellner: The Soviet and the Savage." *Current Anthropology* 16 (4): 604.

Dugaron, Semen. 2005a. "Boevoi Put' zabaikal'tsev: Stalingradskaia bitva" [Wartime path of the Zabaikalians: battle for Stalingrad]. *Tainy Buriatii,* 2005.

———. 2005b. "Boevoi Put' Zabaikal'tsev:Berlinskaia Operatsiia" [Wartime path of the Zabaikalians: Operation Berlin]. *Tainy Buriatii,* 2005.

Dugarov, Dashinima. 1991. *Istoricheskie Korni Beloro Shamanstva (Na Materiale Obriadovogo Folk'lora Buriat)* [Historical roots of white shamanism (on materials of ritual folklore of the Buryats)]. Moscow: Nauka.

———. 2002. "Foreword." In *Shanar: Dedication Ritual of a Buryat Shaman in Siberia as Conducted by Bayir Rinchinov.* New York: Parabola Books.

Dugarova, Radzhana. 2005. " 'My dovodim molitvy lydei do bogov': istorii buriatskikh shamanok" ["We bring the prayers of humans to gods": stories of Buryat female shamans]. In *Zhenshchina i vozrozhdenie shamanizma: postsovetskoe prostranstvo na rubezhe tyciacheletii* [Women and the rebirth of shamanism: the post-Soviet world at the turn of the millenium], edited by Valentina Kharitonova, 228–50. Moscow: IEA RAN, 2005.

Durkheim, Emile. 1995. *The Elementary Forms of the Religious Life.* Translated by Karen Fields. New York: The Free Press.

Eliade, Mircea. 1964. 2000. *Shamanizm: Archaiceskie techniki ekstaza.* Moscow: Sofija.

Evans-Pritchard, E. E. 1976. *Witchcraft, Oracles and Magic among the Azande.* Oxford: Oxford University Press.

———.1979 [1940]. *The Nuer.* Oxford: Oxford University Press.

Fanon, Franz. 1991. *Black Skin, White Masks.* New York: Grove Press.

Fedotev, Alexander, and Alexander Fedotor. 1986. "Evolution of Tibetan 'chams Tradition in Central Asia." *The Tibet Journal* 11 (2): 50–55.

Fisher, R. E. 1993. *Buddhist Art and Architecture.* London: Thames & Hudson.

Forsyth, J. 1992. *A History of the Peoples of Siberia: Russia's North Asian Colony, 1581–1990.* Cambridge: Cambridge University Press.

Freeze, G. 1995. "Counter-Reformation in Russian Orthodoxy: Popular Response to Religious Innovation, 1922–1925." *Slavic Review* 54 (2): 305–39.

Gal, Susan. 1991. "Bartók's Funeral: Representations of Europe in Hungarian Political Rhetoric." *American Ethnologist* 18 (3): 440–58.

Galdanova, G. R. 1987. Dolamanistskie Verovaniia Buriat [Pre-lamaist beliefs of the Buryat]. Novosibirsk: Nauka, Sibirskoe Otdelenie.

Galli, Lucia. 2009. "The Tsam Mask-Making Tradition in Post-Socialist Mongolia." *The Tibet Journal* 34 (2): 81–99.

Geertz, Clifford. 1973 *The Interpretation of Cultures.* New York: Basic Books.

Gellner, Ernest, ed. 1980. *Soviet and Western Anthropology.* New York: Columbia University Press.

Gellner, Ernest, Olga Akhmanova, Frank B. Bessac, Yu. V. Bromley, Tamara Dragadze, Stephen P. Dunn, J. L. Fischer, et al. 1975. "The Soviet and the Savage [and Comments and Replies]." *Current Anthropology* 16 (4): 595–617.

Gerasimova, K. M. 1967. *Obnovlencheskoe Dvizhenie Buriatskovo Lamaistskovo Dukhovenstva* [Renovationist movement of the Buryat Lamaist clergy]. Ulan-Ude: Buriatskoe knizhnoe izdatel'stvo.

Germano, David, and Kevin Trainor, eds. 2004. *Embodying the Dharma: Buddhist Relic Veneration in Asia.* Albany: State University of New York Press.

Giuliano, Elise. 2011. *Constructing Grievance: Ethnic Nationallism in Russia's Republics.* Ithaca, NY: Cornell University Press.

Goffman, Erving. 1979. "Footing." *Semiotica* 25 (1/2): 1–29.

Goluboff, Sascha. 2002. *Jewish Russians: Upheavals in a Moscow Synagogue.* Philadelphia: University of Pennsylvania Press.

Graber, Kathryn E. 2012a. "Knowledge and Authority in Shift: A Linguistic Ethnography of Multilingual News Media in the Buryat Territories of Russia." Ph.D., Department of Anthropology, University of Michigan.

———. 2012b. "Public Information: The Shifting Roles of Minority Language News Media in the Buryat Territories of Russia." *LAC Language and Communication* 32 (2): 124–36.

Graber, Kathryn E., and Joseph Long. 2009. "The Dissolution of the Buryat Autonomous Okrugs in Siberia: Notes from the Field." *Inner Asia* 11 (1): 147–55.

Graeber, David. 2015. "Radical Alterity Is Just Another Way of Saying 'Reality': A Reply to Eduardo Viveiros de Castro." *HAU: Journal of Ethnographic Theory* 5 (2): 1–41.

Grant, Bruce. 1995. *In the Soviet House of Culture: A Century of Perestroikas.* Princeton, NJ: Princeton University Press.

Gray, Patty A. 2005. *The Predicament of Chukotka's Indigenous Movement: Post-Soviet Activism in the Russian Far North.* Cambridge: Cambridge University Press.

Grimes, Ronald L. 1992. "Reinventing Ritual." *Soundings: An Interdisciplinary Journal* 75 (1): 21–41.

———. 2013. *The Craft of Ritual Studies.* Oxford; New York: Oxford University Press.

Gyatso, Janet. 1996. "Drawn from the Tibetan Treasury: The GTer Ma Literature." In *Tibetan Literature: Studies in Genre*, edited by Jose Cabezon and Roger Jackson, 147–69. Ithaca, NY: Snow Lion.

Halbwachs, Maurice. 1992. *On Collective Memory*. Translated by Lewis A. Coser. Chicago: University of Chicago Press.

Hallowell, A. Irving. 1940. "The Spirits of the Dead in Saulteaux Life and Thought." *The Journal of the Royal Anthropological Institute of Great Britain and Ireland* 70 (1): 29.

Handman, Courtney. 2016. "Figures of History: Interpreting Jewish Pasts in Christian Papua New Guinea." *HAU: Journal of Ethnographic Theory* 6 (1): 237–60.

Hann, Chris. 2006. "Introduction: Faith, Power and Civility after Socialism." In *The Postsocialist Religious Question: Faith and Power in Central Asia and East-Central Europe*, edited by Chris Hann, 11: 1–27. Halle Studies in the Anthropology of Eurasia. Berlin: LIT Verlag.

———, ed. 2010. *Religion, Identity, Postsocialism: The Halle Focus Group 2003–2010*. Halle/Saale: The Max Planck Institute for Social Anthropology.

Hann, Chris, and Mathijs Pelkmans. 2009. "Realigning Religion and Power in Central Asia: Islam, Nation-State and (Post) Socialism." *Europe-Asia Studies* 61 (9): 1517–41.

Hartley, Janet M. 2014. *Siberia: A History of the People*. New Haven, CT: Yale University Press.

Hellbeck, Jochen. 2006. *Revolution on My Mind: Writing a Diary Under Stalin*. Cambridge, MA: Harvard University Press.

Hirsch, Francine. 2005. *Empire of Nations: Ethnographic Knowledge and the Making of the Soviet Union*. Ithaca, NY: Cornell University Press.

Hobsbawm, E., and T. Ranger. 1983. *The Invention of Tradition*. Cambridge: Cambridge University Press.

Hodges, Matt. 2010. "The Time of the Interval: Historicity, Modernity, and Epoch in Rural France." *American Ethnologist* 37 (1): 115–31.

Holland, Edward C. 2014. "Religious Practice and Belief in the Republic of Buryatia: Comparing across Faiths and National Groups." *Nationalities Papers* 42 (1): 165–80.

Hummel, Siegbert, and G. Vogliotti. 1997. "The White Old Man." *The Tibet Journal* 22 (4): 59–70.

Humphrey, Caroline. 1989. "Population Trends, Ethnicity and Religion among the Buryats." In *The Development of Siberia: People and Resources*, edited by Alan Wood and R. A. French, 147–76. New York: St. Martin's Press.

———. 1998. *Marx Went Away—But Karl Stayed Behind*. Ann Arbor: University of Michigan Press.

———. 2002a. *The Unmaking of Soviet Life: Everyday Economies after Socialism*. Ithaca, NY: Cornell University Press.

———. 2002b. "Stalin and the Blue Elephant: Paranoia and Complicity in Postcommunist Metahistories." *Diogenes* 49 (2): 26–34.

Humphrey, Caroline, and Urgunge Onon. 1996. *Shamans and Elders: Experience, Knowledge and Power among the Daur Mongols.* Oxford: Clarendon Press, Oxford University Press.

Humphrey, Caroline, and Hurelbaatar Ujeed. 2013. *A Monastery in Time: The Making of Mongolian Buddhism.* Chicago: University of Chicago Press.

Hundley, Helen Sharon. 1984. "Speransky and the Buriats: Administrative Reform in Nineteenth Century Russia." Ph.D. dissertation, Department of History, University of Illinois at Urbana-Champaign.

Imithenov, A. B., and E. M. Egorov, eds. 2001. *Ulan-Ude: History and Modern Day.* Ulan-Ude: The Buryat Scientific Center SB RAS Publishers, by request of the City Administration of Ulan-Ude.

"Indigenous Peoples, Indigenous Voices Factsheet." n.d. United Nations Permanent Forum on Indigenous Issues. http://www.un.org/esa/socdev/unpfii/documents/5session_factsheet1.pdf.

Jokic, Zeljko. 2008. "The Wrath of the Forgotten Ongons: Shamanic Sickness, Spirit Embodiment, and Fragmentary Trancescape in Contemporary Buriat Shamanism." *Sibirica* 7 (1): 23–51.

Kappeler, A. 1992. *Russland Als Vielvoelkerreich: Entstehung, Geschichte, Zerfall* [Russia as a multinational empire: development, history, decline]. Munich: C. H. Beck.

Keane, Webb. 1997. "Religious Language." *Annual Review of Anthropology* 26:47–71.

Kelly, John D., and Martha Kaplan. 1990. "History, Structure, and Ritual." *Annual Review of Anthropology* 19:119–50.

Kendall, Laurel. 1985. *Shamans, Housewives and Other Restless Spirits: Women in Korean Ritual Life.* Honolulu: University of Hawaii Press.

———. 2010. *Shamans, Nostalgias, and the IMF: South Korean Popular Religion in Motion.* Honolulu: University of Hawaii Press.

Keshavjee, Salmaan. 2006. "Bleeding Babies in Badakhshan: Symbolism, Materialism, and the Political Economy of Traditional Medicine in Post-Soviet Tajikistan." *Medical Anthropology Quarterly*, New Series, 20 (1): 72–93.

Khalbaeva-Boronova, M. M. 2005. *Buriatiia: Problemy Kompleksnogo Razvitiia Regiona* [Buriatia: problems of general regional development]. Ulan-Ude: Izdatel'stvo Buriatskogo Gosuniversiteta.

Khazanov, A. 1995. *After the USSR: Ethnicity, Nationalism, and Politics in the Commonwealth of Independent States.* Madison: University of Wisconsin Press.

Khodarkovsky, M. 2002. *Russia's Steppe Frontier: The Making of a Colonial Empire, 1500–1800.* Bloomington: Indiana University Press.

Kitagawa, Joseph. 1981. "The Career of Maitreya, with Special Reference to Japan." *History of Religions* 21 (2): 107–25.

Klimovich, Liutsman. 1931. "Religii Byvshikh ugnetennyx Natsii samo-derzhavnoi sluzhili tsarizmu" [Religions of formerly oppressed nations served tsarism]. *Bezbozhnik*, August 1931.

Klin, Boris. 2006. "Zhivee Vsekh Zhivykh-Ne Lenin, a Lama Itigelov" [Itigelov, not Lenin is more alive than all the living]. *Izvestiia*, November 8, 2006. http://www.izvestia.ru/special/article3095502/.

Kolarz, W. 1954. *The Peoples of the Soviet Far East*. New York: Frederick A. Praeger.

Koselleck, R. 1985. *Futures Past: On the Semantics of Historical Time*. Cambridge, MA: MIT Press.

Krader, Lawrence. 1963. *Social Organization of the Mongol-Turkic Pastoral Nomads*. Uralic and Altaic Series 20. The Hague: Indiana University/Mouton & Co.

Krist, Stefan. 2005. "Where Going Back Is a Step Forward: The Re-Traditionalising of Sport Games in Post-Soviet Buriatiia." *Sibirica: Journal of Siberian Studies* 4 (1): 104–15.

———. 2009. "Kickboxing, Breakdance and Pop Music versus Wrestling, Round Dance and Folklore." *Electronic Journal of Folklore* 41:131–42.

Kymlicka, Will. 1995. "Introduction." In *The Rights of Minority Cultures*, 1–27. Oxford: Oxford University Press.

———. 2001. *Politics in the Vernacular: Nationalism, Multiculturalism, and Citizenship*. Oxford: Oxford University Press.

LaClau, E. 1996. "Universalism, Particularism and the Question of Identity." In *The Politics of Difference: Ethnic Premises in a World of Power*, edited by Edwin N. Wilmsen and Patrick McAllister, 45–58. Chicago: University of Chicago Press.

Lambek, M. 2003. *The Weight of the Past: Living with History in Mahajanga, Madagascar*. New York: Palgrave Macmillan.

———. 2016. "On Being Present to History: Historicity and Brigand Spirits in Madagascar." *HAU: Journal of Ethnographic Theory* 6 (1): 317–41.

Lane, Christel. 1981. *The Rites of Rulers: Ritual in Industrial Society—the Soviet Case*. London: Cambridge University Press.

Laruelle, Marlène. 2007. "Religious Revival, Nationalism and the 'Invention of Tradition': Political Tengrism in Central Asia and Tatarstan." *Central Asian Survey* 26 (2): 203–16.

Lemon, Alaina. 2009. "Sympathy for the Weary State? Cold War Chronotopes and Moscow Others." *Comparative Studies in Society and History* 51 (4): 832–64.

Lenin, V. I. 1975a. "Communism and the East: Theses on the National and Colonial Question." In *The Lenin Anthology*, edited by Robert C. Tucker, 619–26. New York: W. W. Norton & Co.

———. 1975b. "The Question of Nationalities or 'Autonomisation.'" In *The Lenin Anthology*, edited by Robert C. Tucker, 719–24. New York: W. W. Norton & Co.

———. 1975c. "The Right of Nations to Self-Determination." In *The Lenin Anthology*, edited by Robert C. Tucker, 153–81. New York: W. W. Norton & Co.

———. 1975d. "Two Cultures in Every National Culture." In *The Lenin Anthology*, edited by Robert C. Tucker, 654–59. New York: W. W. Norton & Co.

Lévi-Strauss, Claude. 1963. *Structural Anthropology*, translated by Claire Jacobson and Grundfest Schoepf. New York: Basic Books.

Lewis, D. C. 2000. *After Atheism: Religion and Ethnicity in Russia and Central Asia.* Richmond: Curzon Press.

Leykin, Inna. 2015. "Rodologia: Genealogy as Therapy in Post-Soviet Russia." *Ethos* 43 (2): 135–64.

Lincoln, W. Bruce. 1993. *The Conquest of a Continent: Siberia and the Russians.* New York: Random House.

Lindquist, Galina. 2005. "Healers, Leaders and Entrepreneurs: Shamanic Revival in Southern Siberia." *Culture and Religion* 6 (2): 263–85.

———. 2006. *Conjuring Hope: Healing and Magic in Contemporary Russia.* New York: Berghahn Books.

Lopez, Donald. 1998. *Prisoners of Shangri-La: Tibetan Buddhism and the West.* Chicago: University of Chicago Press.

Luehrmann, Sonja. 2005. "Recycling Cultural Construction: Desecularization in Postsoviet Mari El." *Religion, State and Society* 33 (1): 27–56.

———. 2011. *Secularism Soviet Style: Teaching Atheism and Religion in a Volga Republic.* Bloomington: Indiana University Press.

Mahmood, Saba. 2011. *Politics of Piety: The Islamic Revival and the Feminist Subject.* Princeton, NJ: Princeton University Press.

Makley, Charlene E. 2007. *The Violence of Liberation: Gender and Tibetan Buddhist Revival in Post-Mao China.* Berkeley: University of California Press.

Manzhigeev, I. A. 1978. *Buriatskie shamanisticheskie i doshamanisticheskie terminy* [Buriat shamanic and pre-shamanic terms]. Moskva: Nauka.

Martin, Dan. 1994. "Pearls from Bones: Relics, Chortens, Tertons and the Signs of Saintly Death in Tibet." *Numen* 41 (3): 273–324.

Martin, Terry. 2001. *The Affirmative Action Empire: Nations and Nationalism in the Soviet Union, 1923–1939.* Ithaca, NY: Cornell University Press.

Mashchekke, V. 1930. "V Tsentre Lamaizma" [In the center of Lamaism]. *Bezbozhnik*, July 1930.

Menzel, Birgit. 2013. "The Occult Underground of Late Soviet Russia." *Aries* 13 (2): 269–88.

Metzo, Katherine. 2008. "Sacred Landscape, Healing Landscape: 'Taking the Waters' in Tunka Valley, Russia." *Sibirica* 7 (1): 51–72.

———. 2011. "Medical Pluralism and Expert Knowledge in Buriatiia." In *The Healing Landscapes of Central and Southeastern Siberia*, edited by David Anderson, 1: 29–44. Patterns of Northern Traditional Healing. Edmonton, Alberta: Canadian Circumpolar Institute (CCI) Press in cooperation with the Centre for the Cross-Cultural Study of Health and Healing, University of Alberta.

Mikhailov, T. M. 2004. "Shamanizm - Drevniaia Religiia Buriat" [Shamanism—Ancient Religion of the Buryats]. In *Buriati*, edited by L. L. Abaeva and N. L. Zhukovskaia, 352–90. Moscow: Nauka.

Mills, Martin A. 2002. *Identity, Ritual and State in Tibetan Buddhism: The Foundations of Authority in Gelukpa Monasticism*. London: Routledge.

Montgomery, Robert W. 2005. *Late Tsarist and Early Soviet Nationality and Cultural Policy: The Buryats and Their Language*. Lewiston, NY: The Edwin Mellen Press.

Mueggler, Erik. 2001. *The Age of Wild Ghosts: Memory, Violence, and Place in Southwest China*. Berkeley: University of California Press.

Murray, Jesse D. 2012. "Building Empire among the Buryats: Conversion Encounters in Russia's Baikal Region 1860's–1917." Ph.D. dissertation, Department of History, University of Illinois at Champaign-Urbana.

Namzhilon, L. 2005. *K Voprosu "O Fenomene Itigelova"* [On the question: About the Etigelov phenomenon]. Ulan-Ude: privately published.

Natsov, Genin-Darma. 1998. *Materialy Po Lamaizmu v Buriatii Chast' 2* [Materials on Lamaism in Buryatia, part 2]. Ulan-Ude: BNTs - SO RAN.

Naumov, Igor V. 2006. *The History of Siberia*, edited by David Collins. London: Routledge.

Nomer Odin Ulan-Ude. 2004. "V Beslane Pogibla Nasha Zemliachka" [Our country-woman died in Beslan]. Newspaper. "Nomer Odin" Ulan-Ude Novosti Buriatii, September 15, 2004. http://gazeta-n1.ru/archive/detail.php?ID=1364.

———. 2017. "Zachem Buriaty Khodili k Petru I" [Why did Buryats go to Peter I] Nomer Odin Ulan-Ude – Novosti Buriatii January 27, 2017. http://m.gazeta-n1.ru/news/47695/.

Norris, Stephen M. 2011. "Memory for Sale: Victory Day 2010 and Russian Remembrance." *The Soviet and Post-Soviet Review* 38 (2): 201–29.

Okuneva, Iak. 1930. "Zemlaia Sovetskaia: V Strane Pastukhov i Okhotnikov Buriato-Mongoliia" [Soviet land: in the country of herders and hunters, Buryat-Mongolia]. *Bezbozhnik*, September 1930.

Oushakine, Serguei Alex. 2000. "Third Europe-Asia Lecture. In the State of Post-Soviet Aphasia: Symbolic Development in Contemporary Russia." *Europe-Asia Studies* 52 (6): 991–1016.

———. 2009. *The Patriotism of Despair: Nation, War, and Loss in Russia*. Ithaca, NY: Cornell University Press.

Palmié, Stephan. 2002. *Wizards and Scientists: Explorations in Afro-Cuban Modernity and Tradition*. Durham, NC: Duke University Press.

Palmié, Stephan, and Charles Stewart. 2016. "Introduction: For an Anthropology of History." *HAU: Journal of Ethnographic Theory* 6 (1): 207–36.

Paxson, Margaret. 2005. *Solovyovo: The Story of Memory in a Russian Village*. Washington, DC/Bloomington: Woodrow Wilson Center Press/Indiana University Press.

Peers, Eleanor. 2009. "Representations of the Buryat in Political and Popular Newspaper Discourse: The Sanctification of Buryat Culture." *Inner Asia* 11 (1): 65–81.

Pelkmans, Mathijs. 2006. *Defending the Border: Identity, Religion, and Modernity in the Republic of Georgia.* Ithaca, NY: Cornell University Press.

Pesmen, Dale. 2000. *Russia and Soul.* Ithaca, NY: Cornell University Press.

Petrone, Karen. 2000. *Life Has Become More Joyous, Comrades: Celebrations in the Time of Stalin.* Bloomington: Indiana University Press.

Petryna, Adriana. 2004. "Biological Citizenship: The Science and Politics of Chernobyl-Exposed Populations." *Osiris*, 2nd series, 19: 250–65.

Phillips, G. D. R. 1942. *Dawn in Siberia: The Mongols of Lake Baikal.* London: Frederick Muller, LTD.

Pipes, Richard. 1997. *The Formation of the Soviet Union: Communism and Nationalism, 1917–1923.* Cambridge, MA: Harvard University Press.

Platz, Stephanie. 1996. "Pasts and Futures: Space, History, and Armenian Identity, 1988–1994." Ph.D. dissertation, Department of Anthropology, University of Chicago.

———. 2000. "The Shape of National Time: Daily Life, History and Identity during Armenia's Transition to Independence, 1991-1994." In *Altering States: Ethnographies of Transition in Eastern Europe and the Former Soviet Union*, edited by Daphne Berdahl, Matti Bunzl, and Martha Lampland, 114–38. Ann Arbor: University of Michigan Press.

Pomus, V. I. 1943. *Buriat Mongolia: A Brief Survey of Political, Economic and Social Progress.* New York: Institute of Pacific Relations.

Pospielsovsky, D. V. 1987. *A History of Marxist-Leninist Atheism and Soviet Antireligious Policies.* Vol. 1. New York: St. Martin's Press.

Povinelli, Elizabeth. 2002. *The Cunning of Recognition: Indigenous Alterities and the Making of Australian Multiculturalism.* Durham, NC: Duke University Press.

———. 2006. *The Empire of Love: Toward a Theory of Intimacy, Genealogy, and Carnality.* Durham, NC: Duke University Press.

Quijada, Justine Buck. 2008. "What If We Don't Know Our Clan? The City Tailgan as New Ritual Form in Buriatiia." *Siberica* 7 (1): 1–22.

———. 2009. "Opening the Roads: History and Religion in Post-Soviet Buryatia." Ph.D. dissertation, Department of Anthropology, University of Chicago.

———. 2011. "Symptoms as Signs in Buriat Shamanic Callings." In *The Healing Landscapes of Central and Southeastern Siberia*, edited by David G. Anderson, 13–27. Patterns of Northern Traditional Healing 1. Edmonton: Canadian Circumpolar Institute (CCI Press) in cooperation with the Centre for the Cross-Cultural Study of Health and Healing, University of Alberta.

Quijada, Justine Buck, Kathryn E. Graber, and Eric Stephen. 2015. "Finding 'Their Own': Revitalising Buryat Culture through Shamanic Practices in Ulan-Ude." *Problems of Post-Communism* 62:258–72.

Quijada, Justine Buck, and Eric Stephen. 2015. "Performing 'Culture': Diverse Audiences at the International Shaman's Conference and Tailgan on Olkhon Island." *Etudes Mongoles et Siberiennes, Centrasiatiques et Tibetaines* 46. https://journals.openedition.org/emscat/2589

Rappaport, Joanne. 1993. *Cumbe Reborn: An Andean Ethnography of History*. Chicago: University of Chicago Press.

Rappaport, Roy. 1992. "Ritual, Time and Eternity." *Zygon* 27 (1): 5.

Renan, E. 1996. "What Is a Nation?" In *Becoming National: A Reader*, edited by G. Eley and R. Suny, 42–55. Oxford: Oxford University Press.

Rifkin, Mark. 2017. *Beyond Settler Time: Temporal Sovereignty and Indigenous Self-Determination*. Durham, NC; London: Duke University Press Books.

Rivkin-Fish, Michele. 2004. "'Change Yourself and the Whole World Will Become Kinder': Russian Activists for Reproductive Health and the Limits of Claims Making for Women." *Medical Anthropology Quarterly*, new series, 18 (3): 281–304.

Rogers, Douglas. 2009. *The Old Faith and the Russian Land: A Historical Ethnography of Ethics in the Urals*. Ithaca, NY: Cornell University Press.

Rolf, Malte. 2013. *Soviet Mass Festivals, 1917–1991*. Pittsburgh, PA: University of Pittsburgh Press.

Routon, Kenneth. 2008. "Conjuring the Past: Slavery and the Historical Imagination in Cuba." *American Ethnologist* 35 (4): 632–49.

Rupen, R. A. 1956. "The Buriat Intelligentsia." *The Far Eastern Quarterly* 15 (3): 383–98.

———. 1964. *Mongols of the Twentieth Century*. Vol. 149. Bloomington: Indiana University / Mouton & Co.

Sablin, Ivan. 2016. *Governing Post-Imperial Siberia and Mongolia, 1911–1924: Buddhism, Socialism and Nationalism in State and Autonomy Building*. London; New York: Routledge.

Samten, Jampa, and Nikolai Tsyrempilov. 2012. *From Tibet Confidentially: Secret Correspondence of 13th Dalai Lama to Agvan Dorzhiev, 1911–1925*. Dharamsala: Library of Tibetan Works & Archives.

Schorkowitz, D. 2001a. *Staat Und Nationalitaeten in Russland: Der Integrationsprozess Der Burjaten Und Kalmucken, 1822–1925* [State and nationality in Russia: the integration process of Buryats and Kalmyks, 1822–1925]. Stuttgart: Franz Steiner Verlag.

———. 2001b. "The Orthodox Church, Lamaism, and Shamanism among the Buriats and Kalmyks, 1825–1925." In *Of Religion and Empire: Missions, Conversion and Tolerance in Tsarist Russia*, edited by Robert Geraci and Michael Khodarkovsky, 201–25. Ithaca, NY: Cornell University Press.

Sharf, Robert. 1992. "The Idolization of Enlightenment: On the Mummification of Ch'an Masters in Medieval China." *History of Religions* 32 (1): 1–31.

Shimamura, Ippei. 2011. *The Roots Seekers: Shamanism and Ethnicity among the Mongol Buriats.* Kanagawa, Japan: Shumpusha Publishing.

Shnirelman, Viktor Aleksandrovich. 2011. *"Porog tolerantnosti": ideologiia i praktika novogo rasizma* [Threshold of tolerance: ideology and practice of the new racism]. Biblioteka zhurnala "Neprikosnovennyi zapas." Antropologiia, filosofiia, politologiia, istoriia. Moskva: Novoe literaturnoe obozrenie.

Silverstein, Michael. 2004. "'Cultural' Concepts and the Language-Culture Nexus." *Current Anthropology* 45 (5): 621–52.

Skinner, Barbara. 1994. "Identity Formation in the Russian Cossack Revival." *Europe-Asia Studies* 46 (6): 1017–37.

Skrynnikova, Tatiana D. 2002. "Shamanism in Inner Asia: Two Archetypes." *Sibirica* 2 (1): 69–87.

———. 2003. "Traditsionnaya Kul'tura i Buddism v Samoidentificatsia Buryat" [Traditional culture and Buddhism in the self-identification of Buryats]. In *Religia i Identichnost' v Rossii* [Religion and identity in Russia], edited by Marietta Stepaniants, 121–52. Moscow: "Vostochnaya literatura" RAN.

Skrynnikova, Tatiana D., S. D. Batomunkuev, and P. K. Varnavskii. 2004. *Buriatskaia etnichnost' v kontekste sotsiokul'turnoi modernizatsii (sovetskii period)* [Buryat ethnicity in the context of sociocultural modernization: Soviet period]. Vol. 2. 3 vols. Ulan-Ude: Izdatel'stvo Buriatskogo Nauchnogo Tsentra CO RAN.

Slezkine, Yuri. 1992. "From Savages to Citizens: The Cultural Revolution in the Soviet Far North." *Slavic Review* 51 (1): 52–76.

———. 1994. *Arctic Mirrors: Russia and the Small Peoples of the North.* Ithaca, NY: Cornell University Press.

———. 1996. "The USSR as a Communal Apartment, or How a Socialist State Promoted Ethnic Particularism." In *Becoming National: A Reader*, edited by G. Eley and R. Suny, 203–38. Oxford: Oxford University Press.

Smith, Jonathan Z. 1978. *Map is not Territory: Studies in the History of Religion.* Leiden: Brill.

Smolkin-Rothrock, Victoria. 2011. "Cosmic Enlightenment: Scientific Atheism and the Soviet Conquest of Space." In *Into the Cosmos: Space Exploration and Soviet Culture*, edited by Asif A. Siddiqi and James T. Andrews, 159–94. Pitt Series in Russian and East European Studies. Pittsburgh, PA: University of Pittsburgh Press.

Snelling, J. 1993. *Buddhism in Russia: The Story of Agvan Dorzhiev, Lhasa's Emissary to the Tsar.* Rockport, MA: Element.

Solomon, S. G. 1993. "The Soviet-German Syphilis Expedition to Buriat Mongolia, 1928: Scientific Research on National Minorities." *Slavic Review* 52 (2): 204–32.

Spivak, Gayatri. 1988. "Can the Subaltern Speak?" In *Marxism and the Interpretation of Culture*, 271–313. Urbana: University of Illinois Press.

Sponberg, Alan, and Helen Hardacre, eds. 1988. *Maitreya, the Future Buddha.* Cambridge: Cambridge University Press.

Strong, John S. 2004. "Buddhist Relics in Comparative Perspective: Beyond the Parallels." In *Embodying the Dharma: Buddhist Relic Veneration in Asia*, edited by David Germano and Kevin Trainor, 27–49. Albany: State University of New York Press.

Suny, Ronald. 1993. *The Revenge of the Past: Nationalism, Revolution and the Collapse of the Soviet Union*. Stanford: Stanford University Press.

Swancutt, Katherine. 2012. *Fortune and the Cursed: The Sliding Scale of Time in Mongolian Divination*. New York; Oxford: Berghahn Books.

Taylor, Charles. 1994. "The Politics of Recognition." In *Multiculturalism: Examining the Politics of Difference*, edited by Amy Gutmann, 25–73. Princeton, NJ: Princeton University Press.

Ten Dyke, E. A. 2000. "Memory, History and Remembrance Work in Dresden." In *Altering States: Ethnographies of Transition in Eastern Europe and the Former Soviet Union*, edited by Daphne Berdahl, Matti Bunzl, and Martha Lampland, 139–57. Ann Arbor: University of Michigan Press.

Tengeri, Mestnaia Religioznaia organizatsiia shamanov. 2005. "Sovremennie Shamani Buriatii" [Modern shamans of Buryatia]. Exhibition catalog, izdanie osushchestvleno pri pomoshchi Tsentra cokhraneniia i razvitiia kul'turnogo nalsediia Buriatii, translated by Justine Buck Quijada. Ulan-Ude, privately published.

Thum, Rian. 2014. *The Sacred Routes of Uyghur History*. Cambridge, MA: Harvard University Press.

Tkacz, V., S. Zhambalov, and W. Phipps. 2002. *Shanar: Dedication Ritual of a Buryat Shaman in Siberia as Conducted by Bayir Rinchinov*. New York: Parabola Books.

Tomlinson, Matt. 2014. *Ritual Textuality: Pattern and Motion in Performance*. New York: Oxford University Press.

Trainor, Kevin. 1997. *Relics, Ritual, and Representation in Buddhism: Rematerialising the Sri Lankan Theravada Tradition*. Cambridge: Cambridge University Press.

Trouillot, M.-R. 1995. *Silencing the Past: Power and the Production of History*. Boston: Beacon Press.

Tsultemin, Uranchimeg. 2015. "The Power and Authority of Maitreya in Mongolia Examined Through Mongolian Art." In *Buddhism in Mongolian History, Culture, and Society*, edited by Vesna A. Wallace, 137–59. New York: Oxford University Press.

Tsyrempilov, Nikolai. 2009. "Za Sviatuiu Dkharmu i Belovo Tsaria. Rossiiskaia Imperiia Glazami Buriatskikh Buddhistov XVIII-Nachala XXb." [For holy dharma and the white tsar. The Russian Empire through the eyes of Buryat Buddhists XVIII–beginning of XXth century]. *Ab Imperio* 2: 105–30.

———. 2012. "'Alien' Lamas: Russian Policy toward Foreign Buddhist Clergy in the Eighteenth to Early Twentieth Centuries." *Inner Asia* 14: 245–55.

———. 2014a. "Buddhist Minority in a Christian Empire: Buryat Religious Survival and Identity Problems in Russia in the 18th – Early 19th Centuries." In *Religion and Ethnicity in Mongolian Societies: Historical and Contemporary Perspectives*, edited by Karenina Kollmar-Paulenz, Seline Reinhardt, and Tatiana Skyrinnikova, 61–79. Wiesbaden: Harrassowitz Verlag.

———. 2014b. *Buddizm I imperiia: buriatskaia buddiiskaia obshchina I Rossiiskoe gosudarstvo v XVIII – nach. XX v.* [Buddhism and empire: the Buriat Buddhist community and Russian state in the 18th–early 20th c.]. Buriat Mongol Nom.

———. 2015. "Noble Paganism." *Inner Asia* 17 (2): 199–224.

Tumarkin, Nina. 1994. *The Living and the Dead: The Rise and Fall of the Cult of World War II in Russia.* New York: Basic Books.

———. 1997. *Lenin Lives! The Lenin Cult in Soviet Russia.* Enlarged edition. Cambridge, MA: Harvard University Press.

Turner, Victor. 1967. *The Forests of Symbols: Aspects of Ndembu Ritual.* Ithaca, NY: Cornell University Press.

Twigg, Judyth L. 1998. "Balancing the State and the Market: Russia's Adoption of Obligatory Medical Insurance." *Europe-Asia Studies* 50 (4): 583–602.

Ulymzhiev, D. 1993. "Dorzhi Banzarov—the First Buryat Scholar." *Mongolian Studies* 16: 55–57.

Urbanaeva, Irina. 1996. *Central Asian Shamanism: Philosophical, Historical, Religious, Ecological Aspects (The Materials of International Baikal Symposium, 20–26 June, 1996).* Ulan-Ude: Russian Academy of Sciences Siberian Branch Buryat Institute of Social Sciences.

van der Port, Mattjis. 2005. "Circling around the Really Real: Spirit Possession Ceremonies and the Search for Authenticity in Bahian Candomble." *Ethos* 33 (2): 149–79.

Verdery, Katherine. 1996. *What Was Socialism, and What Comes Next?* Princeton, NJ: Princeton University Press.

———. 1999. *The Political Lives of Dead Bodies: Reburial and Postsocialist Change.* New York: Columbia University Press.

Vlasova, Irina. 2004. "Ucheniki Risovali ee sredi tsvetov. Geroicheskoe Povedenie Uchitelei Beslanskoi SHkoly Mnogikh Spaslo ot Gibeli" [Students drew her surrounded by flowers: the heroism of a Beslan teacher who saved many from death]. *Novye Izvestiia*, September 23, 2004. http://www.newizv.ru/accidents/2004-09-23/11963-ucheniki-risovali-ee-sredi-cvetov.html.

Vyatkina, K. V. 1964. "The Buryats." In *The Peoples of Siberia*, edited by M. G. Levin and L. P. Potapov, 203–42. Chicago: University of Chicago Press.

Wanner, Catherine. 1998. *Burden of Dreams: History and Identity in Post-Soviet Ukraine.* University Park: Pennsylvania State University Press.

———. 2007. *Communities of the Converted: Ukrainians and Global Evangelism.* Ithaca, NY: Cornell University Press.

———, ed. 2012. *State Secularism and Lived Religion in Soviet Russia and Ukraine.* Oxford: Oxford University Press.

Watson, Rubie. 1994. "Memory, History and Opposition under State Socialism: An Introduction." In *Memory, History and Opposition under State Socialism*, edited by Rubie Watson, 1–20. Santa Fe: School of American Research Press.

Watson, Rubie, ed. 1994. *Memory, History and Opposition under State Socialism*. Santa Fe: School of American Research Press.

Werth, Paul. 2002. *At the Margins of Orthodoxy: Mission, Governance, and Confessional Politics in Russia's Volga-Kama Region, 1827–1905*. Ithaca, NY: Cornell University Press.

———. 2016. *The Tsar's Foreign Faiths: Toleration and the Fate of Religious Freedom in Imperial Russia*. Oxford; New York: Oxford University Press.

Wertsch, James V. 2000. "Narratives as Cultural Tools in Sociocultural Analysis: Official History in Soviet and Post-Soviet Russia." *Ethos* 28 (4): 511–33.

———. 2002. *Voices of Collective Remembering*. Cambridge: Cambridge University Press.

White, Hayden. 1987. *The Content of the Form: Narrative Discourse and Historical Representation*. Baltimore: Johns Hopkins University Press.

White, Hylton. 2013. "Spirit and Society: In Defence of a Critical Anthropology of Religious Life." *Anthropology Southern Africa* 36 (3–4): 139–45.

Wikoff, Naj. 2005. "Letters Home: Naj Wikoff in Ulan Ude, Russia." 2005. http://www.northcountrypublicradio.org/news/naj/naj.html.

Willerslev, Rane. 2007. *Soul Hunters: Hunting, Animism, and Personhood among the Siberian Yukaghirs*. Berkeley: University of California Press.

Winter, J. 1995. *Sites of Memory, Sites of Mourning: The Great War in European Cultural History*. Cambridge: Cambridge University Press.

Wirtz, Kristina. 2011. "Cuban Performances of Blackness as the Timeless Past Still Among Us." *Journal of Linguistic Anthropology* 21 (August): E11–34.

———. 2016. "The Living, the Dead, and the Immanent: Dialogue across Chronotopes." *HAU: Journal of Ethnographic Theory* 6 (1): 343–69.

Yurchak, Alexei. 2006. *Everything Was Forever, Until It Was No More: The Last Soviet Generation*. Princeton, NJ: Princeton University Press.

———. 2015. "Bodies of Lenin." *Representations* 129 (1): 116–157.

Zbarsky, I., and S. Hutchinson. 1998. *Lenin's Embalmers*. London: The Harvill Press.

Zhukovskaia, N. L. 1994. "Khamnigany." In *Narody Rossii - Entsiklopediia* [Peoples of Russia encyclopedia], 380. Moscow: Nauchoe Izdatel'stvo Bol'shaia Rossiiskaia Entsiklopediia.

———. 2004. "Neoshamanism v Buriatii [Neoshamanism in Buryatia]." In *Buriatii* [Buryats], edited by L. L. Abaeva and N. L. Zhukovskaia, 390–96. Narodi i Kul'turi. Moscow: Nauka.

Zigon, Jarrett. 2011. *"HIV Is God's Blessing": Rehabilitating Morality in Neoliberal Russia*. Berkeley: University of California Press.

Zivkovic, Tanya Maria. 2010. "Tibetan Buddhist Embodiment: The Religious Bodies of a Deceased Lama." *Body & Society* 16 (2): 119–42.

Index

www.ingramcontent.com/pod-product-compliance
Lightning Source LLC
Chambersburg PA
CBHW062323040125
19934CB00005B/157